T3-AJK-505

Burt Franklin: Research & Source Works Series 252
Philosophy Mongraph Series 23

THE PHILOSOPHICAL RADICALS

THE PHILOSOPHICAL RADICALS

AND

OTHER ESSAYS

WITH CHAPTERS

ON THE

PHILOSOPHY OF RELIGION IN KANT AND HEGEL

BY

A. SETH PRINGLE-PATTISON

Burt Franklin: Research & Source Works Series 252
Philosophy Mongraph Series 23

Burt Franklin
New York, N. Y.

Published By
BURT FRANKLIN
235 East 44th Street
New York, N. Y. 10017

ORIGINALLY PUBLISHED
EDINBURGH AND LONDON: 1907

Reprinted 1967

This work has been reprinted
on long-life paper

Library of Congress Catalog Card No.: 68-56767

Printed in U.S.A.

TO

THE RIGHT HONOURABLE

RICHARD BURDON HALDANE

A SLIGHT MEMORIAL

OF

EARLY COLLABORATION

AND

CONTINUED FRIENDSHIP

PREFACE.

THE occasion of the four essays which form the first part of the present volume was the publication of certain notable books, such as Leslie Stephen's 'English Utilitarians,' Herbert Spencer's 'Autobiography,' and James Martineau's 'Life and Letters.' But the studies they contain of important thinkers and schools are, I hope, sufficiently careful to merit reproduction in a more permanent form. Advantage has been taken of this republication to re-insert a few passages which had to yield to the exigencies of editorial space, and the argument at these points will be found more complete.

The title of the volume is that of the paper which appeared first in order of time, but the choice is not merely casual. Doctrines and tendencies discussed in connection with the Philosophical Radicals reappear in the papers which follow, and the prominence throughout of the social and political aspects of philosophical theory gives a certain unity to the collection.

I have added to the Essays three book-reviews, written at different times, which, from the nature of the subjects and the scope of the discussion, seemed important enough to interest philosophical students.

The Reprints which constitute the last section of the volume are from books which have been out of print nearly twenty years. In 1881, as the result of studies in Germany, I published a small volume on 'The Development from Kant to Hegel,' an outline of a vast subject. Most of the ground covered in the first part of the book has been worked over afresh in other connections since, and on certain points my views have changed. But in the second part, which traced the development of the philosophy of religion in the hands of Kant and Hegel, and was mainly expository in character, there is little, if anything, which calls for alteration. Religious thought has moved rapidly during the last quarter of a century, and the significance of the historical element in Christianity for religious faith is a subject that has been widely discussed, and is under discussion still. What Kant and Hegel have to say on that question is as fresh and suggestive as ever, and a concise account of their attitude may still be found useful.

I have a special interest in the republication of the last paper, on "Philosophy as Criticism of Categories," owing to the circumstances of its first appearance and the character of its early associates. It was the first paper in a volume of 'Essays in Philosophical Criticism' published in 1883, in somewhat belated connection with the centenary of the 'Critique of Pure Reason.' The volume was dedicated to the memory of Thomas Hill Green, who died in the previous year, and some prefatory pages by Dr Edward Caird contained a fine tribute to the spirit of Green's life and teaching. It was edited by Mr (now The Right Honourable) R. B. Haldane and myself; and the second essay, on "The Relation of Philosophy to Science," was the work of the present Secretary of State for War, in collaboration with his brother, Dr J. S. Haldane. The other contributors were (to give them their later titles) Professor Bernard Bosanquet, Professor W. R. Sorley, Professor W. P. Ker, Professor Henry Jones, Dr James Bonar, Professor T. B. Kilpatrick of Knox College, Toronto, and the late Professor D. G. Ritchie of St Andrews. This, it will be admitted, was a band of which the editors had no reason to be ashamed.

The ideas of the book were then comparatively unfamiliar, and the writing of the youthful authors was often, perhaps, unnecessarily difficult, but the critics were at least unanimous in recognising the sincerity and scientific purpose which animated the volume. My individual contribution is reprinted, apart from a few verbal emendations, in its original form. Naturally there are things which one might wish to express differently. The nature of the universal self, for example, and the difficult question of its relation to the individual selves of experience, obviously require more adequate treatment. But the main argument of the paper seems to me as sound now as it did twenty-five years ago.

I have to thank the editors of 'The Quarterly Review,' 'The Hibbert Journal,' 'The Contemporary Review,' 'The Philosophical Review,' and 'Mind,' for their kind permission to republish the various essays and reviews. My sincere thanks are also due to my friend, Mr R. P. Hardie, for the care with which he has read the proofs.

University of Edinburgh,
May 1907.

CONTENTS.

ESSAYS

THE PHILOSOPHICAL RADICALS.

ONE reflection which will occur to most readers in taking up Mr Leslie Stephen's volumes on 'The English Utilitarians,'[1] is the rapidity with which even the most recent representatives of the school have passed into the region of history. When Mr Leslie Stephen published his 'History of English Thought in the Eighteenth Century,' in 1876, John Stuart Mill was only three years dead, and the echoes had not yet died away of the famous controversy in which he led the attack upon "Intuitionism," as represented by Dean Mansel and Sir William Hamilton. And although the direct political influence of the 'Philosophical Radicals' was even then a comparatively remote tradition, their social and political theories still largely moulded the views of reform and progress held by Liberal and Radical thinkers of the day. John Stuart Mill's parliamentary experience in the previous decade was doubtless of little more than academic interest, but in the closing years of his life he was not only the most prominent English philosopher, but was reverenced as the fountainhead of economic and political wisdom by men like Henry Fawcett, Mr Courtney, and Mr Morley, with whom the future of

[1] The following paper appeared in the 'Quarterly Review' of July 1901, shortly after the publication of 'The English Utilitarians.'

advanced Liberalism seemed to lie. "The foremost instructor of his time in wisdom and goodness," are Mr Morley's words in the fine tribute penned immediately after Mill's death. The elevation of Mill's character, and the loftiness of his aims, are as heartily recognised now as then, but in other respects the aspect of most questions, whether philosophical, ethical, political, or social, has changed so much during the last quarter of a century that "the equable flow of didactic wisdom" in Mill's pages appeals somewhat coldly to the present generation. He must always remain one of the most interesting figures of the nineteenth century in the region of pure intellect, but the interest will be more and more that of a transition figure, in whose inconsistencies we can trace the gradual break-up of the robust and self-sufficient creed of his youth, and the sympathetic anticipation of larger truths. The history of the century is in truth the history of the emergence and rapid growth of problems with which the rigid formulæ of the Philosophical Radicals were quite inadequate to deal.

Mr Stephen's volumes are in his best manner, and are a valuable contribution to the history of English thought. As he tells us in the preface, he was himself a disciple of the school during its last period. This account of the Utilitarians cannot, therefore, be condemned as written by an unsympathetic outsider; and its clear recognition of the shortcomings of the school possesses something of the inexorable justice of history. For the rest, the subject is treated by Mr Stephen in a way which displays his qualities to the best advantage.

"I have devoted," he says, "a much greater proportion of my work to biography and to considerations of political and social conditions than would be appropriate to the history of a philosophy. . . . I am primarily concerned with the history of a school or sect, not with the history of the arguments by which it justifies itself in the court of pure reason. . . . I deal not with philosophers meditating upon Being and not-Being, but with men actively engaged in framing political platforms and carrying on popular agitations."

Many of these bygone platform framers and "leaders of revolts" are obscure enough to us now, and there are quaint, even sordid, figures among them. Mr Leslie Stephen's intimate knowledge of the byways of history and biography gives life and circumstance to his narrative, and his pages are lit up every now and again by humorous detail or flashes of sarcastic wit. As he proceeds, however, he becomes more absorbed in the history of the doctrines themselves, tracing them to their philosophical presuppositions, inherited, as he points out, from Hume, and most clearly expressed in James Mill's 'Analysis of the Human Mind.'

The three volumes are labelled with the names of the thinkers who represent the three generations of the school's existence as an active force in philosophy and politics—Jeremy Bentham, James Mill, and John Stuart Mill. The first was the founder and patriarch of the school; the second was its most active propagandist, and the most vigorous and typical example of its undiluted orthodoxy and supreme self-confidence. John Stuart Mill has begun to part with some of the most characteristic Benthamite tenets; his admissions and compromises mark, as has been already observed, the gradual break-up of the school and its submergence in a deeper tide of thought and feeling. The three volumes thus coincide with the successive stages of the sect — its rise and progress, its forceful activity, its decline and fall. Each volume introduces, besides the principal figure, a number of minor actors.

In the first we have, at some length, an analysis of the political, industrial, and social conditions of England in the latter part of the eighteenth century, which constitute, as it were, the soil and environment in which philosophical radicalism grew up, and which largely explain its vitality as a political force. In the second volume careful account is taken of Malthus and Ricardo, whose doctrines were incorporated as integral parts of Utilitarian theory and bulked largely in popular attacks upon the school; while the third volume, besides chapters on J. S. Mill's contributions to logic and philosophy, touches on the various social and economic controversies which went to mould or modify his political economy, and gives an account of John Austin, Grote, and Buckle, who represented the school in the departments of jurisprudence, history, and philosophy of history respectively.

Utilitarianism can lay no claim to originality in its philosophical principles. Hedonism is as old as ethical speculation, and the genealogy of "the greatest-happiness principle" may be traced back in England through Paley, Hume, and Hutcheson to the chapters of Locke's 'Essay' which deal with morality. Hutcheson not only lays down this principle unreservedly as a test of the moral quality of actions, but contributes also the famous formula of "the greatest happiness of the greatest number." Bentham tells us that he came upon the phrase in Priestley, but Priestley (whose statement, for the rest, is not so precise) had it from Hutcheson, and to Hutcheson it was probably suggested (as Mr Scott has recently pointed out in his excellent Life of that philosopher) by his readings in Cicero, Seneca, Epictetus, and Marcus Aurelius — the watchword of this hedonistic theory being thus traceable, by the irony of history, to the Stoic "citizenship of the world." In Hume the theory is already complete; and we do not wonder, therefore, when Bentham tells us that on reading the third volume of Hume's 'Treatise on Human Nature' he "felt as if scales fell from his eyes." From Hume to J. S. Mill, in fact, the doctrine received no substantial alteration.

"The writings in which Bentham deals explicitly with the general principles of Ethics would hardly entitle him," says Mr Stephen, "to a higher position than that of a disciple of Hume without Hume's subtlety, or of Paley without Paley's singular gift of exposition."

Yet it was under Bentham that the Utilitarians first became a school in any definite sense, and "Benthamism" was for long the current designation of the doctrine. Under his initiative the doctrine passed from being the speculative tenet of this or that philosopher to be the active creed of a band of men bent upon applying it to political and social reform. With him, therefore, the history of 'The English Utilitarians' or 'Philosophical Radicals' begins. The second title, by which the group were long distinguished, sufficiently indicates the nature of the new departure.

The circumstances of English political and social life in the eighteenth century which formed the antecedents of Philosophical Radicalism are interestingly sketched by Mr Stephen in his first volume. He passes in review the anomalies of Parliamentary representation which made the House of Commons seem at times "little more than an exchange for the traffic between the proprietors of votes and the proprietors of offices and pensions"; the chaotic state of English law, accompanied by the absence of any centralised administration; the slothfulness and ignorance of the Universities; the secular and rationalistic spirit of the Church, which had become, in the main, "simply a part of the ruling class told off to perform divine services, to maintain order and respectability and the traditional morality." Everywhere the established order of things rested upon tradition, and represented a series of compromises, not the elaboration of a theory. It was primarily against the irrationality and chaos of the English legal system that Bentham directed his attack, his radicalism growing, as he advanced, till it left few points of "the matchless Constitution" unassailed. Meanwhile the growth of manufactures and commerce meant the rise of great industrial centres and of a new social class; but the great towns were as yet without municipal institutions, and if the merchants were inclined in the main to liberal principles, "it was less from adhesion to any general doctrine than from the fact that the existing restrictions and prejudices generally conflicted with their plain interests." Mr Stephen notes thus early the divergence of interest between the capitalists and the labourers, which was so plainly visible in the later history of Philosophical Radicalism. Urgent social problems were presented by the alarming growth of pauperism, and by the disgraceful state of the prisons revealed by Howard, while the agitation against the slave-trade was a further proof of the growth of humane sentiment. But towards the end of the century, under the influence of the reaction caused by the excesses of the French Revolution, the demand for Parliamentary reform, which had been growing in volume during the earlier part of George III.'s reign, had entirely lost the support of the nation; and even a philanthropic agitation like that against the slave-trade was looked upon with some suspicion, and abolition was not finally carried till 1807.

This part of Mr Stephen's survey may be instructively and agreeably supplemented by Mr Roylance Kent's well-informed and well-written history of 'The English Radicals.' Taking up his subject more exclusively from the political point of view, and including in it all the prominent phases of Radical thought, Mr Kent gives many additional details, often picturesque and suggestive, and helps to elucidate the differences between the Utilitarians and other types of earlier and contemporary Radicalism. Mr Lecky places the birth of English Radicalism in the year 1769, when the conflict between Wilkes and the House of Commons was at its height, and Mr Kent accepts this date as the starting-point of his narrative. The first Radical attack, it will be observed, was directed, not against the Crown or the House of Lords, but against the House of Commons, which, instead of being regarded as the bulwark of popular liberty, appeared to usurp the rights of the electors and to override their most clearly and repeatedly expressed wishes. Wilkes had right on his side; Diderot sent him his congratulations, and Whitefield prayed for his success. The effect of the agitation was to give a strong impulse to political discussion and the practice of holding public meetings. Political societies were founded in London and throughout the country. Parliamentary reform was not, however, a monopoly of the Radicals, and public opinion had so far ripened in 1783, when Pitt moved his famous resolutions, that a few years would in all probability have seen the passing of a Reform Act but for the blow inflicted by the French Revolution on all such movements. But it would have been a different Act from that passed in 1832. The democratic views of the suffrage to which that measure gave partial expression were then held only by a small band of Radical theorists and agitators, the chief of whom were Cartwright and Jebb, Joseph Priestley and Richard Price.[1]

The Revolution exercised a profound effect upon the course of political history in England. When it began, the cause of the reformers appeared full of promise, and we all know how, for a time, the progress of the Revolution was hailed by the more generous spirits. But the licence and cruelty which stained its further course almost extinguished Liberalism in England for a generation. "Till I see," wrote Fox in 1801, "that the public has some dislike (indignation I do not hope for) to absolute power, I see no use in stating in the House of Commons the principles of liberty and justice." While this was the effect on the mass of the nation, the principles of the Revolution were presented in their undiluted and most obnoxious form by the small band of English Jacobins, or, as they may be conveniently called, the Jacobinical Radicals. Of this sect Paine's 'Rights of Man' was the popular gospel, and Godwin's 'Political Justice' the more ponderous oracle. Mr Kent states very clearly the transformation which English Radicalism underwent in their writings. From being a scheme of parliamentary reform, it became a virulent attack upon the Constitution as a whole, and in particular upon the Crown and the House of Lords. "Paine was perhaps the first to make the point of expense a prime argument against the retention of the monarchy." Another point of difference was that of religious opinion and belief. The earlier Radicals had "all professed some form of Christianity, but Paine and Godwin were strong agnostics

[1] According to Bentham, it was a sentence in Priestley's 'Essay on the First Principles of Government' which first suggested to him his principle of "the greatest happiness of the greatest number," and it was a sermon of Price's which called forth Burke's 'Reflections on the French Revolution.

and materialists," and Paine's 'Age of Reason' completed the association of Radicalism and infidelity in the public mind. As Coleridge said, "It was God's mercy to our age that our Jacobins were infidels, and a scandal to all sober Christians. Had they been like the old Puritans, they would have trodden Church and King to dust—at least for a time." The congratulatory addresses of the new Radicals to the French National Convention, and similar performances smacking strongly of treason, roused a storm of popular indignation against these "philosophising serpents," as Walpole called them. The people wanted no French fraternity, said the first Sir Robert Peel to Fox; "they preferred their religion and their legal freedom, with the good roast beef of Old England, to the atheism, the liberty and equality, and the broken breeches and soup-meagre of France." The mob of Birmingham, shouting "No philosophers," burned Priestley's house over his head. Repressive legislation and political prosecutions were the natural outcome of the feelings aroused, and of the general atmosphere of suspicion. At the close of the century English Radicalism had for the time destroyed itself, and even the old Whig party could scarcely muster forty members in the House of Commons. This was the juncture at which the teaching of Bentham became a force in politics. Radicalism had to be reconstituted in England between 1800 and 1832, and this was mainly the work of the Philosophical Radicals. "The uprising of the Philosophical Radicals," says Mr Kent, "was the greatest force, of a purely speculative kind, that had ever been felt in English politics, and nothing ever did so much to democratise our institutions."

It is impossible to follow Mr Leslie Stephen in his genial sketch of the bustling boyish patriarch in whom selfishness had somehow taken the form of benevolence. Bentham was present at the trial of Wilkes, and his first important work was published in the year of the American Declaration of Independence; he was "codifying like any dragon" at the age of 82, and he died on 6th June 1832, the very day before the passing of the Reform Act to which his teaching had so powerfully contributed. Bentham began as a Tory, and his first bit of writing was a pamphlet in defence of Lord Mansfield. The 'Fragment on Government,' published in 1776, attracted the notice of Lord Shelburne, at whose house he met many prominent politicians of the day, and also two men who were to be of the greatest importance in the dissemination of his views—Dumont and Sir Samuel Romilly. It was the publication by Dumont in 1802 of the 'Traités de Législation de M. Jérémie Bentham' which first gave him his wider reputation and influence. Partly translation and partly a vigorous and lucid statement of the pith of Bentham's doctrine in Dumont's own words, the 'Traités' carried his fame into all the countries of Europe. As many copies were sold in St Petersburg as in London, and a magnificent translation was ordered. Russian officials wrote comparing Bentham to Bacon, Newton, and Adam Smith, as the founder of a new science. "The grand Baintham," said the Spanish alcalde to Borrow, showing him all the master's works upon his shelves, "he who has invented laws for all the world. I hope shortly to see them adopted in this unhappy country of ours." Forty thousand copies of Dumont were sold in Paris for the South American trade. Russia, Spain, and South America form an ironical conjunction.

At home Bentham's influence grew more slowly, but had more permanent results. In 1808 he made the acquaintance of James Mill, who was to be the most powerful apostle of Benthamism, both in its philosophical and its political aspects. By that time the Jacobin controversies had receded into the background, and English Radicalism of the old reforming type was again beginning to make itself heard. Sir Francis Burdett was returned to Parliament in 1807, and his motion in favour of reform in 1809 may be regarded as the first serious beginning of the agitation which issued in the first Reform Bill. Bentham continued "scribbling on in his hermitage," as he called it, and taking no direct part in the political struggle; but the politicians came to dine with him at Queen Square Place, and he was thus in touch with most of the Parliamentary reformers, including at a somewhat later date such men as O'Connell and Lord Brougham. The letters of the latter to his "dear grandpapa," and Bentham's notes enclosing "some nice sweet pap of my own making," to "my dear sweet little poppet," are sufficiently curious documents. Bentham purveyed the philosophy of the Radical movement, wrote a 'Catechism of Parliamentary Reform,' and furnished Burdett with the series of resolutions which he proposed in 1818, demanding universal suffrage, annual parliaments, and vote by ballot. In 1824, by which time the "Benthamites" formed a compact and fairly numerous group, he supplied funds to start 'The Westminster Review' as an organ of thorough-going Radicalism.

The development of Bentham's views is an instructive piece of history. His ultimate political conclusions, as embodied, for example, in his 'Constitutional Code,' are practically identical with those of the Jacobins, as deduced from the rights of man. Yet he declared the American version of these rights, in the Declaration of Independence, to be a "hodge-podge of confusion and absurdity," and he wrote a treatise on "Anarchic Fallacies" to expose the French Declaration of Rights. Natural rights, he says, is simple nonsense; natural and imprescriptible rights is "rhetorical nonsense—nonsense upon stilts." The whole abstract and deductive procedure is at fault. As Mr Leslie Stephen summarises his contention:

"The 'rights of man' doctrine confounds a primary logical canon with a statement of fact. The maxim that all men were, or ought to be, equal, asserts correctly that there must not be arbitrary differences. Every inequality should have its justification in a reasonable system. But when this undeniable logical canon is taken to prove that men actually are equal, there is an obvious begging of the question. In point of fact, the theorists immediately proceeded to disfranchise half the race on account of sex, and a third of the remainder on account of infancy."

All political arrangements must therefore be brought to the test of experience; they must be judged by their "utility." Applying this test to existing inequalities, Bentham believes himself to reach inductively the same practical conclusions. The difference in method is characteristic of the national temperament. Still more characteristic is the way in which Bentham was led step by step from an attempt to reform the penal law to a radical reconstruction of political society. It was the tradition of English reformers to start, not from abstract principles, but from an assault upon particular abuses. Bentham himself began life, as we have seen, with Tory sympathies. His original interest (and to the end probably his ruling interest) was codification; he desired to reform the monstrous abuses of the existing penal law, and generally to introduce order into the bewildering chaos of the English legal system. But there was no rancour in his zeal. "I was a great reformist," he says, "but never suspected that the 'people in power' were against reform. I supposed they only wanted to know what was good in order to embrace it." This devout imagination was first shaken by the cool reception which the politicians he met at Lord Lansdowne's gave to his scheme, and was finally shattered by the failure of the Panopticon, the great scheme of prison-reform which occupied him, more or less, for twenty years. As might have been expected, he passed with almost equal naïveté to the opposite extreme. Lawyers of all classes, he now insists, have a common interest in multiplying suits and complicating procedure; and thus a tacit partnership (described as "Judge and Co.") has grown up, which bars every attempt at reform. Hence the unmeasured terms in which he denounces Eldon as worse than Jeffreys, and expresses his belief that the most hopeless of reforms would be to raise a "thorough-paced English lawyer" to the moral level of an average man. But the legal profession did not stand alone; it was in the closest relations with the whole privileged class. Presently he discovered, as Mr Stephen puts it,

"that behind 'Judge & Co.' were George III. and the base Sidmouth, and the whole band of obstructors entrenched within the 'matchless constitution,' and thus his attack upon the abuses of the penal law led him to attack the whole political framework of the country."

Bentham's constitutional gospel follows with charming simplicity from this new insight, when combined with his foundation-principle of utility. The "right and proper end" of government is "the greatest happiness of the greatest number." But, according to the equally primary principle of "self-preference," every man always desires his own greatest happiness, and therefore in every government the governors will legislate for their own advantage.

"Hence the whole problem is to produce a coincidence of the two ends, by securing an identity of interest between governors and governed. To secure that, we have only to identify the two classes, or to put the government in the hands of all. In a monarchy, the ruler aims at the interest of one—himself; in a democracy, its end is the right one—the greatest happiness of the greatest number."

Universal suffrage, annual parliaments, and vote by ballot are easily deducible. Members of Parliament are to be simply "deputies," not "representatives," and they are not to be re-eligible till after an interval, every precaution being thus taken against the possible rise of a class whose interests might be divergent from those of the community as a whole. For the rest, since "all government is in itself one vast evil," let us "minimise confidence"; let all governors be directly responsible, and let us have as little government as possible. Industry in particular should say to government only what Diogenes said to Alexander, "Stand out of my sunshine."

The abstract simplicity of the perfect State corresponds to the abstract simplicity of the philosophical principles from which it was deduced. Unadulterated selfishness as the motive, universal benevolence as the end—these are the two fixed poles of Bentham's thought. They presented themselves to him in the first instance as a solution of his own specific problem, the creation of a science or philosophy of law, as a basis for practical reform. Utility, or the greatest-happiness principle, furnished him with a universal test for the criticism of existing enactments, and the introduction of order and system into the chaos of English "judge-made" law. The other problem of legislation is the encouragement of actions which promote the general happiness and the discouragement of actions which have a contrary tendency. This is solved by an appeal to the universal motive. "Nature has placed mankind under the governance of two sovereign masters, pain and pleasure. It is for them alone to point out what we ought to do, as well as to determine what we shall do." The legislator, therefore, must annex pains or pleasures to those classes of actions which he wishes to discourage or promote. Pains and pleasures, so annexed to courses of action, are called "sanctions," and they should be so manipulated by the legislator that from dictates of self-interest alone a man shall be impelled to conduct which promotes the general happiness.

As has been already hinted, these philosophical principles are in themselves neither very original nor very profound. We have glanced at the source of the greatest-happiness principle: the psychological hedonism with which it was coupled was a commonplace of the schools, and had been current in English philosophy since Locke. The truth is, as Mr Stephen puts it, that Bentham

> "founded not a doctrine but a method; the doctrine, which came to him simply as a general principle, was in his hands a potent instrument applied with most fruitful results to questions of immediate interest. . . . The characteristic of his teaching was not the bare appeal to utility, but the attempt to follow the clue of utility systematically or unflinchingly into every part of the subject."

It is, in short, in the history of legislative theory rather than in philosophy proper that Bentham holds a place. Even his psychology, as seen in his "analysis of the springs of action," is rough and ready. Not unnaturally he extended the principles which he found sufficient to solve his own practical problem, and used them as ultimate principles of explanation in psychology, ethics, and sociology. But working principles, sufficiently exact to yield valuable results in their own sphere, cannot be made absolute in this way without revealing their inadequacy to the task thus thrust upon them. Later criticism and the subsequent history of the Utilitarian school itself have made this abundantly evident in the case of Bentham's abstract scheme of man and society. But this detracts little from his merit in his own sphere, the sphere in which his real work was done,—a sphere in which, as Mr Stephen somewhat cruelly puts it, he "got on very well without philosophy." In the department of law, his success was so great that it has tended perhaps to obscure his merits. With the disappearance of the abuses against which his polemic was directed, and with the general acceptance of the canon by which he judged them, much of his writing is apt to appear superfluous. He has been compared to Samson, who perished in the ruins of the temple he destroyed.

The philosophical defects of Benthamism will be best considered when we have the subsequent development of the school before us. We shall proceed, therefore, briefly to trace its fortunes under the leadership of the Mills, father and son. The twenty years between 1820 and 1840 may be set down as the period during which the Utilitarians exercised their most direct influence upon English politics. They were during that time not only a group of thinkers with common principles, in constant communication with one another, but also a compact political party with clearly defined aims, active both in Parliament and in the press. Their organisation in this twofold capacity was unquestionably due in the main to the vigorous but repellent personality of James Mill. Bentham himself exerted his influence almost entirely through his writings, and even of them Sydney Smith wittily said that, while learned economists have doubted "whether it be necessary that there should be a middleman between the cultivator and the possessor of the soil, neither gods, men, nor booksellers can doubt the necessity of a middleman between Mr Bentham and the public." Mill was much more than such a middleman; he was at once the systematiser and the prophet of the Benthamite faith. And there is some truth in Höffding's[1] description of him as "the intellectual father of the first parliamentary reform." The best account of Philosophical Radicalism in the days of its confident youth is still to be found in his son's 'Autobiography.'

"The school," he says, "had no other existence than what was constituted by the fact that my father's writings and conversation drew round him a certain number of young men who had already imbibed, or who imbibed from him, a greater or smaller portion of his very decided political and philosophical opinions. . . . Bentham is a much greater name in history. But my father exercised a far greater personal ascendancy. I have never known any one who could do such ample justice to his best thoughts in colloquial discussion."

This is confirmed by the accounts of Grote and Mrs Grote. Mill goes on to indicate the chief articles of the creed which they held in common.

"It was not mere Benthamism," he says, "but rather a combination of Bentham's point of view with that of the modern

---

[1] In his 'History of Modern Philosophy' Höffding gives a remarkably fresh and well-written account of the Utilitarian thinkers. As a Dane, Professor Höffding perhaps takes a more cosmopolitan view of the progress of European thought than is to be found in the otherwise admirable histories of philosophy made in Germany. The seventy pages of the English translation which deal with Bentham and the Mills, Carlyle and Sir W. Hamilton, are a model of accurate statement, sympathetic appreciation, and incisive criticism.

political economy and with the Hartleian metaphysics. Malthus's population-principle was quite as much a banner and point of union among us as any opinion specially belonging to Bentham. This great doctrine, originally brought forward as an argument against the indefinite improvability of human affairs, we took up with an ardent zeal in the contrary sense, as indicating the sole means of realising that improvability."

The Hartleian metaphysics, as it is here called, was James Mill's special contribution to the general body of doctrine. Bentham, as has been seen, was not a trained psychologist, nor was he interested in such questions. To Mill, on the contrary, as a Scotchman—one of the Scotch "feelosophers" so passionately denounced by Cobbett—these investigations were part of his national inheritance. If he had time, he said in 1817, he could write a book which "would make the human mind as plain as the road from Charing Cross to St Paul's." In the doctrine of Association, as applied by Hobbes, Hume, and especially by Hartley, he thought he had found the instrument which effected this result; and in his 'Analysis of the Phenomena of the Human Mind,' published in 1829, he supplied the world, as he conceived, with the book in question. He furnished the school at any rate with an official philosophy in which the very vigour and clearness of the exposition force into relief the startling inadequacy of its account of conscious experience. James Mill also provided the school with a complete political theory in a powerful series of articles written for the supplement of the 'Encyclopædia Britannica' between 1816 and 1823, and printed as a volume in 1824. As regards political economy, the Philosophical Radicals looked upon themselves throughout as the special champions of the science. Macaulay, indeed, accused them of discrediting it by the ostentatious way in which they took it under their protection. Ricardo became acquainted with Mill in 1811, and was induced by him to publish his 'Principles of Political Economy' in 1817. Malthus's 'Essay on Population' had appeared in 1798, and in a second, amended, edition in 1803. The controversies which gathered round these two names are closely associated with the history of the Philosophical Radicals. By their rigid interpretation of the doctrines in question, and their uncompromising application of them in the discussion of practical questions, they were probably responsible for a large measure of the odium which the doctrines aroused in many quarters, and which in turn reacted unfavourably upon the general political influence of the party. The decline of Philosophical Radicalism was indeed, from a variety of causes, as rapid as its rise.

But between 1810 and 1830 the party was still in process of consolidation. Able recruits were yearly gathering to its banners, and its members were full of the most unbounded confidence in the sufficiency of their own principles, and in the speedy triumph of these principles over the mass of ignorance and prejudice which was all that their magisterial assumption permitted them to see in the forces opposed to them. Among the practical workers in the cause, the most notable was perhaps Francis Place, the tailor, whose shop at Charing Cross was the centre of Radical activity in the Westminster constituency. Since the days of Wilkes, Radicalism had migrated from the City to Westminster, as it was later to move to Manchester and Birmingham. Place carried two Radical candidates for Westminster against the Whigs as early as 1807; and one of these, Sir Francis Burdett, retained his seat for thirty years. In the press, yeoman service was done by John Black of 'The Morning Chronicle,' and later by Albany Fonblanque on 'The Examiner.' Among members of Parliament, in addition to Sir Francis Burdett and Sir John Hobhouse, members for Westminster, there were Joseph Hume, a school-fellow of James Mill's, who, after he entered Parliament in 1818, made himself, as Mr Kent puts it, "the self-appointed auditor of the national accounts," and Roebuck, whose parliamentary career, however, only began in 1832 and eventually led him into other company. Sir William Molesworth's activity, as member of Parliament and one of the wealthy supporters of the cause, also belonged to the years after 1832. The intellectual leaders of the movement, besides James Mill and Ricardo, were Grote, who was introduced to Mill by Ricardo in 1817, and who, with Mrs Grote, represented to the end the strictest sect of Philosophical Radicalism; John Austin, the philosophical jurist, and Charles Austin, his younger brother, whose brilliant oratory in the Cambridge Union introduced Benthamism to the younger members of that University and brought several recruits to the standard. Finally, there was John Stuart Mill, trained from his earliest youth for the apostolic succession, and already in 1823 or 1824 beginning to be a leader among the younger men. In 1824 the foundation of 'The Westminster Review' and James Mill's formidable onslaught in the first number upon 'The Edinburgh Review' and the Whig policy called general attention to the new party.

"So formidable an attack on the Whig party and policy," says J. S. Mill, "had never before been made, nor had so great a blow been ever struck, in this country, for Radicalism. . . . At a time when the current was already setting strongly towards reform, it is not strange that attention should have been aroused by the regular appearance in controversy of what seemed a new school of writers, claiming to be the legislators and theorists of this new tendency. The air of strong conviction with which they wrote, the boldness with which they tilted against the very front of both the existing political parties, their uncompromising profession of opposition to many of the generally received opinions, and the suspicion they lay under of holding others still more heterodox than they professed; the talent and verve of at least my father's articles, and the appearance of a corps behind him sufficient to carry on a Review, and, finally, the fact that the Review was bought and read, made the so-called Bentham school in philosophy and politics fill a greater place in the public mind than it had held before, or has ever again held since other equally earnest schools of thought have arisen in England."

Down to 1832, and later, the Utilitarians unquestionably claimed, as Mill puts it, to be "the legislators and theorists" of the new tendency. They attacked both the great political parties with equal bitterness as representing the aristocratic principle in government; but their special bitterness, hatred, and contempt seemed reserved for the Whigs, with whom they were compelled to cooperate. The Whig creed was a "see-saw," and the Whigs themselves were selfish "trimmers." This was the gist of Mill's attacks in 'The Westminster Review,' and the feeling grew more intense with the approach of a successful termination of the agitation. The Radicals, who, as Mr Stephen says, had some grounds for considering themselves to be the "steel of the lance," saw the Whig politicians stepping forward to receive both the reward and the credit of their labours. The Whig legend of the Reform Bill is different. Macaulay, then in the first flush of his Cambridge reputation, ridiculed the claim of the Utilitarians to be the defenders of the true political faith. He would draw a broad line between judicious reformers and a "sect which, having derived all its influence from the countenance which they have imprudently bestowed upon it, hates them with the deadly hatred of ingratitude." He is afraid of "the discredit of their alliance." No party was ever so unpopular. "It had already disgusted people with political economy, and would disgust them with parliamentary reform if it could associate itself in public opinion with the cause."

This is obviously unjust to the real influence of the Utilitarians, in leavening political opinion and pushing on the cause of reform, but it is a wholesome reminder of the fate that awaits any extreme party in English politics. The Philosophical Radicals had apparently expected that, after the first instalment of reform in 1832, they would increasingly dominate the Liberal policy of the future. Nothing could have been more unlike what actually happened. As the crisis actually approached, and the tide of feeling rose throughout the country, the Utilitarians were more or less lost in the crowd. Several of the party were returned to the first reformed Parliament. Besides Hume, Hobhouse, and Sir Francis Burdett, there were Grote, Roebuck, Charles Buller, Sir William Molesworth, and some others. The hopes of Mill and his father ran high. But none of them made any figure in the house. "On the whole," says Mill, reviewing this period in his 'Autobiography,' "they did very little to promote any opinions," and soon sank into "a mere *côté gauche* of the Whig party." "I laboured," he adds, "from this time till 1839, both by personal influence with some of them and by writings, to put ideas into their heads and purposes into their hearts. I did some good with Charles Buller and Sir William Molesworth. On the whole, however, my attempt was vain." With more irritation he describes them in a contemporary letter, some as full of crotchets, others as fastidious and overloaded with petty scrupulosity, and all devoid of energy, except Roebuck and Buller, while "Roebuck has no judgment, Buller no patient, persevering industry." They gave, in fact, too much ground for the English prejudice that "philosophical" means unpractical; while the centrifugal tendency, so curiously characteristic of all bodies of "advanced" theorists, soon showed itself in dissensions and mutual recriminations. "I tell you what it is coming to," Charles Buller remarked one night to Grote; "in no very long time from this, you and I will have to 'tell' Molesworth." As Buller and Molesworth both died prematurely, there was thus at least some plausibility in Macaulay's witty description of the party as consisting of "Grote and his wife." Sir Francis Burdett became a Tory of the Tories, Sir John Hobhouse took office with the Whigs, and Roebuck became a law unto himself. Thus, by 1840, says Mr Stephen, the Philosophical Radicals, who had expected to lead the van, were almost disbanded. "Grote, the ablest of Mill's friends, retired from Parliament to devote himself to the 'History of Greece,' about the same time as Mill set to work upon the completion of his 'Logic.'"

In the 'Autobiography,' Mill finds a partial explanation of this result in the fact that the years after 1832 were essentially a period of reaction, the public mind desiring rest after the Reform excitement, and being disinclined to listen to schemes involving further change. He also attributes it to the want of a leader:

"some man of philosophic attainments and popular talents who could have used the House of Commons as a rostra or a teacher's chair for instructing and impelling the public mind, and would either have forced the Whigs to receive their measures from him or have taken the lead of the Reform party out of their hands."

His father, he thinks, would have been such a leader had he been in Parliament. But these considerations do not reach to the root of the matter. No doubt the presence of a man with the concentrated force of James Mill might have given more unity and fighting spirit to the band; but the main cause of the decline of the Philosophical Radicals was the abstract and negative character of their views, and the want of insight and sympathy which they displayed in dealing with the concrete questions which now pressed for solution. The "condition-of-England question," as Carlyle called it in his 'Chartism,' had become clamant. The great industrial revolution and the development of capitalism had broken up the old organisation of society in many directions, bringing in its train many crying evils which have only gradually been rectified or mitigated. In the most different quarters men were trying to diagnose the evils and proposing remedies. Among the Conservatives, Southey and Coleridge were feeling after a more adequate theory of the State and its functions, and insisting on the importance of the national Church as the organ of sound religion and morality. Among the non-philosophical Radicals, Cobbett was raging against the degradation of the peasantry, and denouncing the economists and all their works. Owen and his followers, tracing distress to the development of the manufacturing system, looked towards Socialism for the remedy. Popular feeling was inflamed by hideous stories of child-labour and white slavery in factories and mines, and practical philanthropists like Lord Shaftesbury were promoting the Factory Laws to safeguard the human rights of women and children. The workmen themselves were seeking to organise trade-unions for the protection of their interests and the improvement of their position. But all these signs of the times were lost upon the "paralytic Radicals," as Carlyle sarcastically called them. They either refused to admit the existence of the evils, or pronounced them to be the inevitable results of economic laws. "Laissez-faire" and unlimited competition were bound, they held, to work out the best results, if only the people would lay to heart the teaching of Malthus, and restrain the increase of population. Some of the Utilitarians, it is true, were better than their creed, and supported the factory legislation, but the school was opposed to it on principle. The Utilitarians were, in fact, as we have seen, the chief elaborators of the classical political economy, and they accepted its doctrines, not as abstractions and laws of tendency provisionally true in given circumstances, but as an absolute theory of society. They preached these doctrines as the one scheme of social salvation, in opposition to "sentimentalists" of every colour. Small wonder that the dumb instinct of the multitude turned from men who were always preaching that nothing could or should be done; and that the guidance of popular aspirations passed into other hands.

"The Philosophical Radicals," says Mr Stephen, "represented rather intellectual scorn for old prejudices and clumsy administration than any keen sympathy with the sufferings of the poor. The harsher side of the old Utilitarianism was therefore emphasised by them, and Mill's attempts to enlarge and soften its teaching were regarded by his critics with a certain suspicion. Their philosophy suited neither party. To the class which still retained the leading position in politics they appeared as destructives, and to the classes which were turning towards Chartism they appeared as the most chilling critics of popular aspiration."

One of the most striking features of the Philosophical Radical movement, indeed, was its complete failure to enlist the support of the working classes. The effect of the Reform Bill had been to throw political power into the hands of the middle class; and the working classes, who had looked for far-reaching social changes as the result of the agitation, and who now sat, as Carlyle puts it, at a Barmecide feast, conceived a deep distrust of their would-be representatives in Parliament. This was the origin of the Chartist movement, and though the aims of the Chartists were largely embraced in the Radical programme, there was no solidarity between the two parties. The Chartist agitation was a movement of the working classes themselves, carried on in a lower social stratum than that to which the Philosophical Radicals appealed. The Utilitarians mostly belonged themselves to the middle class—even to the prosperous ranks of that class—and, philosophers as they were, were firmly convinced of the superior wisdom and virtue of their own class. This is almost naïvely expressed by James Mill in his 'Essay on Government,' in which he deduces "from the principles of human nature" that the lower orders hold up the middle class as a model to be imitated by their children, and "account it an honour" to adopt its opinion. Consequently, however far the franchise were extended, it is this class—which has produced the most distinguished ornaments of art, science, and even of legislation—which will ultimately decide upon political questions. "The great majority of the people," he concludes, "never cease to be guided by that rank." Twenty years later J. S. Mill, in an article[1] deploring the failure of the Radicals to secure the sympathy of the working classes, still emphatically maintains that the motto of every Radical should be government for the working classes by means of the middle classes. The ideal of such govern-

[1] 'Westminster Review,' April 1839.

ment would of course, in Mill's conception, be the redress of practical grievances; but unfortunately the working classes and their Radical pedagogues were not agreed upon the remedies for the social and industrial ills they complained of. "They could not," says Mr Leslie Stephen, "see a philanthropy which was hidden behind Malthus and Ricardo, and which proposed to improve their position by removing privileges, indeed, but not by diminishing competition." The Utilitarians, therefore, disappeared from public life as a distinct party, although their economic doctrine survived in Cobden and the Manchester school, and was successfully applied by them to commercial legislation. But the Free-trade movement was essentially a manufacturers' agitation, and, apart from political economy, and a hatred of the aristocratic or land-owning class, Cobden and his friends had little in common with the Philosophical Radicals who preceded them.

The year 1840 may be said to mark the end of Utilitarian Radicalism, as preached by its founders with logical consistency and with an intellectual intolerance born of implicit confidence in the all-sufficiency of their own social scheme. By that time J. S. Mill, opening his mind to various contemporay influences, had freely acknowledged the defects and one-sidedness of his inherited creed in the notable articles on "Bentham" and "Coleridge" which appeared in 'The London and Westminster Review' for 1838 and 1840 respectively. So early as 1829, he says in his 'Autobiography,' he found the fabric of his old opinions giving way, and, as he never allowed it to fall to pieces, he was "incessantly occupied in weaving it anew." Macaulay's attack on the 'Essay on Government' convinced him that his father's premises were "too narrow, and included but a small number of the general truths on which, in politics, the important consequences depend." Through the writings of Coleridge, and through the Coleridgians with whom he was in personal intercourse, through Carlyle also and others, he had become acquainted with the modern philosophy of history, and accepted the position that "all questions of political institutions are relative, not absolute, and that different stages of human progress not only *will* have, but *ought* to have, different institutions." About this time, also, he came strongly under the influence of the St Simonian school, and accepted from them the theory of an alternation in the history of human progress between "organic" and "critical" periods. "Their criticisms on the common doctrines of Liberalism seemed to me full of important truth; and it was partly by their writings that my eyes were opened to the very limited and temporary value of the old political economy." They gave him, in other words, his first impulse in a socialistic direction. A Utilitarian who can talk in this way of "the common doctrines of Liberalism," who has "ceased to consider representative democracy as an absolute principle," and who looks even upon political economy as of "limited and temporary value," has already left the landmarks of his youth far behind him; and a series of articles on "The Spirit of the Age," written by Mill in 1831, caused Carlyle, when he read them at Craigenputtock, to say to himself, "Here is a new Mystic," and led him, on coming up to London the same autumn, to make inquiry for the author. But so long as his father lived Mill felt himself under restraint. He felt it the part both of prudence and piety to conceal, wherever practicable, how far he had wandered from the paternal creed. "My father," he says, "was not one with whom calm and full explanations on fundamental points of doctrine could be expected, at least with one whom he might consider as in some sort a deserter from his standard." As a dutiful son, therefore, John Mill made the most of their general agreement on the political questions of the day. But after his father's death in 1836 he proceeded to liberate his soul in the two striking articles already referred to. These articles are truly remarkable for the insight and sympathy they display. It may almost be said that they already embody the most important criticisms that have been made upon Benthamism by succeeding thinkers, while they contain acknowledgments of the truths contended for by Bentham's opponents which could hardly be better stated by these opponents themselves.

In short, if Mill, at the time when this expansion of his ideas first began, had been an independent and solitary thinker, instead of being, as he was, one of a band of active propagandists, and pledged by all that he held most sacred to carry on the leadership of the school, one is tempted to think that the course of English philosophy in the nineteenth century might have been widely different. If he had been free from the jealous supervision of his father and the stricter members of the sect, and had given free scope to the train of reflection on which he had now entered, the revision of his philosophical principles might have been so thorough that he would have realised that "higher unity" of Bentham and Coleridge to which he pointed as the complete philosophy. But, as it was, his method of incessantly weaving the new into the fabric of the old, and thus maintaining a semblance of continuity and consistency, made such a thorough revision impossible. The old groundwork remained, and the new elements appeared as incongruous patches. Instead of presenting a new synthesis, Mill introduces modifications and additions without perceiving their total inconsistency with principles which he nevertheless refuses to abandon; and hence the bankruptcy of Associationism and the old Utilitarianism was not declared till nearly half a century later. This may be explained to a large extent by the fact that the changes which his social theories underwent never led him to reconsider the atomistic doctrine of Sensationalism and Associationism which he had accepted from his father as a theory of knowledge. It was late in life—in connection with the Hamiltonian controversy—that he returned to deal more systematically with these matters; and the polemical nature of the occasion precluded any reconsideration of fundamentals. He was the English champion of one set of views, as Hamilton was of the other; and, although in the course of the discussion his candour led him to make important admissions, it was without any consciousness of their combined effect upon the structure of his philosophic edifice. His father's systematic training had, in fact, done its work more thoroughly than he was aware of; and accordingly his subsequent works show him closer to his father's and Bentham's point of view than might have been expected from his critical attitude in the thirties. Those articles, written while he was still in close intercourse with Carlyle, Maurice, Sterling, and others, mark the point of his closest approximation to other ways of thinking: at bottom, however, they implied no breaking away from his moorings, but only (as he himself says) an attempt "to give a wider basis and a more free and genial character to Radical speculations." Later, he tells us that, except as regards his gradual advance in the direction of Socialism, he "completely turned back from what there had been of excess in his reaction against Benthamism."

Mill says of his father that "as Brutus was the last of the Romans, so was he the last of the eighteenth century; he continued its thought and sentiment into the nineteenth (though not unmodified nor unimproved), partaking neither in the good nor in the bad influences of the reaction against the eighteenth century, which was the great characteristic of the first half of the nineteenth." Similarly, in his account of the widening of his own mental horizon, he treats Benthamism throughout as synonymous with eighteenth-century thought. "The French *philosophes* of the eighteenth century" were, he says, the example which he and his youthful companions sought to emulate in the salad days of 1824. This affiliation is beyond dispute. James Mill reproduces the psychological metaphysics of Hume, while Bentham repeats the selfish and hedonistic ethics of Helvetius. Without any disparagement of that much maligned but indispensable and meritorious period, it will be admitted that the eighteenth century represents in philosophy the principle of analysis; that its analysis of man and society is conducted in an abstract fashion without reference to the teaching of history; and that the philosophers are throughout individualists, alike in their presuppositions and in their resulting dogmatic teaching—individualists often of so pronounced a type as to be more accurately described as Atomists or Anarchists. Mill mentions "the Hartleian metaphysics" as the philosophical groundwork of the Utilitarian creed. But Hartley's doctrine is, in the main, simply that of the association of ideas done into terms of physiology; the seminal mind of the eighteenth century, in this as in so much else, is David Hume. James Mill's 'Analysis,' dropping Hartley's obsolete physiology, offers us sensations *plus* associations as a complete explanation of the mind and its operations, reproducing with almost startling exactitude Hume's fundamental positions in the 'Treatise.' The work is, indeed, as Höffding says, the most systematic attempt ever made to explain all mental phenomena by the association of ideas—all associations, moreover, being reduced to contiguity. Our experience, according to Mill's analysis, consists of sensations and ideas which are copies of sensations; both may be spoken of as feelings, a term which includes every phenomenon of mind. Consciousness is a succession of such sensations and ideas, which are conceived, both by Hume and by Mill, as separable atoms. There is no *logical* connection between ideas; but, when two occur together, or in close succession, an association tends to establish itself between them, so that the one afterwards suggests the other.

The ideas, in Mill as in Hume, appear to be not only separable atoms but to be self-subsistent entities, which somehow cohere, and when aggregated into a cluster constitute the mind. J. S. Mill remarks that his father's theory of Predication (as "simply a contrivance for marking this order of ideas") omits all reference to belief. Now to believe is actively to judge or to make some assertion about reality; but mental activity and reality are conceptions for which Mill, like Hume, has no place. Belief can be no more than lively suggestion of one idea by another in the course of their rapid self-initiated transit. In other words, Mill omits the active function of thought altogether, and leaves us with a dance of passively apprehended images, which weave their mazes till they form in time a "lively idea" of a mind or apprehending self, and of a real world which that self apprehends. Like Hume, he has, in the course of his analysis, got rid both of objective reality and of the mind itself; the two, indeed, stand or fall together. But it is hard, as Mr Stephen says, in unconscious reminiscence of Reid, "to conceive of mere loose 'ideas' going about in the universe at large and sticking accidentally to others. After all, the human being is in a true sense also an organised whole, and his constitution must be taken into account in discussing the laws of 'ideation.'" When J. S. Mill's candour long afterwards impelled him to his famous admission that the mind is more than a series of feelings, it was felt instinctively that he had surrendered the key of the position. The question of Judgment or Belief is, indeed, as he partly saw in his comments on his father's theory, the crucial question for such a philosophy.

As already indicated, James Mill would fain reduce all association (and therefore all relation) to the principle of contiguity or accidental collocation. Even resemblance, which Hume had retained as one of the fundamental laws of association, makes Mill uncomfortable, because it is a relation which seems to depend on the intrinsic nature of the ideas themselves. He suggests that resemblance is, after all, really a particular case of the law of frequency. "I believe it will be found that we are accustomed to see like things together. When we see a tree, we generally see more trees than one; a sheep, more sheep than one; a man, more men than one." His loyal son and editor, in disavowing this extraordinary suggestion, is driven to remark that we are also much accustomed to see like things separate and to see unlike things together. Clearly, as Mr Stephen wittily puts it, sheep are not seen to be like because they often compose a flock, but are considered a flock because they are seen to be like. James Mill himself, it is fair to say, does not insist on this reduction, but the attempt is significant, for it helps to explain (or at least falls into line with) what J. S. Mill tells us was his father's "fundamental doctrine" in psychology—"the formation of all human character by circumstances through the universal Principle of Association, and the consequent unlimited possibility of improving the moral and intellectual condition of mankind by education." If the individuals with which we start have no character or nature of their own, and if there are no connections between them discoverable by reason, but only associations due to chance coincidences, then undoubtedly (to vary Hume's famous dictum) anything may be made out of anything. James Mill, in his article on "Education," does, as a matter of fact, go nearly the whole way with the doctrine of Helvetius that all the differences between men are due to education, including under that word "all the circumstances that act during the first months, perhaps the first moments, of existence." This is substantially the doctrine of the school from first to last. J. S. Mill remarks on Bentham's complete neglect of national character as a factor in moulding and explaining the social arrangements of a people. "Bentham's idea of the world," he says, "is that of a collection of persons pursuing each his separate interest or pleasure, the prevention of whom from jostling one another more than is unavoidable may be attempted by hopes and fears derived from three sources—the law, religion, and public opinion." That is to say, the material of the legislator consists of abstract or colourless units — the "average man" actuated by the universal motive. By a sufficiently skilful manipulation of hopes and fears, and the consequent weaving of proper associations, any result may be attained. In this spirit, as Mr Stephen points out, Bentham professed himself as ready to legislate for Hindostan as for his own parish, and he was eager to make codes not only for England, Spain, and Russia, but for Morocco. And J. S. Mill himself, in spite of his censure of Bentham, speaks towards the close of his life of "the irresistible proofs that by far the greater part of the marked distinction of human character, *whether between individuals, races, or sexes,* are such as not only might but naturally would be produced by differences in circumstances."[1]

Indissoluble or inseparable association comes in, finally, to explain, as J. S. Mill says, "all the mental incompatibilities, the impossibilities of thought, of which so much is made by a certain class of metaphysician." After explaining in this way the supposed necessity of mathematical axioms, J. S. Mill proposed to treat the principle of contradiction itself as just "one of our first and most familiar generalisations from experience." In other words, we have found as a fact that "belief and disbelief are two different mental states excluding each other," just as "we also find that light and darkness, sound and silence, any positive phenomenon whatever and its negative, are distinct phenomena, pointedly contrasted, and the one always absent where the other is present." The law is, therefore, "a generalisation from all these facts." It is, in short, an association arising out of frequently repeated collocations of facts, and to that extent itself a mere matter of fact, something that we find to be so, but which embodies no insight of reason, no necessity of thought. The antipathy to logical or rational necessity could go no farther than this attempt to make the law of contradiction itself an accident of experience. In the same way, even resemblance as a perceived relation sticks in James

[1] In fairness it ought to be added that this doctrine of the fluidity of all distinctions, because due to external circumstances, and the consequent indefinite modifiability of character, was the source of some of the best features of the Utilitarians as well as of their limitations. It explains their enthusiastic belief in education as an instrument of social progress, and their optimistic view of the unlimited possibilities of future advance.

Mill's throat. To feel two things to be alike, he argues, is the same thing as to have the two feelings. Separate units, accidentally combined, thus constitute, on the conjoint testimony of father and son, absolutely the whole stock-in-trade of the empirical philosophy.

Bentham's ethics are the counterpart of this psychological atomism. Just as the mind or self is pulverised into separate and accidentally associated states, so each man, considered ethically, is a purely self-regarding creature, connected by no natural bonds of cohesion with his fellows, but actuated solely by the desire to attain selfish pleasure or escape selfish pain. Virtue being, nevertheless, defined as the promotion of the greatest happiness of the greatest number, the problem of ethics becomes, in Carlyle's phrase, "Given a world of knaves, to educe an Honesty from their united action," or, as Mr Stephen puts it, to make universal cohesion out of universal repulsion. This is achieved by means of "sanctions," that is, pains and pleasures annexed to actions, which make it a man's private interest to promote the public good. Bentham is entirely occupied with this jurisprudential question of arranging "tutelary motives," so that self-interest shall lead in the direction of benevolence. Dealing only with the overt act, and disregarding, as from the legal point of view he must, the motives which led to it, it is apparently indifferent to him whether a course of action be the outcome of selfish calculation or disinterested benevolence; and, as J. S. Mill confesses, the training of the affections and the will in the latter direction is a blank in his system. "Man is never recognised by him," says Mill, "as a being capable of pursuing spiritual perfection as an end, of desiring for its own sake the conformity of his own character to his standard of excellence, without hope of good or fear of evil from other source than his own inward consciousness." Such a view, it is hardly necessary to add, amounts to a complete neglect of what constitutes virtuous action as such, and consequently to the disappearance of ethics as in any way distinguished from law.

The actual emergence of disinterestedly benevolent sentiments, and the logical justification of universal benevolence on a basis of universal selfishness, become, therefore, the special problems of the Utilitarian school. To Bentham himself the necessity of reconciling Benevolence and Prudence, and so justifying his own ethical principle, seems hardly to have presented itself as a difficulty. This was due, no doubt, partly to his purely external view of obligation, partly to a vague belief in the actual harmony of individual and social interests, properly understood—an idea which he found prominently set forth in Helvetius, and which, in the economic sphere, pervades the work of Adam Smith. The more analytic mind of James Mill perceived the necessity of some kind of logical justification, and his answer is the theory of "mental chemistry" or indissoluble association, by which actions, originally performed from motives of self-interest, may come to be performed for their own sake, as the miser comes to love gold without any thought of converting it to use. In his son's 'Utilitarianism' the question is prominent. As might have been expected from his criticism of Bentham, J. S. Mill lays great stress on the necessity of a disinterested love of virtue as a mark of the truly virtuous man. He will not surrender the fundamental tenet of the school that "actions and dispositions are only virtuous because they promote another end than virtue," but he not only recognises as a psychological fact the possibility that virtue may become to the individual a good in itself; he holds that "the mind is not in a right state, not in a state conformable to Utility, not in the state most conducive to the general happiness unless it does love virtue in this manner." We have thus a parallel to the general paradox of hedonism that pleasure is only gained when it is not directly pursued. The solution is sought by Mill very much on his father's lines by bringing association into play. He lays stress also upon the social feelings of mankind as affording a natural basis of sentiment for Utilitarian morality. "The social state," he says, "is at once so natural, so necessary, and so habitual to man, that except in some unusual circumstances, or by an effort of voluntary abstraction, he never conceives himself otherwise than as member of a body." Mill is thus, as usual, on the point of discarding the picture of the abstract individual which gives rise to the whole difficulty. But, as his manner uniformly is, he refuses to take the final step which his successive admissions have necessitated; and Nemesis overtakes him a few pages farther on, when he endeavours to pass from "egoistic" to "universalistic hedonism" by the notorious "fallacy of composition" so often commented on. "Each person's happiness is a good to that person, and the general happiness, therefore, a good to the aggregate of all persons." The 'Utilitarianism,' accordingly, like all Mill's works, only marks a stage in the dissolution of the school, or if to be preferred, in the transcendence by the school of its original opinions. It was at least convincing as to the impossibility of justifying the Utilitarian end on the basis of egoistic hedonism. The closest reasoner of the school—if, indeed, so broad and cautious a thinker as the late Professor Sidgwick may be ranked among the adherents of any school—proceeded, therefore, to take the final step of dissociating the two. By placing benevolence alongside of prudence, and accepting it as "the most certain and comprehensive of intuitions," he must be held, in spite of certain characteristic reserves, to abandon definitively the ethical atomism of the original doctrine.

To what extent can such a theory as that of Bentham and the Philosophical Radicals explain the structure and functions of society? Mr Leslie Stephen hardly improves upon the answer which J. S. Mill gave in 1838:—

"It can teach the means of organising and regulating the merely *business* part of the social arrangements. . . . It will enable a society which has attained a certain state of spiritual development, and the maintenance of which in that state is otherwise provided for, to prescribe the rules by which it may protect its material interests. It will do nothing (except sometimes as an instrument in the hands of a higher doctrine) for the spiritual interests of society, nor does it suffice of itself even for the material interests. That which alone causes any material interests to exist, which alone enables any body of human beings to exist as a society, is national character. A philosophy of laws and institutions not founded on a philosophy of national character is an absurdity."

Bentham would probably have retorted that to talk in this strain of national character is to lapse into "mysticism" and "vague generalities"; for does not his legitimate disciple, Nassau Senior, tell us that "a State is nothing more than the aggregate of individual men who inhabit a certain country"? Nevertheless Mill in this passage lays his finger upon the point where the Benthamite theory of society breaks down. Given a society and a government of some sort, utility, in the hands of the reforming critic, may furnish an important practical test of any of its particular institutions and arrangements.

But you cannot apply such a test to the existence of the social organism itself. It was, no doubt, as Mr Stephen suggests, a dim perception of this truth that prompted the theory of the Social Contract, which it is difficult to believe was ever regarded by its authors as embodying a historical fact. We may perhaps understand them to mean by it that the existence of society is, as Kant might have said, the result of "an intelligible act," or, to put it more simply, that it is the necessary presupposition of all further thought on these subjects. The modern view of the relation of the individual to society has obviated the necessity of having recourse to such a fiction. Through the influence of Hegel and of Comte, and partly through the reaction of biological conceptions upon philosophy and general thinking, the nineteenth century has seen the definitive abandonment of the individualistic or atomistic view of that relation. To Mr Leslie Stephen himself belongs the credit of having, in his 'Science of Ethics,' worked out with much impressiveness, from a Utilitarian basis, the conception of the organic nature of society, and the impossibility, therefore, of treating the moral individual apart from the society whose product he is, or apart from the race whose history he inherits in the instincts and habits which make him human. With equal emphasis, from another point of view, T. H. Green (who holds, against hedonistic theories of every shade, that the moral end must be formulated in terms of self-realisation) insists that the self to be realised is social, and that the moral ideal is therefore the idea of "a common good." This is "an ultimate fact of human history—a fact without which there would not be such a history." Instead of being the unit from which we must start, the individual, it has been said, is a late product of evolution; and it is only, therefore, within certain spheres and with certain limitations that we can, by a convenient abstraction, discuss his conduct and qualities apart from the "social tissue" in which he is, as it were, embedded, or out of which, rather, he is woven. If this be so, it is only with such qualifications that we can speak of an opposition between self-regarding and social qualities; and we are spared the impossible task of explaining how one of these abstractions produces the other—how pure selfishness gives rise to pure benevolence. We do not even require to justify Benevolence at the bar of Prudence. The cohesion of the race is secured by organic instincts which reach deep down beneath any such antithesis.

"How wonderful it all is! Built not by saints and angels, but by the work of men's hands; cemented with men's honest blood and with a world of tears; welded by the best brains of centuries past; not without the taint and reproach incidental to all human work, but constructed on the whole with pure and splendid purpose; human, and not yet wholly human, for the most heedless and the most cynical must see the finger of the Divine."

These fine words, spoken by Lord Rosebery of the narrower case of the British Empire, may still more fitly be applied to the fabric of human civilisation itself, reared upon a meagre basis of animal needs and impulses by the nameless generations of the past. To this vast process of unconscious reason the Utilitarians were strangely blind. Like most reformers, they saw in the past only the incorporated spirit of evil, the fountain of unnumbered abuses. Every abuse they attacked appeared to them due to some "sinister interest," which had called it into being originally, and now opposed its removal. A little historical sense might have taught them that in many cases, perhaps in most, what had *become* an abuse had begun by serving a useful purpose, while its persistence after its usefulness had ceased was often due more to the forces of inertia, and even to a mistaken but intelligible sense of loyalty, than to any definitely sinister interest on the part of individuals or classes. It might even have occurred to them that the long or extensive prevalence of any opinion is itself a presumption that it is not altogether a fallacy. But Bentham and his followers contemptuously dismissed, under the sweeping phrase of "vague generalities," whatever their foot-rule of provable utility did not enable them to measure. "He did not heed," says J. S. Mill in his critical essay, "or rather, the nature of his mind prevented it from occurring to him, that these generalities contained the whole unanalysed experience of the human race."

Mill signalises his father's unbounded confidence in the influence of reason over the minds of mankind, and in so doing he touches both the strength and the weakness of the Utilitarian position. Meagrely enough supported by the records of its constructive application in political and social history, this confidence in the power of conscious reflection is none the less a noble and a necessary faith in the ultimate power of clear intelligence. In a sense, this faith can only be surrendered if we capitulate to the powers of irrationality and chaos. It is the claim of the free human spirit eternally to criticise its own procedure and all the institutions in which it has embodied itself. Only by this unceasing criticism can the fabric of human institutions be kept sweet and clean, and be continuously adapted, with some measure of success, to new times and new needs. And in the hands of reformers, utility, as the most practical test of rationality, may be applied with potent and beneficent effect to laws and customs which, useful in their day, have survived their usefulness and become a useless anachronism, a harmful restriction, or a crying injustice. There is no doubt that, in this sense, Utilitarianism rendered services of the most important kind to the true interests of mankind. T. H. Green does not hesitate to call it the moral theory which has been of most public service in modern Europe. "Whatever the errors arising from its hedonistic psychology, no other theory has been available, for the social and political reformer, containing so much truth with such ready applicability. No other has offered so commanding a point of view from which to criticise the precepts and institutions presented as authoritative." To this extent, the Utilitarians undoubtedly represent the principle of modern thought and the freedom of the human mind. In their assaults upon indefensible privileges, unreasoned prejudices, and blind appeals to tradition, the truth has been with them, and they have prevailed. Law has been simplified, commercial activity has been freed from its fetters, privileges have been swept away, and the political machine reconstructed in accordance with Radical ideals. And yet the Radical Utopia has not been realised; the state of public opinion on fundamental points of social and national policy is as far removed as can well be conceived from that contemplated by Bentham and his followers. The Utilitarians had, in a striking degree, the defects of their qualities. The reason they invoked with so much confidence was abstract and unhistorical, and, as a consequence, their insight failed them when they had to deal in any way with the unseen foundations of society or the hidden springs of national life. In these cases their criticisms have recoiled, with fatal effect, upon themselves. Philosophical Radicalism was, in short, essentially a negative and critical movement, and its strength departed from it just in proportion as its critical attack was successful. When effect was given to its legitimate criticisms, whatever hold it had upon popular support was lost, for it had no constructive suggestions to offer in the work of social organisation. Its impotence in this respect arose, as has been seen, from the inadequacy of its philosophic basis.

MR KIDD ON WESTERN CIVILISATION.[1]

IN 'Social Evolution' Mr Kidd stated some wholesome truths in a fresh and vigorous manner, which was none the less effective because the statement was often paradoxical in form, and depended sometimes on forced antithesis. Clothed in the all-conquering phraseology of biological evolution, his views on the nature and factors of social progress attracted an amount of public attention which was fully justified, on the whole, by the knowledge of social phenomena and the power of comprehensive generalisation which the volume displayed. It had an adventitious popularity in certain circles because, by the connection it asserted between religion and the very doctrine of natural selection on which modern biology rests, it seemed to turn the tables upon the anti-religious dogmatism which masquerades as science. The "ultra-rational sanctions" of morality and social progress on which the book insisted, proved a palatable phrase to the defenders of supernatural dogma. Provoking undue heat and animosity in those of the opposite camp, the phrase led them, perhaps, to do less than justice to what there was of solid truth in Mr Kidd's interpretations of history and of the present

[1] The following discussion of Mr Kidd's historical generalisations appeared in 'The Contemporary Review,' June 1902.

trend of social movement. The book thus stimulated discussion in many quarters; and as it partook itself of the nature of a *brochure* or manifesto, it naturally foreshadowed an attempt on the part of the author to work out a system of social philosophy on the basis of the ideas therein enunciated. This task Mr Kidd has now essayed in his 'Principles of Western Civilisation,' which purports to be only "the first volume of a system of evolutionary philosophy," and thus inevitably challenges comparison with Mr Spencer's undertaking. Unfortunately, it cannot be said that in the eight years' interval Mr Kidd's thought has gained in lucidity or convincingness. In applying the ideas of his previous book, he has invented a cumbrous and (as it seems to me) singularly unfortunate terminology, in which he disguises them almost beyond recognition, and which is repeated on page after page almost as if he were reciting the words of an inspired creed, and were fearful of deviating in the smallest particular from the exact words of the formula. Mr Kidd is, moreover, himself so impressed with the importance of his message, and by accumulating his adjectives labours so insistently to produce the same impression upon his readers, that in the parts of the volume dealing with his philosophical generalisations, the style becomes turgid and inflated, sometimes to the verge of meaninglessness, and only recovers sanity when it touches earth, so to speak, in the later chapters dealing with historical facts and present-day social conditions.

What, then, are the ideas, common to the two books, in which Mr Kidd believes that he has found the key to the history of mankind? The main theses of 'Social Evolution' were (1) that human society, like animal life everywhere, progresses only through the stress of competition—the ceaseless rivalry of race with race, of individual with individual—in virtue of which, according to the operation of natural selection, the unfit are weeded out, and only the fittest maintain themselves and survive to propagate their kind; (2) that this upward movement is being carried on at the expense of the individual, and of the present generation as a whole, in the interest of the efficiency of the stock and of the generations that are to follow, and is thus flatly at variance with the enlightened self-interest of the individuals of whom, at any given moment, the social organism consists. Self-interest would teach them to conserve their own material interests by easing the stress of competition in every possible way,—notably, for example, by artificially restricting the growth of population and the consequent pressure upon the means of subsistence. To these promptings of self-interest Mr Kidd restricts the term "reason," which he accordingly describes as "the most profoundly individualistic, anti-social, and anti-evolutionary of all human qualities." "Reason has nothing to do with any existence but the present, which it insists it is our duty to ourselves to make the most of." (3) It follows immediately from this definition of terms that there is no rational sanction for progress—that in submitting to the conditions of the social and evolutionary process, man is swayed entirely by the "ultra-rational" sanctions which religion in its various forms, and Christianity pre-eminently, supplies. Religion, therefore, instead of being a survival from primitive savagery, to be gradually merged in rational insight, appears as the eternal and necessary counterpart or complement of reason, the cohesive force in society which antagonises the disintegrative tendencies of the individual reason and ensures the possibility of progress. Thus, "we understand how an ultra-rational sanction for the sacrifice of the interests of the individuals to those of the social organism has been a feature common to all religions; we see also why the conception of sacrifice has occupied such a central place in nearly all beliefs, and why the tendency of religion has been to surround this principle with the most impressive and stupendous of sanctions."

Applying this scheme to the facts of Western Civilisation, Mr Kidd finds the characteristic feature of that civilisation to be the altruism with which it was so powerfully inoculated at the Christian era, and the "development of a stupendous system of other-worldliness," in which reason, as a faculty of independent judgment, came near to extinction, and "the super-rational sanction for conduct attained a strength and universality unknown in the Roman and Greek civilisations." Proceeding to contrast modern with ancient civilisation, he points out that in the latter the tribe or state was the unit, and the struggle for existence operated mainly between these groups: the survival of a group or society depended, therefore, on its efficiency as a fighting organisation. In modern societies this external competition of state with state no doubt continues to operate; but a marked and growing feature of modern societies is the relative independence possessed by the individual,—an independence characteristic of an industrial as distinguished from a military organisation. Mr Kidd, therefore, in dealing with them concentrates his attention on what has been called intra-group competition—*i.e.*, competition for economic goods between individuals of the same society. Here his position is peculiar and worthy of note. As might be expected from the quasi-religious sanction with which he invests the struggle for existence, as the divinely appointed instrument of progress, he sees in this internal rivalry, which keeps all the powers of individuals at their utmost tension, the most precious instrument of social efficiency and the ultimate cause of progress. "So far from our civilisation tending to produce an interruption of, or an exception to, the cosmic process which has been in progress from the beginning of life, its distinctive and characteristic feature must be found in the exceptional degree to which it has furthered it." The direction of advance among the modern nations has been, he points out, towards "the political and social enfranchisement of the masses," so that "the fact of our time, which overshadows all others, is the arrival of Democracy." But democracy means essentially "participation in the rivalry of existence on equal terms." The democratic ideal is "a condition of society in which the whole mass of excluded people will be at last brought into the rivalry of existence on a footing of equality of opportunity." Thus "the significance of the entire order of social change in progress among the Western peoples consists, in short, in the single fact that this cosmic process tends thereby to acquire amongst us the fullest, highest, and completest expression it has ever reached in the history of the race." Notwithstanding this laudation of unlimited competition, it presently appears, however, that this divinely appointed instrument cannot be trusted to work alone, and religion is invoked on the opposite side as a controlling and modifying force. It is significant of the looseness with which the term religion is used that, whereas it appeared, to begin with, as the consecration of the struggle, Mr Kidd now proceeds to argue, in effect, that the process of Western Civilisation is the story of the gradual success of Christian ideals in tempering the ruthless action of natural selection. For presumably "the power-holding classes" obtained their position through the operation of natural selection, by reason of their greater social efficiency. There is nothing in that cosmic principle which should induce them to part with one jot or tittle of the power and privilege they have acquired. The true moral of the situation is drawn by Nietzsche, when he urges them to improve their advantage to the utmost, and to cultivate the "Uebermensch" on the labours of a subject population. Yet, as Mr Kidd tells us, the course of Civilisation has been marked by the breaking down of privileges one after another; and the tendency of recent legislation in particular has been "to strengthen and equip at the general expense the lower and weaker against the higher and wealthier classes of the community." This is traced by Mr Kidd, with much truth, to "the immense fund of altruistic feeling with which our Western Societies have been equipped," or, in simpler language, to the feeling of human brotherhood which first found full expression in the teaching of Christ. The presence of this element he finds to be the characteristic feature of Western Civilisation, and one that opens out possibilities of progress which were closed to states of the antique pattern.

These, then, are the ideas upon which Mr Kidd draws in his present volume. He has not, so far as I can see, added in any way to the stock; but those on which he here concentrates attention reappear under quasi-philosophical titles which are intended to magnify their importance, but which in reality, I cannot but think, tend to obscure their real meaning.

He begins as before by connecting his work with the theory of evolution, calling attention to the transformation which the doctrine of evolution by natural selection has effected in all departments of knowledge, and especially in those which deal with man in society. As we have seen, he calls his work expressly "a system of evolutionary philosophy," and professes in it to draw the ultimate consequences, hitherto unperceived, of the scientific theory when applied to social phenomena. These consequences, he contends almost on every page of his book, are so "momentous," so "extraordinary," so "vast," so "remarkable," so "gigantic," "enormous," and "stupendous," that he appears to labour under a sense of almost prophetic importance in being the first to enunciate them. His first thesis is that the evolutionary process works everywhere in the interests of the future,—that is to say, in the interests of the species or type, not in the interest of "existing individuals considered either separately as individuals or collectively as members of political society." The recognition of this fact involves, he maintains, "a shifting of the centre of significance in the evolutionary hypothesis." Social philosophy has been governed hitherto by the idea of "the ascendancy of the interest of the present"; but in the evolutionary process truly interpreted the evolutionary centre of the process is seen to be in the future, and its meaning therefore can never be grasped by "any theory of utilitarian politics in the State." This is what he intends by the ever-repeated phrase that the meaning of the process is "projected beyond the limits of merely political consciousness." And under the title of "The Principle of Projected Efficiency"—a title surely singularly unfortunate and ill-adapted to express the author's meaning—this idea becomes the keynote of the book. It is next identified with the principle of Western—*i.e.*, modern or Christian—as contrasted with ancient, civilisation; and thus the social evolution of mankind falls into two great periods, ancient or pre-Christian civilisation, based entirely, according to Mr Kidd, on the ascendancy of the present, and Western or Christian civilisation, based on the ascendancy of the future. Political and social writers before Mr Kidd have not recognised the significance of this remarkable antithesis, and consequently their speculations continually tend to revert to an antique standard. This declension of thought from the governing principle of our civilisation is also to be noted in the practical sphere in many current ideas and tendencies. But in proportion as a society or nation refuses, for considerations of immediate interest or personal ease, to take upon itself the burden of the world-process, to that extent it falls behind in the selective struggle for the inheritance of the earth. This is the ultimate principle of division between dead or dying nations and those to which the future belongs. The English-speaking peoples (with the possible addition of the Germans) represent in this respect most truly the underlying principle of Western civilisation.

Such is a brief and, I think, a fair outline of Mr Kidd's argument. What meaning and value can we attach to it as a theory of human history and progress? In what sense is it true, in the first place, that evolution works for the future and not for the present? And, secondly, what connection is there between this fact, if it be a fact, and the principles of the Christian religion?

In regard to the first point, no one would think of denying—it is indeed a commonplace—that natural selection works towards the improvement (or, to be quite strict, towards the modification) of the species or type, and that the individual or the present generation may be regarded, in any given case, as simply a link between the past and the future—a material, as it were, in which the developing principle is working out ends which do not yet appear. It is surely quite without foundation to suppose, as Mr Kidd intimates, that Darwin and the earlier Darwinians were blind to this fact: it is the very essence of their doctrine. Of course Darwin constantly describes natural selection as taking advantage of variations which are beneficial *to the creature itself.* But how otherwise could he express the fact? It is because the variation is beneficial to the individual that it is preserved and accumulated for future generations. If it were not beneficial to the individual in the first instance, natural selection would have no material to work upon. It does not follow from this statement of plain fact that Darwin or any other evolutionist regarded the present individual or the present generation as a *terminus ad quem:* the procession of the generations is the presupposition of all evolutional thought. And, in truth, Mr Kidd's exclusive insistence on the aspect of futurity involves a much more serious risk of distorting the true significance of the theory. Pressing into his service the striking essay in which Weismann treats the death of the individual as a device in the interest of the species—to prevent stagnation and provide for variation, adaptation, and progress—and referring to such facts as the growing burden of parenthood which accompanies growing complexity of structure in the individual, Mr Kidd discerns "a principle of inherent necessity in the evolutionary process, compelling ever towards the sacrifice on a vast scale of the present and the individual in the interests of the future and the universal." "It is the burden of the generations to come which controls the whole process." The meaning of the drama of life "remains continually projected beyond the content of the present." "The interests of the individual in those adjustments 'profitable to itself' . . . have actually no place except in so far as they are included in, and have contributed to this larger end in the future." "The winning qualities in the evolutionary process must of necessity be those qualities by which the interests of the existing individuals have been most effectively subordinated to those of the generations yet to be born." And applying the same idea to different types of social order, he says, "The interests of all the visible world around us can have no place except in so far as they are included in the larger interests of a future to which they are entirely subordinated."

Now if it is an abstraction to speak of the individual or the present as if it were an ultimate and independent and self-explaining goal, it is equally an abstraction to treat it in this way as merely the *matrix* of that which is to be. The consequences of such a mode of presentation are instructively exemplified in Mr Kidd's own theory. For we are embarked, in that case, upon what philosophers call the infinite progress. The present generations are sacrificed (if we are to speak of sacrifice) to the interests of those that are to follow, but *they* cannot be said, any more than their predecessors, to reap the fruit of those sacrifices. They are the victims of the same stress and strain in the interest of the hungry generations to come, whose feet are at the door, but who will likewise be sent empty away from the Barmecide feast of existence. Once embarked upon this process, there is no possibility of stopping anywhere; and when the idea is realised, it reduces the cosmic process to a manifest futility, making it the pursuit of a goal which is nowhere reached, and to which in strictness, owing to the conditions of the case, we never make any nearer approach. But the illusion results from the abstraction to which we originally committed ourselves. The present, it must be repeated, is not a *terminus ad quem*; but it is, at any given point, the term in which existence is summed, the heir of the past as well as the womb of the future. Past and future are alike projections from its reality. It is the heir in possession. It lives its own life and realises its own satisfaction. And it may not be amiss to remark that the common way of speaking of the generations of the past as sacrificed to produce the present stage of evolutionary progress is largely misleading. We import thereby a mistaken pathos into the situation. Every generation realises all the satisfaction of which its nature and its life-conditions render it capable. If in many respects the life of a past generation appears poor and mean, compared with the opportunities and capacities of which we are conscious, we do well to remember that our life-conditions would have appeared to the ancestors we compassionate vastly more "stale, flat, and unprofitable" than theirs appear to us. Nor must we forget in such an estimate those "joys in widest commonalty spread"—spread as wide, indeed, as the bounds of animal life itself—the joys of love and battle and the more passive pleasures of elemental being.

> "Is it so small a thing
> To have enjoyed the sun,
> To have lived light in the spring,
> To have loved, to have thought, to have done,
> To have advanced true friends, and beat down baffling foes?"

It is impossible, therefore, to separate the present and the future as Mr Kidd does. His argument (though I do not think he intends this) sometimes conveys the impression that the efficiency of a stock in the future is purchased at the price of its efficiency in the present. This is, of course, in the teeth both of science and of logic. It is only through its efficiency in the present that any community or race can vindicate itself before the bar of natural selection and win the promise of the future. Natural selection, that is to say, works equally for the present and the future, according as we look at it, but always primarily for the present, and for the future only so far as its conditions are identical with those of the present, or are being continuously modified in the direction hitherto observed. Should any fundamental change of conditions ensue, natural selection would discriminate in favour of the race which could most rapidly retrace its steps along the course of development it had hitherto followed. Natural selection, indeed, can never do anything more than justify the "whatever is" of actual fact. In a sense, therefore, it would be more correct to say that natural selection never carries us a step beyond the present: it deals with conditions as they arise, but is in itself entirely blind, so far as any foresight of the future is concerned. Looked at as a natural law of causation, in short, the principle of natural selection is always at work, and always at work in precisely the same way. It is impossible, therefore, to use it as a principle of division between periods of human history, and to divide that history into two epochs, in the first of which natural selection works for the efficiency of the existing political or social organisation, in the second of which it works for the efficiency of society in the future. Whatever difference there may be between Ancient and Western civilisation, Mr Kidd's mode of arriving at this dichotomy in human history cannot be accepted as satisfactory.

But if natural selection possesses in itself no principle of guidance—seeing that in one sense everything, just as it is, may be traced to the operation of natural selection—how does Mr Kidd come to assign to it the philosophical importance he does? What he really has in view seems to be something quite different from natural selection strictly so called—to be, in fact, a teleological interpretation of the cosmic process. Natural selection, or the survival of the fittest, it cannot be too clearly understood, supplies us with no standards of value—not merely no standards of ethical comparison, but no basis for comparing different stages of the process as better or worse in any respect whatever, save that of adaptation to the immediate environment. Such adaptation may mean retrogression as well as development; it may mean, that is to say, what we, with our inveterate habit of so judging, *call* retrogression or development. But natural selection itself gives us only a sequence of events, not in a strict sense an evolution. Given, however, the last term of the series (for our present purposes man as so far evolved), and assuming the value (in ethical or other terms) of the result, it is always possible for us to regard the sequence of events which terminated thus, as travailing towards this birth, or, in Bacon's large phrase, guided by a "divine marshal" towards this issue. Such a teleological interpretation may be entirely immanent in character, implying no interference *ab extra* with the mechanical operation of natural selection; but it derives its warrant, not from that scientific principle, but from a conviction of the absolute worth of the end attained—a conviction strong enough to determine us to interpret the whole process in the light of its culmination. The sequence of events, so viewed, becomes then, throughout, a chain of means and ends. The forces which have been operative, either continuously or at critical junctures in human history, appear as the main factors which have contributed to produce the result. This is what is meant by a philosophy of history. It is a philosophy of history in this sense, and depending on these assumptions, which Mr Kidd professes to give us.

When history is thus conceived as the working out of an end, it at once becomes evident that the means employed in its realisation are such as often completely transcend the short-sighted calculation of the human actors through whom at any given epoch the purpose is being accomplished. God, as the theologians say, makes the wrath of man to serve Him. Or, to put it more generally, the shaping spirit of the future uses the blind instincts of men, their follies and obstinacies, their light desires, to beat out the fabric of the years to come.

> "Our indiscretion sometimes serves us well,
> When our deep plots do pall: and that should teach us
> There's a divinity that shapes our ends,
> Rough-hew them how we will."

The blindness of human beings and of nations to the true issues of their actions is a commonplace of the moralist and historian. Sometimes it meets us in an encouraging form. Saul, the son of Kish, who went out to seek his father's asses, and found a kingdom, has been often quoted; and the handful of British traders who laid the foundations of our Indian Empire is also not a new comparison. On the other side, there is a passage in J. A. Symonds's biography, in a letter to the late Professor Sidgwick, in which he gives poignant expression to the helplessness of the best-deduced political principles to aid a people in the crisis of their fate. "We cannot apply what we have learned, and the green tree of life laughs at our gray theories. Nay, worse, the unexpected evolutions of the organism force us to doubt what we confidently thought we had learned. Surely England has reached a crisis at which, if ever, principles ought to suggest the way to right solution. And yet none are applicable. Sternly, blindly, patiently, sufferingly, we shall have to live it out, just like the meanest mollusc."

Mr Kidd concentrates on the contrast, so often emphasised by psychologists and moralists, between self-preserving and race-preserving activities. The living being is a mass of impulses and instincts, of whose origin he can give no account, and whose purpose in the scheme of things is hid from him. His nature being what it is, the satisfaction of all his impulses and instincts is necessarily, so far as it goes, a source of pleasure; and the unreflecting individual is thus impelled by an inner force to the performance of the one set of functions no less than the other. But the accounts of egoism and altruism are far from easy to balance, when the calculating reason appears upon the scene. The Pessimists have expended perhaps a disproportionate amount of time and labour in proving that *if the individual is taken in isolation from his kind*, the balance of pleasure and pain will in most cases come out on the wrong side. The sexual and parental impulses and instincts may be taken, without injustice, as the central fact in animal life; but it is due to the wiles of the Unconscious, insatiately bent on its own ends (so runs the argument), that the individual fails to perceive, or perceives too late, that he has been duped in the interest of the generations to come. No bountiful Venus, *hominum divomque voluptas*, but an insatiate mother of longing and woe, she blinds one generation after another to the clearest teachings of reason. The *rôle* of the Unconscious in human affairs, and in the cosmic process generally, furnished Von Hartmann some forty years ago (as it had done Schopenhauer before him) with a system of philosophy; and though handled in a different interest, the facts adduced, and the line of argument pursued, bear frequently an instructive resemblance to what we find in Mr Kidd. There is the same contrast in both between the selfish hedonistic reason and the ends of the cosmic process, though these ends are viewed by Mr Kidd as the perfection of wisdom and by pessimism as the perfection of folly. And in both cases the argument turns upon the power of reflection which comes with reason. Man can say to himself, in a sense in which no animal can, "Pleasure, be thou my good." For with the gift of reflection which makes him man, he acquires the power of self-control, the power of guiding his instincts and impulses; and while this power is the source of all upward progress towards the human virtues and graces, it also implies the capacity of manipulating his instincts in the interests of selfish indulgence, and, so applied, it may sink him lower than the brutes from which he springs.

Without following the process of the selfish reason to the lower depths of moral degradation, Mr Kidd, both in this book and in 'Social Evolution,' returns repeatedly to the population question. Taking, as he does, a pronouncedly optimistic view of the world-process and the ends to which it moves—seeing also, as a practical politician, the way in which the natural increase of population has worked in the past to secure the future of the English-speaking races—the tendency towards artificial restriction of the birth-rate presents itself to him as a dereliction, so to speak, from cosmic duty. It means at all events the deliberate resolve, on the part of an individual or community, to limit its horizon to considerations of its own comfort and wellbeing. And to that extent it may be fairly taken as a symptom of the degeneracy of the race in which it appears. Such a race must have an ever-dwindling share in the future of mankind; and Mr Kidd is at least right in insisting that society has never been founded, and will never be maintained, on a basis of individual self-interest or pleasure. This furnishes him with a text from which he preaches, in a way which is bound to be useful, against two apparently opposite, but at bottom closely related, tendencies of modern thought and practice.

In designating his first chapter "The Close of an Era," Mr Kidd expressly indicates that it is the Utilitarian theory of society and of the State, as expounded by the Philosophical Radicals, and as preached and practised by the Manchester School of economists and politicians, which he regards as having reached its term. These doctrines of political enfranchisement, combined with unlimited economic competition and social *laissez-faire*, may not always have been expressed with precision or held with consistency; but they have formed, as he points out, the common creed of the older Liberalism and Radicalism. On the political side it is no exaggeration to say, as he does, that "the political party in England which has been most closely identified with the cause of progress in the past inherited . . . the greatest tradition in politics which our civilisation has produced"; and its principles may claim in this respect to have conquered the world. But, as he says again, "the great Utilitarian movement of the nineteenth century has run its course"; "the basis of the old Radicalism has gone." "There has been no system of ideas that has ever held the mind of the world, from which the intellectual basis has been so completely struck away." To students of philosophy and to philosophical students of history and society, this conclusion can hardly be called novel. The doctrines of individual freedom and human equality which made modern Liberalism a power conquering and to conquer were, in their origin, ethical ideas, embodying fundamental principles of our civilisation; but it was their fate to be interpreted and formulated in terms of abstract individualism, by men who had been bred on the philosophy of pure sensationalism which dominated the eighteenth century, and found its classical expression in Hume. Reducing experience to isolated impressions and ideas, adhering to one another in consequence of casual collocation, this philosophy treats society as an aggregate of mutually exclusive units, each pursuing as sole end his own individual pleasure. The problem of Utilitarian ethics and politics thus takes the form of evolving social and benevolent action from the play of individual selfishness, or, as Carlyle puts it, "given a world of knaves to educe an Honesty from their united action." Mr Leslie Stephen has recently, in his volumes on 'English Utilitarianism,' ably exposed the bankruptcy of this system of thought as applied to social affairs. Utility, he says in effect, may be a valuable practical test of many political arrangements or social institutions, but you cannot apply such a test to the existence of the social organism itself. The origin and maintenance of society depend on cohesive forces which cannot be weighed in such a balance. Mr Stephen laid stress chiefly on the defects of this system of thought as a social philosophy; but its social consequences depend on the fundamental defects of its theory of knowledge, and these the prolonged criticism of modern Idealism may claim to have effectively exposed long before Mr Stephen wrote. The influence of such criticism is slow and cumulative in its effects, but perhaps Mr Kidd's relegation of this whole system of ideas to the past may be taken as a sign that this lesson has at last gone home to the general consciousness. And it is no small advantage, it may be added, to have this conclusion so vigorously enforced in a book which is bound to be widely read by many whose contact with philosophical ideas is mainly at second-hand.

But in bracketing with the Manchester School the apparently opposite ideals of Marxian Socialism and Social Democracy, Mr Kidd performs, perhaps, a more timely service; and in condemning them upon the same grounds, he shows the philosophical power of detecting a single underlying principle in its diverse manifestations. The point of resemblance is their exclusive preoccupation with the conditions of material wellbeing. Political Economy was central, as is well known, in the thought of the Utilitarian Radicals, and formed the gospel of the Manchester School. It is the same economic interpretation of history which dominates modern Socialism. The process of human development is regarded as determined entirely by economic conditions, and assumes the aspect of a war of interests between existing members of society. The conflict of labour and capital sums up for Marx the significance of the human record; and his sole ideal is the adjustment of the conflict by the extinction of the antithesis and the cessation of the personal struggle for existence. The ideal is thus concerned purely with the distribution of material goods, or, as Mr Kidd likes to put it, with the material interests of the present. While, as we shall see, entirely in sympathy with many so-called socialistic proposals, Mr Kidd censures this profoundly materialistic conception of human good on which the systems of aggressive Socialism are founded, and which is so frankly expressed in the anti-religious ideals of Social Democracy in Germany and elsewhere. He finds there systematised and formulated the spirit of practical materialism which is fostered by many influences and in many quarters at the present time, and in which he recognises, not without reason, the great and growing danger of our civilisation. As regards the socialistic contention, he had already pointed out in 'Social Evolution' that if the economic factor were indeed the only operative factor, the forces at work would long since have reached the equilibrium demanded by their inherent tendencies. "If we are to have nothing but materialistic selfishness on the one side, leagued against equally materialistic selfishness on the other, then the power-holding classes, being still immeasurably the stronger, would be quite capable of taking care of themselves, and would indeed be very foolish if they did not do so." The very existence of the socialistic propaganda would be inconceivable but for the presence of humanitarian factors quite other than the economic. In spite of the avowed materialism of what may be called its official principles, Socialism, as an active force in practical reform, really rests upon ethical, or, as Mr Kidd prefers to call them, religious principles, which set limits in human affairs to the ruthless operation of natural selection, as it is seen at work in the animal world. The more equal distribution of material goods is claimed as the indispensable substructure of a more truly human life. In this at least consists the appeal of socialistic ideas to the conscience of the modern world.

All this is excellent. It is when Mr Kidd proceeds to connect these valuable criticisms with his twofold division of human history, founded on his distinction between the ascendancy of the present and the ascendancy of the future, that we begin to feel that we have left solid ground behind us. In one sense, we have seen, in considering the action of natural selection, that the ascendancy of the present represents nothing objectionable —is indeed the inevitable condition of all human effort. On the other hand, if the ascendancy of the present means the recognition of none but material ends, and the acknowledgment of no principle of action but individual self-interest, then surely few generalisations could be more rash than to seek to affix this label either to pre-Christian civilisation as a whole, or to Greek and Roman civilisation in particular. Yet the ground on which Utilitarianism and official Socialism are condemned is repeatedly stated as being that they represent the principles of the older civilisation, and have not become conscious of the forces operative in our own. Splendid patriotism and devoted affection—not to mention more homely virtues—were assuredly as little absent from the ancient world as were ideals of truth and goodness, far transcending the conditions of material well-being. The pagan ideal undoubtedly differed in many ways from the Christian, but all human virtue must have a common basis, and the old phrase "anima naturaliter Christiana" is perhaps nearer the truth than Mr Kidd's laboured antithesis. The old civilisation no doubt ended in practical materialism and a recrudescence of the grossest superstition, but these were the causes of its death, not the forces which made it great.

If we press the parallel between the social atomism of the Utilitarian theory and the principles of ancient civilisation, the want of coherence springs at once to light; for in antiquity the State rather than the individual is the unit. That is to say, the cohesive forces of society are so strong that, within the ancient State, the individual does not attain the full measure of development of which he is capable. The individual in this sense is a modern product. This is, of course, one of the commonplaces of philosophical history, and Mr Kidd is far from being unaware of it. Indeed he uses this very fact of the overshadowing influence of the

State as one of the points in his contrast between ancient and Western civilisation. Both impeachments, it would seem, can hardly be true; but Mr Kidd passes from one to the other through the assumption which he apparently makes that the ends of a State are necessarily material in their character. In so doing he falls back upon the idea, already criticised, of the materialistic basis of ancient civilisation. But here, again, the antithesis will not bear analysis. The State, as such, certainly deals to a large extent with externals; and, in the conflict of State with State for sovereignty and predominance, the materialistic aspect of its functions must necessarily fill the eye. But it is the ethical virtues, nurtured by the State in its citizens, which in the long-run (as Mr Kidd himself is not slow to argue) decide such conflicts. And there must be something wrong with an antithesis which would compel us to rank the Athens of Pericles or the Rome of Hannibal's day as representative of materialism, and (let us say) Chicago or the Rand as the exponent of Western idealism. The patriotism of Sparta and Rome or the ethical outlook of Sophocles cannot be put on one side as qualities which refer to a limited present, while modern communities live under "the shadow of the infinite future."

The difference between ancient and modern civilisation is not the difference between selfishness and altruism, nor yet that between action for the present and action for the future. Profound differences there obviously are, and Mr Kidd is right in connecting them with the influence of Christian sentiment; but the nature of that influence may surely be much more simply and unambiguously expressed. It seems almost a deliberate perversity to represent the message of Christianity as a call to self-sacrifice for the future of the race. The early Christians did not believe in any future for the race; they looked for the speedy conclusion of this mundane drama. The future in which they did believe was a future for the individual in another world. The interests of *this* future were certainly of such transcendent importance in their eyes, that they quite overshadowed the passing concerns of the present life. This is the primary (though not, I admit, the deepest) meaning of the Christian antithesis between the things that are unseen and eternal and the things that are seen and temporal. To Christian sentiment the interests of future generations are no more a satisfying object of devotion than the interests of the present generation: both belong to the same plane of existence—the world that now is. The destiny to be realised is outside the world-process altogether. Mr Kidd's statements of the central principle of Christianity are so highly generalised—one might almost say, so studiously vague—that they might cover either interpretation of the future. "We have present," he says, "in that religion, underlying all its phases, however varied, however obscure, one central phenomenon which constitutes not only the essential fact of its inner life, but the distinctive principle to which its evolutionary significance is related. It is the opening in the individual mind of the terms of a profound antithesis, of which the characteristic feature always remains the same—namely, that it is incapable of being bridged or closed by any principle operating merely within the limits of present consciousness." Statements like this are hardly calculated to convey a very definite idea of Christian teaching; but knowing what we know of historical Christianity, it would be just possible to interpret the "profound antithesis" referred to in the Christian sense. Mr Kidd, however, so far as one can see, has no interest in that interpretation. Present and future, all through his volume, mean present and future in the mundane history of the race; and to that sense he seems to pass through the ambiguous middle term of the "infinite." The eternal world of Christian faith is often described as the infinite in contrast with the finite; and the procession of future generations may also be spoken of as infinite (in another sense), seeing that it never comes to an end. When Mr Kidd speaks of the Christian era as "the epoch in which the present and the finite begin to pass under the control of the future and the infinite," the two meanings seem to become interchangeable in his mind; and it is certain that the whole of the rest of his argument depends upon a supposed antithesis to which the most typically religious minds of Christendom would have been profoundly indifferent. It is almost incredible that Mr Kidd should leave the matter thus ambiguous; but it is upon this ambiguity, mainly, that the identification of the supposed principle of Projected Efficiency with the central phenomenon of the Christian religion depends for its plausibility.

What are, let us ask ourselves, the Christian ideas which have worked like a slow leaven in modern civilisation? If we try to answer this question very generally, but at the same time as simply as possible, should we not say that the most fundamental idea, in a social regard, was the idea of a perfectly universal human brotherhood based on the doctrine of a common divine sonship? This was the principle that burst the bonds of the antique state. To those who learned the lesson of Jesus there was "neither Greek nor Jew, circumcision nor uncircumcision, Barbarian, Scythian, bond nor free." Though not enunciated for the first time by Jesus, no one will deny that through his life and teaching this idea first became a vital force in world-history. The brotherhood of all was intimately associated with—might indeed be said to be based upon—the new and infinite worth recognised in each. In Christianity the individual steps out of the limitations of a merely civic or national existence, not in the negative sense of Epicureanism or Stoicism, but as one who while in the world is raised above it, as one whose fellowship is with God, and who is the heir of eternal life. As the compassion of Christ went out towards universal man, so the same thought is perpetuated in the mystical dogmas in which the Church enshrined his teaching. The doctrine of the Incarnation invests with sacredness for evermore the human flesh in which God himself had deigned to dwell. When Gregory the First urged upon the conscience of Christendom the manumission of slaves, it was, in his own noble words, because "redemptor noster, totius conditor naturæ, humanum carnem voluerit assumere." Similarly, oppression and cruelty become sin, because they are an offence against those for whom Christ died. And the mystical unity of all men with Christ becomes their unity with one another: "Inasmuch as ye did it unto the least of these little ones, ye did it unto me." On the one hand, there is thus a raising of the whole scale of values. Human life is invested with a new significance. In view of his eternal destiny and infinite capacities, man is removed from the category of natural things which are born and live their season, and perish, so to speak, in the using. A single human soul outweighs to the Christian thinker the whole material system. And, on the other hand, this intensification of the value of each individual is extended to every member of the human family. The slave takes his place beside the free man; the new-born infant, the weakling, the deformed, the aged and hopelessly diseased, are all alike invested with the sacredness of a divine humanity. Practices, therefore, such as infanticide, which the harsher pagan world had sanctioned without remorse, became at once impossible to the Christian conscience. And though the pagan hardness long perpetuated itself in institutions and laws, and is far from being yet extinct, Mr Kidd is right in connecting with Christian sentiment the gradual amelioration in modern times of the general human lot, and in particular the striking increase of genuine concern for the lot of the suffering and the oppressed. But in the new "philanthropy" there is no thought of any antithesis between present and future generations. It is simply man as man who has become invested with claims to consideration which the sentiment of the ancient world restricted to the citizen. The way had been prepared for such a revolution in feeling by the ideas of the later Stoics and by the world-wide extension of Roman citizenship; but Christianity alone impressed it upon the world, and gave the feeling its warmth and its absolute universality.

This Christian doctrine of the "rights of man" has undoubtedly worked in our civilisation towards political enfranchisement and social betterment. Democracy may be something of a catchword, but in a large sense Mr Kidd is fully justified in connecting the general movement of modern political thought with the ethical and religious conceptions in which our civilisation is rooted. And there is one part of his argument, in the chapters on "The Position in Modern Thought" and "Western Liberalism," which is full of suggestion and warning. Quoting Sir Henry Maine, he points out that the modern doctrines of popular government are essentially of English origin, and may be said to have been evolved in the political struggles of the seventeenth century. These doctrines may all be conveniently resolved into "the claim of the native equality of all men." But "by the men with whom the assertion of 'natural right' originated in England, the doctrine of the native equality of men was most certainly not accepted as a first principle. It had no meaning apart by itself. We see that it was accepted at the time, as it was accepted later in Locke's writings, only as a corollary to a conception of the relationship in which men were held to stand to a meaning in their lives which transcended the meaning of the interests included within the limits of political consciousness." Later, however, in the French thinkers who heralded the Revolution, in Bentham, in the social philosophy of J. S. Mill, and in the current theories of Social Democracy, the doctrine of equality has become detached from the ethical considerations which originally gave it force. It is presented as a first principle or self-evident truth on which these writers base their theory of the State. And as they do not start from ethical conceptions, their theory tends to contemplate the State exclusively in its economic or material aspect; their chief topic and problem is the conflict of rival interests and their reconciliation on the basis of self-interest. This may not be entirely true of a writer like Mill, but in the theories of social democracy which start from Marx the logical outcome of the matter is seen in the frank acceptance of a purely "materialistic interpretation of history."

But when humanity is emptied in this fashion of ethical content, and the claim to equality is advanced as an abstract doctrine on behalf of the self-seeking individual, what cogency does it possess? Does it not justly provoke the furious scorn which Nietzsche heaped upon it? For a right is an ethical idea, and can be vindicated only by an ethical view of human capacity and destiny. If history is reduced to a mere struggle for power and gain, then strength is the only law, and *beati possidentes* the only creed. Mr Kidd has done good service, I think, in calling attention to the process of degradation which the principles of modern Liberalism have undergone in being separated from their ethico-religious presuppositions, and to their inherent inability, when thus separated, to cope with a materialistic gospel of force, or with the many dangers which threaten our modern society from the unscrupulous pursuit of wealth, the immense accumulations of capital, and the hardening effects of selfish luxury. I have already commented on the injustice of Mr Kidd's attempt to identify the materialistic interpretation of history with "a return to the standpoint of the ancient world." It would be more correct to describe it as a reappearance among the Western peoples of the same canker which blighted the ancient civilisation. But apart from this misrepresentation, Mr Kidd utters a well-timed warning. His book is a reminder of ideals which have moulded and directed our civilisation in the past, and which he rightly maintains to be essential to its continued existence.

In the same spirit he criticises the opposition of the older Utilitarians and the Manchester School to the humanitarian legislation of their day as a declension from the social consciousness of Christendom. He praises them for their "profound instinct that the future of the world belongs to the principle of free competition"; but despite his former criticisms of official Socialism, he recognises in socialistic theories an expression of "the equally profound instinct that the conditions of *laissez-faire* are nothing more or less than conditions of barbarism." They are conditions, moreover, which defeat their own object; for competition, if left to itself and allowed to go on to the bitter end, leads to the monopoly of the strongest, and so abrogates the conditions of free competition on which social health depends. He cites as examples the gigantic Trusts which have sprung up in the United States, and which threaten in the near future to become matters of national, and even international, concern. It is impossible for any civilised State to permit the conscienceless use of such tremendous resources for the exploitation of the community in the selfish interest of a capitalistic ring. This leads Mr Kidd naturally to a definition of his own standpoint in practical politics. He is prepared to see the attitude of *laissez-faire* abandoned in many directions, and he sympathises to that extent, as we have seen, with much that the survivors of the old Radicalism condemn as socialistic. But the interference must be prompted throughout by ethical considerations, and must never be such as to kill the principle of free competition, in which he recognises from first to last the salvation of society. His programme, in short, is not strikingly original, but possesses the English virtues of moderation and good sense—though in his ideal of competitive stress and strain he seems to reflect the nervous tension of American life rather than the temperament of the parent stock. So insistent is his emphasis in the later chapters on the "free conflict of forces" as the guarantee of political, intellectual, and religious wellbeing, that at times he seems to preach competition for competition's sake, just as, in his idea of the relation of the present to the future, he seemed to fall into the idea of sacrifice for sacrifice's sake. Applying the idea of a competitive struggle for survival to intellectual beliefs and moral conceptions as well as to more material spheres, he envisages the ideal social state as that of "a fair, open, and free rivalry of all the forces within the social consciousness—a rivalry in which the best organisations, the best methods, the best skill, the best government, and the best standards of action and belief shall have the right of universal opportunity." In some of his statements the ideal appears to cut at the very notion of truth as something which claims universal allegiance. But it would be more just to Mr Kidd to say that it is his confidence in the omnipotence of truth which inspires his optimistic forecast of the ultimate issue of such a conflict. Does he, after all, say more than Kant said, when he spoke of the age on which we had entered as the age of criticism, in which every doctrine, practice, or belief must establish its right to continued existence? Both simply draw the last consequences of the principle of Protestantism and of modern scientific thought. Mr Kidd's ideal of universal toleration as the ultimate safeguard of truth itself compares advantageously with the mediæval authority with which Comte seemed anxious to invest his scientific and spiritual hierarchy. In his contention that the principle of toleration is itself, like the doctrine of human equality, the product of ethical and religious conviction rather than an abstract truth of reason, Mr Kidd returns to the fundamental idea of his book that the fabric of human society rests ultimately on ethical conceptions, and that the history of mankind is essentially the development of man's ethical ideals. It is the forcible and often fresh presentation of this perennial truth, rather than any new philosophical construction of history, which gives the book its vitality. For the main formula which Mr Kidd seeks to establish as a philosophical law of human development seems both ambiguous and misleading. But so many have apparently made up their minds of late that man does live by bread alone, that even the paradoxes of the book may have their use in stirring the turbid waters of popular thought.

MARTINEAU'S PHILOSOPHY.[1]

IN attempting any estimate of Martineau's work, it is particularly desirable to bear in mind the long period over which his intellectual activity extended. The dates of his life almost coincided with those of the nineteenth century. He was born the year after Kant died, and two years before Hegel published his first volume. When he left college, in 1827, Hegel was still teaching in Berlin and Goethe was still alive at Weimar; in France, Cousin was at the height of his reputation as a philosophical lecturer, and Comte had not yet published the first volume of the 'Philosophie Positive'; while, at home, James Mill was leading the Philosophical Radicals to victory in 'The Westminster Review,' and his son had just discovered the future designation of the school in a novel of Galt's. The elder Mill's 'Analysis of the Human Mind,' and Sir William Hamilton's celebrated article on the Philosophy of the Unconditioned, landmarks in the history of two different schools, did not

[1] This paper appeared in 'The Hibbert Journal' of April 1903. I am indebted throughout to Professor Upton's luminous account of Martineau's Philosophy in the second volume of the 'Life.' Professor Upton not only furnishes all the material for a critical estimate of Martineau's place in English thought, but himself touches with discriminating hand the weak no less than the strong points of his master's system.

appear till two years later. During the twenties, as Professor Upton says, what philosophical interest existed in the British Isles "was divided between the Hartleyan empirical school and the Scotch school of so-called 'common-sense'"; and young Martineau was brought up by his college preceptors on Belsham's 'Elements of Mental and Moral Philosophy,' which popularised the associationist and necessarian tradition of Hartley and Priestley. In the philosophical classes which the young minister gathered round him in Liverpool in the thirties, the text-books were James Mill's 'Analysis' and Dr Thomas Brown's 'Essay on Cause and Effect.' In his first article in 1833, devoted to Priestley, he talks of "the piercing analysis of Brown or James Mill, before whose gaze the most intricate and delicate of human emotions and the most evanescent trains of human ratiocination are arrested, questioned, and made to marshal themselves in their true places amid the nimble evolutions of the mind." Before he was appointed professor, however, in 1840, he had already fought his way, under the imperative pressure of conscience, to the clearly defined ethical position which he ever afterwards occupied. And as the change of view in ethics was necessarily accompanied by a revision of the doctrine of causation, Professor Upton goes the length of saying that "his philosophical teaching remained for the rest of his long life substantially unaltered. The modifications which it underwent were all the outcome of, and in harmony with, the basal principles which he adopted in 1839."

The date carries us back to a time when Hamilton had only been three years in his Edinburgh Chair and John Stuart Mill was still at work upon his 'Logic.' It is not without significance, therefore, that although Martineau's 'Study of Religion' was published in 1887, we are told in the first sentence that the word Religion will be used throughout "in the sense which it invariably bore *half a century ago*." The fact is not without significance, I mean, if we are to form a true judgment of the value of Martineau's work. His philosophical *books* all appeared towards the close of the century, but the ideas they contained had been formulated forty or fifty years before, and had indeed been operative in English thought for a generation, through the author's college teaching and numerous important articles and addresses. This would be true even if we date his complete philosophical equipment from the fifteen months he spent in Germany in 1848-49, the effects of which he so eloquently describes in the Preface to the 'Types of Ethical Theory,' speaking of it as "a kind of second education," and "a new intellectual birth." In 1848, it is important to remember, the 'Origin of Species' was still eleven years ahead, and, so far as Great Britain was concerned, the serious study of Kant and Hegel had yet to begin. In Germany it was, on the whole, ebb-tide in philosophy. The great idealistic movement in the beginning of the century had temporarily spent its force, and was discredited in the land of its birth by the extravagances of some of its adherents. Martineau did not come under its influence, and thus his thought was formed and matured independently of the two great influences which have transformed English thought within the last forty years.

His most productive period was during the fifties and sixties. During these decades he contributed to the 'Prospective' and 'National Review' what Professor Upton justly describes as "a splendid series of articles, as finished in expression as they are powerful in thought, dealing with the chief philosophical thinkers and movements of the time." He appears impartially as the critic of Hamilton and Mill, of Comte and Newman, of the agnosticism of Spencer and Mansel. In these articles, and in the still more celebrated criticisms of modern materialism called forth by Tyndall's Belfast address in the seventies, we may probably recognise his most direct influence on contemporary thought, before the cumulative effect produced by the publication, in advanced age, of his two systematic treatises and the garnered harvest of his 'Essays, Reviews, and Addresses.' There are imperishable principles that persist through every change of philosophical dialect or fashion, but on other parts of a philosopher's work the time-spirit has his will. The famous battle of the Intuitionalists and Sensationalists round Hamilton's body in the sixties no longer tempts us to break a lance on either side. Its very echoes have grown strangely faint. Professor Upton comments aptly on the sudden transformation of philosophical issues which followed these heated encounters. "Just at the time when the followers of Hamilton and those of Mill and Bain were thus vehemently contending with each other, and Dr Martineau was holding his own independently of both, two fresh and quite unexpected claimants for philosophical supremacy appeared upon the scene. Of these one sprang into birth on British soil, the other was of German extraction. The motto of the former was "Evolution and Heredity"; that of the latter the "Absolute Reality of Thought"; but each of them vigorously attacked the fundamental principles both of the Edinburgh Intuitionalists and of the London Sensationalists; and it is one of the most dramatic events in the history of philosophical thought that, in less than twenty years, these newcomers had between them managed to dethrone and dispossess both of the pretenders to philosophic rule with whom Dr Martineau had, in previous years, such brilliant encounters. From this circumstance it comes about that Dr Martineau's earlier polemics, powerful as they were, have now not much more than a literary and historical interest."[1]

The services of Martineau to spiritual philosophy in England during the nineteenth century cannot easily, I think, be over-estimated. These services seem to me, however, to be to a large extent independent of the specific form which the fundamental doctrines of such a philosophy assume in his own theory. His peculiar theory of conscience has grave defects, and I question whether any one maintains it at the present day. But his splendid insistence on the moral life and its implications, as furnishing the key to human existence and man's relation to the divine — the massive resistance which he offered to every attempt to explain ethical experience by other than ethical categories, whether baldly physical or of the metaphysical kind that are but physical in disguise,—these are in the spirit of Butler and of Kant, and greatly helped to raise English thought from its inherited hedonism and necessarianism. Even should his doctrine of Freedom itself be found to require modification, it was ethically true as against the necessarianism from which it emancipated Martineau himself and all who have listened to his searching and persuasive pleading. So, again, his own doctrine of Cause may be open to serious philosophical criticism, but his distinction between ordered sequence and real agency, and his demonstration of the impossibility of reducing the latter to the former, enabled him to dissect the sophisms which are apt to gather round the term "law." His exposure

[1] 'Life and Letters,' ii. 358.

of the fundamental absurdity of a mindless universe, his timely reminder of the true scope and meaning of evolution, and his impassioned vindication of moral right as "no local essence," but allegiance "due to one eternal Perfection which penetrates the moral structure of all worlds," made his addresses on 'Modern Materialism' more effective than any other utterances in stemming the dangerous tide of turbid materialistic speculation to which the Darwinian doctrine at first gave rise. The clearness and beauty of Martineau's style, the rhetorical force of his pleading, the ethical passion and spiritual dignity of the man, combined to make him an ideal champion of the spiritual view of the world in a time of transition and intellectual insecurity. For myself, I cannot but think that it is on such imperishable services to the common cause of Idealism, rather than on the peculiar features which differentiate his own treatment from other systems, that Martineau's place in the history of English thought will ultimately depend. So that when Professor Upton speaks of "the systems of Hegel, of Lotze, and of James Martineau" as the three philosophical systems which are most likely by their contributions to mould the philosophy of religion of the twentieth century, I feel as if the word system were almost out of place in connection with Martineau's influence, and as if this juxtaposition of the three thinkers suggested claims which it might be difficult to establish. For we find Professor Upton himself acknowledging on important points the defects of his master's "formulated philosophy," the "intellectual framework" of which, he considers, did not do justice to important aspects of truth which, in less systematic moments, find expression in "some of his divinest utterances." But it is by the adequacy of his "intellectual framework" that the philosopher, *qua* philosopher, takes a distinctive place in the historic series. It was some perception of this which led R. H. Hutton, another old pupil, to write in his memorial article in 'The Spectator': "We doubt whether the historian of the English thought of our time will credit Martineau with any distinct modification of the theological or philosophical opinions of this age. It was something that went below opinion; it was a revelation of spiritual character and power." The turn of expression hardly does justice to Martineau's clear-cut thought and great intellectual force; yet in the end this estimate may perhaps be found nearer the mark than any more far-reaching claim.

It is as the vindicator and, one may almost say, as the prophet of Theism that Martineau is widely honoured. Thus Professor J. E. Carpenter, in an eloquent tribute at the unveiling of a memorial in Little Portland Street Chapel, described his philosophical achievement as essentially a revolt against "the interpretation of the universe by a mechanical Deism." "He discovered a new philosophy and a new religion which brought the human spirit into immediate communion with the living God, placed His authority within the soul, and transformed the infinite spaces of the universe from lonely immensities into the presence-chamber of the everlasting Mind." Martineau's own characterisation of Deism, in the 'Study of Religion,' as an imperfect Theism which scarcely passes into a religion, may be accepted as justifying this estimate of his philosophical intention. And, indeed, as regards the external universe, what Martineau did was substantially to substitute Berkeley's conception for Locke's, reducing its ordered sequences of events to the organised expression of continuously active Divine Will, while in the sphere of ethics and religion he insisted on the immediate presence of the Divine to the human soul. But although the intention of his philosophy doubtless is to provide us with a doctrine of Theism which shall rise above the externalities of Deism, and conserve all that is true in the counter-error of Pantheism, it is only in his deepest religious utterances that he completely emancipates himself from deistic presuppositions. His intellectual scheme of the world was much more under the influence of his individualistic and deistic training than he was himself aware of; and the defects of his "formulated philosophy"—its frequent rigidity and externality and its exaggerated anthropomorphism—are nearly all traceable to this source.

As we have already seen, Professor Upton considers that his main positions had been reached as early as 1839, and that his teaching remained substantially unaltered after that date. The terms in which Martineau himself speaks of his "Annus Mirabilis" in Germany ten years later do not seem to me inconsistent with this statement. There is no evidence that he experienced "a new intellectual birth" in the sense of a revolution in his own philosophical convictions. He made a careful study of Kant, and also read Plato and Hegel side by side. Ancient and modern philosophy shed light upon each other, and of Greek philosophy especially he got quite a new impression. "I seemed to pierce through what had been words before, into contact with living thought, and the bleak grammatical text was aglow with luminous philosophy. It was essentially the gift of fresh conceptions, . . . and, once gained, was more or less available throughout the history of philosophy, and lifted the darkness from the pages of Kant and even Hegel. It was impossible to resist or distrust this gradual widening of apprehension: it was as much a fact as the sight of the Alps I had never visited before. . . . The metaphysic of the world had come home to me." He returned, therefore, with a mind indefinitely richer for this companionship with the masters of them that know, and with his own philosophical powers strengthened by the long wrestle with their meaning. He could not have spoken as he afterwards did, with the same largeness of utterance and the same confidence or knowledge, had he not been lifted by contact with "the metaphysic of the world" above the parochialism of contemporary English thought. But still the result was comparable, after all, to the enlarging effect of foreign travel. It must be remembered that he was already forty-three years of age; and his fifteen months of study, though they enabled him to base his philosophy more broadly, did not alter the lines on which it was already laid down.

Neither from Kant nor Hegel can he be shown to have assimilated any formative ideas. Trendelenburg was not the best guide to what was really vital in Kant's analysis of knowledge; and Martineau appears in his books to adopt the psychological interpretation of the Kantian theory which makes it substantially a variety of Intuitionalism. He is mainly concerned to refute the subjectivism and relativism of the theory, and this is done largely in the spirit of Natural Realism. As for Hegel, he must be said to have remained entirely outside the system, so far as sympathy was concerned and the more intimate understanding that is born of sympathy. In that respect he was unfortunate in the date of his visit. The reaction against Hegel had set in, and though Martineau studied him conscientiously, he may easily have been led to regard him as a spent force. It was a quarter of a century later before Hegelianism began to be a power in English thought, and by that time Martineau was close upon his seventieth year. "Strange to say," Professor

Upton tells us "he never fully realised the powerful attraction which Absolute Idealism has for many minds, nor at all anticipated the lengthened influence it was destined to exert on both sides of the Atlantic." This want of sympathy is to some extent an indication of defective speculative insight, and is only explicable by the pronounced individualism of Martineau's own view, which resulted from the exclusively ethical cast of his mind and the relics of an imperfectly transformed deistic theory. He was at least much nearer the deistic than the pantheistic extreme, and had all his life long quite an exaggerated apprehension of anything that could be considered to savour of Pantheism. Even Professor Upton's modest criticisms and amendments on his own theory he considered "sometimes came dangerously near to Pantheism." Now however valuable Martineau's "Ethical Individualism" may be as a protest against certain tendencies within the Hegelian school, "the historic pabulum" in Hegel (to use Dr Stirling's apt phrase) is so rich that to remain entirely outside his "way of ideas" is a voluntary impoverishment of thought, which cannot be made good from any other source.

In issuing his 'Study of Religion' in 1887, Martineau remarked with a touch of sadness, in the closing words of his Preface, that he was well aware that the volumes were in conflict with the prevailing opinions and tendencies of the time. The same note is heard occasionally in his correspondence. The isolation which he felt was not altogether imaginary, and it arose mainly from the circumstance that the two greatest intellectual influences of the century had left his scheme of thought practically unaffected. Professor Carpenter comments on the significance of the fact that "his essential work as a thinker was done before the production of the 'Origin of Species,'" and we have just seen his attitude to Hegel and modern Idealism. The result was that when he abandoned the associationism and necessarianism of his youth, the theory he adopted was, in essentials, akin to the Intuitionalism of the Scottish philosophers. In Ethics, it is explicitly to "the writers of the Scottish school and their editors, critics and disciples in Paris," that he refers as being, with Butler, the only faithful adherents of what he calls the "idio-psychological" method. They alone "have declined to betray their science to the physiologist on the one hand and the ontologist on the other." ('Types of Ethical Theory,' i. 19.) Ethics to him, as to them, is the science which collects and vindicates "our ethical intuitions," or "the particular averments of the moral consciousness." "Our moral verdicts," he says, "are the enunciation of what is given us ready-made and has only to pass through us into speech. . . . We have nothing to seek by logical process, but only to give forth what we find." ('Study,' ii. 6.) Martineau's pages, like Hamilton's, abound with appeals to "the veracity of consciousness,"—though at a pinch both Martineau and Hamilton are found interpreting the responses of the oracle in a sense which might astonish the ordinary man. In regard to the external world, the doctrine of Natural Realism is maintained, quite in Hamilton's manner, on the faith of "the intuitive witness borne by consciousness to the presence of a world beyond the contents of that consciousness." ('Study,' i. 133.) Martineau, while sympathising with Professor Laurie's supposed "return to Dualism," finds fault with him because he does not "accept the non-ego, as, like the ego, immediately known in the act of perception." (i. 191.) "Our reference of a perception to an object in independent space and time" is "an intuitive apprehension of what is," and to doubt it is a "surrender of the reliance which we inevitably place on the veracity of our own faculties." (i. 77.) In short, "the idealist's superior airs towards the natural postulates and the direct working of the honest understanding are seldom unattended by intellectual error and moral wrong." (i. 80.)

But to present the task of philosophy in this way is surely to demonstrate unwittingly its perfect uselessness; for if we have only to "trust in the *bona fides* of our intuitive witnesses" to find ourselves in possession of truth, why should we trouble further? The service of metaphysics, Dr Chalmers once wrote,[1] is "not to supply a new but only to certify and authenticate an old instrument of observation, given ready-made to all men by the hand of nature, and which all men could have confidently and successfully made use of without the necessity of being told so by a right metaphysics, had not a wrong metaphysics cast obscuration on the dictates and disturbed the confidence of nature." "The child sees an apple on the table and affirms an apple to be there. A Berkeleian philosopher labours to disprove the assertion. A second metaphysician arises and repels the sophistry of the first." And so the child keeps his apple. It is not often that the position is stated with such naïveté, but Martineau comes near saying the same thing when, in the Preface to his 'Study of Religion,' he speaks of the metaphysical investigation as winning at last "only the very position which common-sense had assumed at first," and when he describes metaphysics—his own, be it observed, not any species of what Chalmers calls "wrong metaphysics"—as "but medicine for sickly minds, which the healthy may well fling away as they would 'apples of Sodom.'" "I believe," he adds, "in the permanent necessity of the philosophic schools which torment the wits of mankind." The critical process, however, "gives no

[1] 'North British Review,' vi. 275-279.

new revelation, but *reinstates us where we intuitively stood*, only with certainty secured that the ground is not hollow beneath us." ('Life,' ii. 217.)

There is, of course, an important truth in the view that, as Tucker put it, philosophy may be likened to Achilles' spear which healed the wounds it had itself inflicted. One great function of good metaphysics is to oust bad metaphysics and disprove its pretensions. In a sense, it is even true that a true philosophy will be found to justify the principles of common-sense—that is to say, the beliefs upon which we all act in practical life. But it vindicates their "veracity" for the purposes of that life, and not as oracles of ultimate truth. The philosophical problem—the question, that is, how we may most truly express the ultimate nature of reality—cannot even be stated, till we have left the hard and fast distinctions of common-sense far behind us. If the question is to be solved at all, it must be, not by accepting these categories and distinctions as final, but by allowing the free play of reflection upon them to disclose their inadequacy and to show us the way to a higher truth. In the particular case of Ethics a similar criticism holds. "To interpret, to vindicate and systematise the moral sentiments," says Martineau, "constitutes the business of this department of thought" ('Types,' i. 1). If to vindicate the moral sentiments meant to vindicate our ethical experience as a foundation of inference as to the nature of reality; if to "systematise" meant to investigate, like Sidgwick, what common-sense really believes about morality; and if to "interpret" meant to bring to self-consciousness the principles which have unconsciously guided its formation and progress, and to relate the ethical life to other aspects of reality,—then, indeed, the definition would be as comprehensive and as unexceptionable as could be desired. But the Intuitional Method, it is obvious, understands by vindication the acceptance of "the particular averments of the moral consciousness" as immediate oracles; and, in that case, the task of systematisation and interpretation seems to become comparatively unimportant, if not superfluous. It is certain, at least, that Intuitional moralists as a rule devote little attention to this part of their work.

To this Intuitionalism, and to what I have called the survivals of Deism in his thought, the main defects of Martineau's ethical theory are traceable. His volumes abound in passages of keen psychological analysis, of rare moral insight and spiritual beauty; but his specific theory of Conscience, as in every case intuitively deciding between two conflicting motives, never, I think, made any converts, and is not really maintainable, either on psychological or on philosophical grounds. What is true and suggestive in it is that the moral choice is not so much between an absolutely good and an absolutely bad, as between a better and a worse; though the choice of the better is, in the particular circumstances, the absolutely right for me, and the choice of the worse would be the absolutely bad. We may also, perhaps, arrange the "springs of action," as Martineau does, in an ethical order of merit as "higher" and "lower"; the appetites, for example, coming near the bottom of the scale, the love of power or ambition a good deal higher, the primary affections higher still, and compassion and reverence at the top of the list. Martineau supplies such a list in considerable detail; and his theory is that, whenever any of the propensions, passions, affections or sentiments thus classified comes into conflict with one higher in the scale, right volition consists in choosing the "higher" in preference to the "lower." But Sidgwick conclusively argues that, although this will probably be true as a general rule, and the scale of motives may therefore be useful as serving to "indicate in a rough and general way the kind of desires which it is usually best to encourage and indulge, in comparison with other kinds which are ordinarily likely to compete and collide with them," still it cannot be maintained that any such "universal relation of higher or lower subsists between any pair of impulses as is here affirmed." Common-sense would rather hold "that, in all or most cases, a natural impulse has its proper sphere, within which it should be normally operative, and that the question whether a motive commonly judged higher should yield to a lower, is one that cannot be answered decisively in the general way in which Martineau answers it." "Love of ease and pleasure," for example, comes nearly lowest in Martineau's list, and "love of gain" and "love of culture" much higher; but we often find men prompted by the latter motives to shorten unduly their hours of recreation. The answer must depend in every case on the particular conditions and circumstances of the conflict. And hence it is impossible to evade Sidgwick's general conclusion that the comparison ultimately decisive is "not a comparison between the motives primarily conflicting, but between the effects of the different lines of conduct to which they respectively prompt, considered in relation to whatever we regard as the ultimate end of reasonable action."[1] But if we accept this conclusion, it also disposes of the notion of a special faculty issuing immediate decisions on the moral question at issue. The apprehension of the superior worth of a principle is, according to Martineau, "no mediate discovery of which we can give an account, but is immediately inherent in

[1] 'The Ethics of Green, Spencer, and Martineau,' pp. 359-361. This conclusion is accepted by Professor Upton, 'Life and Letters,' ii. 395.

the very experience of the principles themselves,—a revelation inseparable from their appearance side by side. By simply entering the stage together and catching the inner eye, they disclose their respective worth and credentials." Or, as he puts it elsewhere, "there is no analysis or research required; the claims are decided by a glance at their face." To this the reply is, that if by Conscience is understood what it usually means in ordinary speech, the response of the trained moral nature in view of any ethical alternative, then every one will admit that conscience acts with much of the swiftness and certainty of an instinct, and furnishes in most cases an infallible touchstone of the nature described. But apart from experience of the effects of action—as regards the individual, apart from moral training and the ethical heritage of humanity—I am totally unable to conceive the existence of such a power of immediate or abstract judgment as Martineau's theory seems to imply.

Martineau's extreme Intuitionalism here was, in one sense, a natural consequence of the individualism which so strongly marks his ethical theory. "Ethical Individualism" is the term which Professor Upton uses more than once as giving "the keynote of his moral philosophy." It springs from his intense realisation of the personal character of the moral life, and is one great source of his power as a moral teacher. But in the region of theory it leaves him committed to untenable abstractions. The idea of conscience as an infallible faculty in each individual is closely connected with the view of mankind as a collection of isolated or self-sufficient individuals. Martineau does scant justice to the social aspect of morality—the extent, that is, to which our actual conscience is the creature of authority, moulded by inherited institutions and customs, the product, in a word, of the age-long "education of the human race." This view may be presented so baldly as to reduce morality to an affair of external sanctions, a sense of punishability—which would mean the elimination of the moral element from conduct altogether—and, in his reaction from this false form of statement, Martineau is carried to the extreme of treating the individual as sufficient unto himself. But it is not really open to doubt that we are men and moral beings at all, only as we share in the corporate and inherited life of humanity. We are quite literally members one of another, and the subjective conscience is, in its main contents, the organ of the objective ethos which has shaped itself in human history and lies around us from our infancy. It would be unfair to say that Martineau nowhere recognises this unity of mankind. He could not have been the great religious teacher he was, had he not recognised it. There is a passage in the second volume of his 'Types of Ethical Theory' which expresses the true view so finely that I will venture to quote it, even at the risk of seeming to cut the ground from under the foregoing criticisms. He is describing the transformation of conscience "into social consensus and religion."

"This process so implicates together the agent and his fellows that we can scarce divide the casual factors into individual and social, inner and outer: *bodily*, no doubt, he stands there by himself, while his family are grouped separately round him; but *spiritually*, he is not *himself* without them; and this reveals itself by a kind of moral amputation, if death should snatch them away, and put his *selfdom* to the test of loneliness. It is the same with the larger groups which enclose him in their sympathetic embrace. His *country* is not external to him: he is woven into it by sensitive fibres that answer to all its good or ill: its life-blood courses through his veins, inseparably mingled with his own. The social union is most inadequately represented as a compact or tacit bargain subsisting among separate units, agreeing to combine for specific purposes and for limited times, and then disbanding again to their several isolations. It is no such forensic abstraction, devised as a cement for mechanically conceived components; but a concrete though spiritual form of life, penetrating and partly constituting all persons belonging to it, so that only as fractions of it do they become human integers themselves."—('Types of Ethical Theory,' ii. 373.)

But it is to be noted that this eloquent acknowledgment only appears as an afterword, in the act of passing beyond ethics to a religious standpoint, and though doubtless coexisting with it in the author's mind, is not really harmonised with the exclusive individualism of the formulated ethical theory. Moreover, it can be shown that although he rises above it in the utterances of personal religious feeling, his individualism invades his theory of religion itself. His ethical individualism leads him to an ethical Deism which treats God consistently as "another person." There is no part of Martineau's theory which is more characteristic, or on which he lays more stress, than his doctrine of Obligation. It is probably his chief contribution to the theistic argument; for in Obligation he sees, as it were, the meeting-place of the human and the Divine. "In morals, it is God and self that stand face to face." But the explanation he offers of the feeling of Obligation is that "the Moral Law is *imposed by an authority foreign to our personality*, and is open, not to be canvassed, but only to be obeyed or disobeyed."[1] Professor Caldecott justly remarks on this as "an expression so forbidding that, were it not for the fact that it is italicised, one would have ignored it as a lapsus."[2] But it is impossible to ignore it, for to Martineau it is just

[1] 'Study,' ii. 7. [2] 'Philosophy of Religion,' p. 346.

this feature of the ethical consciousness which carries us on to religion, and gives us an immediate certainty of the Divine existence. It forms the pivot of his argument, against Sidgwick and Green, that the law cannot be self-imposed. "It takes two," he says, "to establish an obligation. *To whom*, then, is the alleged obligation upon the agent? You will say, perhaps, it is to *himself* that the obligation lies to choose the more fruitful lot. By the hypothesis, however, he is the person that *bears* the obligation, and cannot also be the person whose presence *imposes it:* it is impossible to be at once the upper and the nether millstone. Personality is unitary, and in occupying one side of a given relation is unable to be also in the other."[1] He concludes, therefore, that "if the sense of authority means anything, it means the discernment of something *higher than we*, having claims on our *self*, therefore no mere part of it. . . . If I rightly interpret this sentiment, I cannot therefore stop within my own limits, but am irresistibly carried on to the recognition of another than I, . . . *another Person*, greater and higher and of deeper insight."[2]

This position is in the sharpest contrast to the Kantian doctrine of the autonomy of the will, which is surely one of Kant's most valuable contributions to modern thought. A man can be bound only by the enactment of his own self-legislative will. So long as the law comes to me from without, I can demand its warrant and evade its claims; but I cannot escape from my own law — from the law which is the expression of my necessary will. Martineau himself follows this more excellent way in the Introduction to his 'Study of Religion,' where he is discussing the relation of Ethics to Religion. "Without an internal enactment in the soul, to which the external

[1] 'Types,' ii. 100. [2] Ibid., ii. 97.

mandate brings its appeal," he says, "the consciousness of Right is impossible, and the human world is susceptible of government only as a menagerie." And it is undeniable, he further admits, that "conscience may act as human before it is discovered to be divine. . . . Ethics, therefore, have practical existence and operation prior to any explicit religious belief: the law of right is inwoven with the very tissue of our nature, and throbs in the movements of our experience, and cannot be escaped by any one till he can fly from himself."[1] But if that is so, then the bindingness of moral rules cannot depend essentially on the fact that they emanate from "another Person," and consequently Martineau's theological version of the ethical consciousness cannot be true as it stands. He is, of course, absolutely right in insisting on the objective nature of the moral law, and in rejecting the notion that the law is in any way constituted, or made authoritative, by the subjective act of recognition. Duty may, therefore, not unfitly be spoken of as the law of God revealed in the consciousness of the individual who recognises it. But the difficulties of Martineau's theory all arise from the sheer separation which he appears to make between the self of the moral being and its divine source, conceived in this connection as an objectively legislating Will. This appears from the hypothetical examples to which he has recourse to justify his position. He supposes "the case of one lone man in an atheistic universe,"[2] and asks whether there could "really exist any authority of higher over lower within the enclosure of his detached personality"; and he not unreasonably concludes that "an insulated nature,"[3] "an absolutely solitary individual," cannot be conceived as the seat of

[1] 'Study,' i. 21, 22.

[2] 'Types,' ii. 97.

[3] Ibid., ii. 96, 99.

authority at all. But such an individual is a *non-ens*, the creature of a theory, and is certainly improperly spoken of as a self or a person. If any being were shut up, in Martineau's phrase, "within the enclosure of his detached personality," he would be a self-contained universe to himself, or rather he would be one bare point of mere existence. If intelligences were simply mutually exclusive points of subjectivity, then indeed they could not be the seats and depositaries of an objective law; they could not be the subjects of law at all. Consciousness of imperfection, the capacity for progress, and the pursuit of perfection, are alike possible to man only through the universal life of thought and goodness in which he shares, and which, at once an indwelling presence and an unattainable ideal, draws him "on and always on." Personality is not "unitary" in Martineau's sense, as occupying one side of a relation and unable to be also on the other. The very capacity of knowledge and morality implies that the person is not so confined, but is capable of regarding himself and all other beings from what Martineau well names "the station of the Father of Spirits." [1]

It is only, therefore, after discarding the intuitionalism, and the abstract individualism and deism of the theory, that it can be accepted as a true account of the ethical consciousness and its implications. These may be the features most distinctive of Martineau, the technical philosopher, but they were not the inspiration of the religious thinker and seer who habitually spoke of God as "the Soul of all souls." Professor Upton has very clearly pointed out the coexistence in Martineau's writings of "two modes of conceiving God, one of which is deistic or Hebraic, while the other is distinctly and intensely Christian." [2] The first mode represents God as

[1] 'Types,' ii. 98.

[2] 'Life,' ii. 475.

"another and higher person"; the second represents Him as "the Soul of souls." The former conception rests upon an *inferential* knowledge of God, derived either from the experience of God's resistance to our will through the forces of Nature, or from God's felt restraint upon us in the voice of Conscience. In both cases, the Supreme Being is regarded as completely separated from the human soul, and His existence and character are apprehended and demonstrated by a process of reasoning. This rationalistic or deistic view Professor Upton acknowledges to be mainly in the foreground in the formulated philosophy, but he strongly contends that in the other view — "in the apprehension of God as the Infinite, including all finite existences, as the immanent Absolute who progressively manifests his character in the Ideals of Truth, Beauty, Righteousness, and Love, we have the inmost essence of Dr Martineau's religious philosophy,"[1] and that without this "both his philosophy and his sermons would lose much of their characteristic depth and beauty."[2] I most readily believe this, and only regret that this "mystical," or, as I should prefer to call it, speculative, insight found such inadequate expression in his formal theory. Professor Upton suggests by way of explanation that, although in 1841 Martineau explicitly treats the moral and spiritual affections as "constituting a participation in the divine nature," he soon afterwards became alarmed by the danger to which such a doctrine is exposed of gliding easily into Pantheism. Certain it is that, during the greater part of his life, he seemed dominated by an almost morbid dread of this particular form of error, and, in his professorial and critical *rôle*, exhibited an almost striking insensibility to the great speculative

[1] 'Life,' ii. 479. [2] Ibid., ii. 477.

truth it embodies. His 'Study of Spinoza,' for example, contains an admirable "Life," and much acute and incisive criticism of technical doctrine, but the criticism is entirely from the outside. The failure to appreciate the inner motives of Spinoza's thought and the secret of his power over some of our greatest thinkers and poets is complete. One cannot help recalling a significant sentence of Hegel's in which he represents the philosophy of Spinoza as the test of speculative initiation. "When one begins to philosophise one must first be a Spinozist; the soul must bathe in this æther of the one Substance in which everything that had been held as true has disappeared." It does not appear as if Martineau, so far as his intellect was concerned, had ever submitted to this immersion.

I am afraid that a somewhat similar line of criticism is forced upon us in regard to his Libertarian interpretation of moral freedom. He is right, in my view, in saying that "the language of ethics when translated into necessarian formulas parts with all conceptions distinctly moral, and becomes simply description of phenomena in natural history. It tells us what has been, what is, what probably will be; but not (unless in an altered sense) what *ought to be*."[1] So far as he insisted on the inadequacy of such a version of moral action, Martineau rendered a service to English thought. Kant has shown once for all that moral action is inseparable from the idea of freedom. Freedom is the category of morality. But he has also indicated, in his obscurely expressed distinction between the empirical and the intelligible character, that the recognition of this has nothing to do with the question of causality, as that is investigated by science. The simple truth is that *that question is not*

[1] 'Study,' ii. 318, quoted in 'Life,' ii. 467.

raised by the ethical consciousness at all. For the moral agent to entangle himself in questions of this sort would be, *ipso facto*, to lapse from the moral point of view; and as a matter of fact he does not do so. Kant stated the truth in a paradox, when he described the moral act as essentially timeless. The moral agent is, as it were, timelessly face to face with his law or ideal, and the moral consciousness considers only the relation of the will to the law. The fact that the law can present itself to him is sufficient proof that he possesses the capacity to realise its demands: it could not otherwise be a motive for him at all. As ethical being, there reside in him all the capacities of his race. What he ought to be, that he might be, and he judges his act accordingly, both while it is in process of contemplation and when he looks back, it may be remorsefully, upon his choice. Should he really seek to excuse himself in the sequel, by trying to show that it was impossible for a man with his particular antecedents to act otherwise than he did, he is regarding the action entirely from an external and non-moral (which for him in the circumstances is an immoral) point of view.

I do not find, therefore, that the unsophisticated conscience, when face to face with a moral alternative, looks either behind, to assert necessity, or before, to assert contingency. It does not seem to me to make any report as to perfectly "open alternatives," if by alternatives we mean events one of which is going to happen. In order to do this, it would be necessary for the agent to give up the personal problem in whose solution he is engaged, and to begin to contemplate himself, *ab extra*, as a finite object or sum of forces. This is the position which the ordinary necessarian theoriser takes up, and it is the position which science must assume in dealing with the empirical individual as a calculable factor in the production of events. Science, looking at the moral action merely as an event in time, limits itself to the question of its relation to its antecedents. The moral quality of the action is no longer under consideration. And to the scientific question only one answer—that of Determinism—is possible. The initial error of Libertarianism is that it accepts battle on the necessarian terms, and then seeks to evade the consequences by a distinction between the character and "the self which has the character," attributing to the latter a power "at will" to "determine himself to either branch of an alternative."[1] But a characterless self is an abstraction of which it is impossible to predicate agency; to regard it as issuing its fiat for the one branch or for the other is to throw us back on the liberty of indifference. A self over and above the concrete self of character is no more a reality than a thing apart from all its qualities; or, to put it otherwise, it is the abstraction of form without matter, and can do no work in the real world. It is impossible to load the scales in this way; and by treating the self as abstract will, Libertarianism, no less than Determinism, though in a different way, deprives the act of its moral quality. May we not say that the moral consciousness escapes the dilemma of ordinary Libertarianism and Determinism just because it does not, like them, regard the self as an "insulated" or merely finite being with a definite equipment, whose equation may be found in terms of character and environment, and who may therefore be treated as a measurable and definitely calculable force interacting with other forces? Such a conception belongs entirely to the plane of mechanics, and has all the abstractness of that science.

[1] 'Study,' ii. 309.

Just because he is not a punctual or self-contained unity, but, in virtue of his reason, a sharer in a universal life, the potentialities of an ethical being are infinite. All things are possible to him — not as a finite individual at any given moment of time (the ethical consciousness guarantees no miracles), but eternally possible to every son of man. The absolute claim of the moral ideal, and its infinitely regenerative power in breaking the yoke of the past, seem to me the real facts to which the moral consciousness testifies. Both Libertarianism and Determinism misrepresent them by insisting on applying to them the categories of mechanism and temporal succession.

I have left myself no space to deal with Martineau's doctrine of Cause and his theory of the material world. But that is perhaps the less to be regretted, seeing that Professor Upton acknowledges that this part of Martineau's system does not "exert the same convincing force" as his more specifically religious utterances. I will confine myself, therefore, to reminding the reader that the theory is based on the assertion of our own noumenal causality, as revealed in the consciousness of effort, and the acknowledgment in the same act of a counter cause, opposed to and controlling our activity. This is Martineau's Natural Dualism, which, however, he at once proceeds to interpret in a Berkeleian sense. The Cause revealed to me in nature can only be a Will, for no other real cause is known to me; phenomenal causation, so called, is relation of events but not agency. There are no second causes except created spirits like myself; in nature we have simply the continual forthputting of the divine causality, according to certain laws laid down by God once for all. The theory is thus, in all essentials, Berkeley's short and easy method with the materialists and sceptics of his day — the argument that God is immediately present to us in the phenomena of sense, as their efficient and regulating cause. Now there is certainly a perennial attractiveness about Berkeley's theory, from the way in which it seems to bring God near to us, and to make the doctrine of his immanence a reality. It seems very simple to unify the forces of nature in this way, and regard them all as the expression of a noumenal Will behind them. But further reflection shows that to represent the divine causality as the direct forthputting of a force, of which we become aware in the experience of "resistance to our will," is to conceive God on the level of mechanical science merely as a cause of motion—the very error for which Socrates blamed Anaxagoras. We cannot, in truth, without the grossest anthropomorphism, relate physical phenomena directly to God by the category of cause, as that is used in dynamics, or conceive God and man as two forces pushing against one another. We must not fly off at once, as Bacon warned us, to the highest generalities. The complete inappropriateness of such a conception in an ultimate metaphysical reference is further seen by the difficulties which Martineau encounters in connection with space. The divine agency, it turns out, requires a datum. "I think of a cause," he says, "as needing something else in order to work—*i.e.*, some *condition* present with it; as constituting one term of a *relation*, and as being a cause only by reason of its so standing." He accordingly accepts such a "coexisting datum" in the form of "space, ready to have forces thrown into any of its points";[1] and in his college lectures he treats space and time as "the infinite, uncreated, eternal data which constitute the negative conditions of all beings and all phenomena."[2] But the

[1] 'Study,' i. 406. [2] 'Life,' ii. 284.

conception of God as a Being projecting causal energy into space, and as "committing" himself once for all to certain general laws of operation, the unfortunate individual results of which he is thenceforward powerless to obviate, is, I fear, too deistic and anthropomorphic to carry conviction or consolation to the present age. And it is not surprising that Professor Upton finds the doctrine of space in particular "a perplexing feature in Dr Martineau's cosmical philosophy."

It seems strangely inconsistent with much of the foregoing criticism to find Martineau himself protesting, "If there is one modern tendency more than another against which I have striven through life with the united earnestness of natural instinct and deliberate conviction, it is the extreme individualism which turns our foremost politics, philosophy, religion into a humiliating caricature."[1] For it has been chiefly the relics of individualism and deism in his theory that have been commented on. But that merely shows how far the intellectual framework of a man's beliefs may come short of embodying the animating principle of his thought, and how subtly pervasive is the influence of inherited conceptions which we imagine ourselves to have outgrown and even to be combating. In one of his essays,[2] Martineau distinguishes between the Religion of Causation, the Religion of Conscience, and the Religion of the Spirit as three aspects or stages, of which the third alone presents God and man in their true relations. Man, from this final point of view, is no longer "a spiritual island planted out in the natural deep of things," but lives in a communion where every moral ideal or spiritual affection appears as a movement of "the all-quickening Spirit"—a revelation of "the common essence of God and man,

[1] 'Life,' i. 373. [2] 'Essays, Reviews, and Addresses,' iv. 578-580.

the divine element that spreads its margin into us." Unfortunately, in his formal philosophy, Martineau remains almost entirely on the level of the first and second stages, adopting the defective terminology of contemporary Intuitionism and the Philosophy of Commonsense. Hence the critic of his "system" feels himself in the ungrateful position, described in an apt phrase by Martineau himself, of "saying Amen to the faith but picking holes in the dialectic." The deepest expression of his thought is really to be found in his religious writings, and in those passages of his philosophical books which are written under the same inspiration. He was of the lineage of the prophets and the saints rather than that of the great speculative thinkers. Yet it is easy to undervalue his specifically philosophical work, and I should much regret if the criticisms into which I have been led tended to encourage such a view. On a previous page of this article, I have already recorded my sense of his imperishable services to the common cause of Idealism. As a thinker, his defects were to a large extent the defects of his qualities. His insistence on the supreme place of the ethical life was like a trumpet-call to rally men from a naturalistic absorption in the world of things and events that happen. His jealous reservation of the personal sphere in man, even from the influx of the divine, though it may have obscured his own speculative outlook, was a wholesome corrective of panlogistic and purely pantheistic tendencies within the Hegelian school. In a more general reference, his exposure of the futility of "ideals" which are not faiths in "the everlasting Real," his noble confidence in Reason, and his unclouded assurance of the immortal destiny of the spirit, made him a beacon of hope to multitudes in a troubled century. "The true," he writes, "is always the divine; depend upon it, the facts of the universe will not prove profane." And in 1898, at the extreme verge of human life, he writes to a correspondent: "I only know that duty and love look more divine, and the spiritual life more surely immortal, than when I spoke of them with less experience." With what better words can one lay down one's pen?

HERBERT SPENCER: THE MAN AND HIS WORK.[1]

IT was eminently in accordance with the fitness of things that the philosopher of evolution should end by writing the evolution of himself, and in spite of its ponderous length and other palpable faults, the result is a very interesting human document. If Spinoza said that he would treat of God and the mind exactly as if he were concerned with lines, planes, and solids, Spencer analyses himself in these pages much as he might dissect a natural history specimen. If we add to the outspoken candour of its self-analysis the unconscious revelations of mind and character of which it is full, and the details which it furnishes of his early upbringing and the history of his ideas, it is manifest that the two volumes give us a much more intimate knowledge than we have hitherto possessed, both of the antecedents of the man and the *milieu* in which his work was produced. Consequently they must be an important aid to a better estimate of that work, both in its strength and its limitations. The history of an idea or a set of ideas is often the best criticism that can be offered. Of the 'Autobiography' itself, as a literary product, it would be easy to speak too harshly. Some allowance must be made for the circum-

[1] The following estimate of Spencer and his work appeared in the 'Quarterly Review' of July 1904, shortly after the publication of the 'Autobiography.'

stances of its composition. Dictated as a rough outline of facts as early as 1875, it was taken up again in 1886 after the last and most serious breakdown in Spencer's health, when more serious mental work was impossible. A little time was spent daily in putting the memoranda into shape; but even this was not done in chronological order. Haunted, as he was apt to be, by the thought that he might not survive to complete the record, he decided to take up first the sections which he deemed of most importance, passing thus freely backward and forward from one period of his life to another, and gradually filling up the gaps of the narrative as destiny proved kinder than his fears.

Such a desultory mode of composition explains many redundancies and repetitions; and the ebb-tide of mental energy during which much of it took shape may also explain the frequent slackness of style and the prolixity of non-significant detail through which the reader has often to plough his way. There is a lack of proportion in the narrative, especially as it advances in the second volume. Sometimes it is as if the writer were at the mercy of his memoranda, and we have a chronicle of itineraries and incidents which have no interest beyond the fact that they happened at a certain date, and help Spencer to block out the blank spaces of his memory. At other points, an association of ideas betrays him into general reflections, and he airs for a page or two some of his favourite "nonconformities," with which readers of his works are already sufficiently familiar. It is at times, an unkind reader might say in the author's style, as if the centres of inhibition had temporarily abdicated their function. Shall we say that such causes as these help to explain the 1098 pages to which the volumes run, or must this damning fact be ascribed to an egotism so massive and unconscious that it loses all the pettiness of ordinary vanity? Spencer makes an excuse for the egotistic suggestion which the autobiographical form necessarily involves, but it does not seem to have occurred to him that the scale of his posthumous monument would be taken as the true measure of his self-absorption.

But after all these grave deductions have been made, the 'Autobiography' somehow succeeds in holding the reader's interest, and even engaging his sympathy. It lies in the nature of the man who is its subject, that we find in it neither the beautiful simplicity of character which charms us in Darwin, nor the vivid personality which gives light and animation to Huxley's 'Life.' Spencer's story owes its attraction chiefly to its frankness, to the transparent honesty of the narrator, and the absence of all affectation or pose. Paradoxical as the statement may seem in view of Spencer's achievement, the mind here portrayed, save for the command of scientific facts and the wonderful faculty of generalisation, is commonplace in the range of its ideas; neither intellectually nor morally is the nature touched to the finest issues. Almost uneducated, except for a fair acquaintance with mathematics and the scientific knowledge which his own tastes led him to acquire, with the prejudices and limitations of middle-class English Nonconformity, but untouched by its religion, Spencer appears in the early part of his life as a somewhat ordinary young man. His ideals and habits did not differ perceptibly from those of hundreds of intelligent and straight-living Englishmen of his class. And to the end, in spite of his cosmic outlook, there remains this strong admixture of the British Philistine, giving a touch almost of banality to some of his sayings and doings. But just because the picture is so faithfully drawn, giving us the man in his habit as he lived, with all his limitations and prejudices (and his consciousness of these limitations, expressed sometimes with a passing regret, but oftener with a childish pride in them), with all his irritating pedantries and the shallowness of his emotional nature—we can balance against these defects his high integrity and unflinching moral courage, his boundless faith in knowledge and his power of conceiving a great ideal and carrying it through countless difficulties to ultimate realisation, and a certain boyish simplicity of character as well as other gentler human traits, such as his fondness for children, his dependence upon the society of his kind, and his capacity to form and maintain some life-long friendships. A kindly feeling for the narrator grows as we proceed, and most unprejudiced readers will close the book with a genuine respect and esteem for the philosopher in his human aspect.

For the student of Spencer's personality and ideas, the opening chapters of his 'natural history,' in which he depicts the stock of which he came and the social surroundings in which his early years were passed, are probably the most valuable. This account of his ancestry—in particular, the picture of his father and of the uncle who superintended his education—gives us already, "in large letters," some of the most striking intellectual and moral features which we associate with the philosopher. Spencer sums up the outstanding characteristics of the race as "independence, self-asserting judgment, the tendency to nonconformity, and the unrestrained display of their sentiments and opinions, more especially in respect of political, social, and ethical matters." "A general absence of reticence" and "a tendency to disagree" are, perhaps, simpler and more illuminative phrases. Wesleyanism was traditional in the family, but "they dissented more or less from that form of dissent." In the case of Spencer's father, "his repugnance to all living authority" led him to the Quakers' meeting-house—not, according to his son, because he had adopted any of their special tenets, "but the system was congruous to his nature, in respect of its complete individualism and absence of ecclesiastical government." Among negative traits of the family, accompanying those mentioned above, Spencer instances

> "a comparatively small interest in gossip. Their conversation ever tended towards the impersonal. . . . There was no considerable leaning towards literature. Their discussions never referred to poetry or fiction or the drama. Nor was the reading of history carried to any extent by them. And though in early life they were all musical, the æsthetic in general had no great attractions. It was rather the scientific interpretations and moral aspects of things which occupied their thoughts."

Ethical and political discussion were the very breath of their nostrils, and they were all reformers of a radical type.

The notes we get of Spencer's desultory and fragmentary education are also instructive. He had a boy's taste for natural history; and through helping his father to prepare experiments for his pupils, he gained some acquaintance with physics and chemistry, and interest sufficient to carry him through a popular manual of the latter subject. In a skipping way, he read a good deal in the medical and scientific periodicals lying about the house, besides books of travel and history from the various libraries of the town. During the years of his more systematic education under his uncle, the chief feature of the boy was his repugnance to language-study and his leaky memory in that direction. To mathematics he took more kindly. The sum of his acquirements when he returned home at the age of sixteen was meagre enough.

"A fair amount of mathematics had been acquired, and the accompanying discipline had strengthened the reasoning powers. In the acquisition of languages but trifling success had been achieved; in French nothing beyond the early part of the grammar and a few pages of a phrase-book; in Greek a little grammar, I suppose, and such knowledge as resulted from rendering into English a few chapters of the New Testament; and in Latin some small ability to translate the easy books given to beginners —always, however, with more or less blundering. Education at Hinton was not wide in its range. No history was read; there was no culture in general literature; nor had the concrete sciences any place in our course. Poetry and fiction were left out entirely."

For the three and a half years following this, up till his twenty-first birthday, he was learning his profession as an engineer, and actively engaged on the London and Birmingham and other railways then in course of construction. During these important years his mental development continued in the same course. His mathematical studies were carried farther, and his letters to his father at this time were filled with geometrical problems and solutions. He did not, however, proceed to the higher developments of the subject, for at a later period we hear of his succumbing to his "constitutional idleness" in an attempt to master the differential calculus. The letters also discuss mechanical problems, and contain speculations on various questions in physics. Some lectures on chemistry in the town where he was placed prompted a resumption of that study; and the collection of the fossils disclosed by the railway cuttings through the blue lias clay led to some study of geology and to the purchase of Lyell's 'Principles,' then recently published. But beyond these scientific and practical interests there is no record of those stirrings of the higher life of the imagination, or those impulses towards the deeper problems of philosophy and religion which commonly visit thoughtful youth in these years. Spencer, indeed, makes at this time the impression of a matter-of-fact young Englishman of an inventive turn of mind and with a distinct bent towards reflection on physical problems, but without much emotional depth of nature or delicacy of feeling, and with an almost singular absence in his composition of what Carlyle used to call the "mystical" element—that is to say, the specifically religious and metaphysical impulse. The religious beliefs in which he had been brought up were slowly losing their hold upon him without any sense of mental crisis, obviously because they had never been held with any emotional tenacity,—had never, indeed, satisfied in his case any personal need. The creed of Christendom, he says in a passage which, by the shallowness of its analysis, sufficiently exemplifies his own defective endowment, was

"evidently alien to my nature, both emotional and intellectual. To many, and apparently to most, religious worship yields a species of pleasure. To me it never did so; unless, indeed, I count as such the emotion produced by sacred music. . . . But the expressions of adoration of a personal being, the utterance of laudations and the humble professions of obedience, never found in me any echoes."

At the age of twenty-one he gave up his engineering appointment, in order to devote himself to working out the idea of an electro-magnetic engine which his father had conceived. But within a month it became apparent that the idea could not be practically applied. The next seven years of his life were of an unsettled and desultory character. More than once he was glad to accept temporary engineering engagements, but with the exception of about eighteen months thus occupied, the time was passed in "speculating and experimenting, leading to no practical results." The idea underlying his restless intellectual activity was the hope of making some discovery or perfecting some mechanical device which might yield a commercial return. But though some of the ideas looked promising enough, and one contrivance was actually patented, the labour was in vain so far as its immediate purpose was concerned. The range of these speculations and experiments, however, gives a vivid impression of the mental "discursiveness" on which Spencer dwells with some complacence as a characteristic trait.[1] In addition to these scientific interests, there also persisted in the young man the family bias towards social and political reflection; and his first appearance as an author in 1842 was in the department of political ethics. A visit to Hinton in that year, and a renewal of political conversations with his uncle, suggested a series of letters to 'The Nonconformist' newspaper embodying their common views. His uncle gave him a letter of introduction to Mr Edward Miall, under whose editorship the paper had recently been established as an organ of the advanced dissenters, and a series of twelve 'Letters on the Proper Sphere of Government' appeared in the same year.

[1] "The products of mental action are seen to range from a doctrine of State-functions to a levelling-staff; from the genesis of religious ideas to a watch-escapement; from the circulation in plants to an invalid bed; from the law of organic symmetry to planing machinery; from principles of ethics to a velocimeter; from a metaphysical doctrine to a binding-pin; from a classification of the sciences to an improved fishing-rod joint; from the general Law of Evolution to a better mode of dressing artificial flies" ('Autobiography,' ii. 435). At the point we have reached most of these larger speculations were still in the future, but in addition to the appliances mentioned, we hear of plans for an improvement of the printing-press, for an improved method of typefounding, a rationalised system of letters for printing, a scheme for a universal language on a monosyllabic basis, and the outline of a duodecimal system of notation.

These 'Letters,' republished as a pamphlet in 1843, are not to be taken, perhaps, as expressing more than what he calls "the mental attitude of the Spencers." The principles expounded were those which he drew in with the air he breathed; in the language of his own philosophy, they might almost be styled connate. The 'Letters' elaborate the definition of the State which he had volunteered to a friend the year before—"a national institution for preventing one man from infringing upon the rights of another"; and they apply the theory of individualism with the rigour and vigour of two-and-twenty. Even war is excluded from the sphere of government interference, and is to be conducted as a private enterprise on joint-stock principles. Spencer is fain to confess, in the light of later reflection, that here he has gone too far, though, as he characteristically adds, he might have cited in support of his argument "the case of the Iroquois league"! But although modified in particulars, the 'Letters' give us in their first form ideas which controlled the whole course of Spencer's political philosophy; and to the writing of them he traces himself, in a natural development, the successive stages of his subsequent authorship.

"Had they never been written, 'Social Statics,' which originated in them, would not even have been thought of. Had there been no 'Social Statics,' those lines of inquiry which led to the 'Principles of Psychology' would have remained unexplored. And without that study of life in general, initiated by the writing of these works, leading, presently, to the study of the relations between its phenomena and those of the inorganic world, there would have been no 'System of Synthetic Philosophy'" (i. 212).

The train of thought initiated in the 'Letters' was followed out at intervals during the years that followed, and latterly became Spencer's chief intellectual interest. Thus in 1843 he writes: "I have been reading Bentham's works, and mean to attack his principles shortly"—a purpose executed in 1850 in the opening pages of 'Social Statics.' As he explains the matter himself, he had become dissatisfied with the 'Letters,'—

"not so much with the conclusions set forth as with the foundations on which they stood. The analytical tendency had begun to show itself. What was the common principle involved in these conclusions? Whence was derived their ultimate justification? Answers to these questions had become clear to me; and it was the desire to publish them which moved me to write" (i. 305).

Accordingly, in the early months of 1846 we find him beginning a course of reading with a view to his projected book. Characteristically, however, he "paid little attention to what had been written either upon ethics or politics. The books I did read were those which promised to furnish illustrative material." By April 1847 he had collected a large mass of matter for his 'Moral Philosophy,' and it was "beginning to ferment violently." By September of the same year he was able to send thirty pages of the Introduction to his father; and during 1848, while his future hung in suspense, he was thinking out other chapters as he rambled through the fields round Derby,—his thinking being done then, as always, he tells us, mainly while walking. So uncertain did the future seem in the beginning of 1848, that there was talk of emigration to New Zealand. Another scheme ventilated was that he should join his father in starting a school, to be conducted on enlightened educational principles. But before the end of the year his appointment as sub-editor of 'The Economist' relieved him from the necessity of considering such alternatives. The record of his life henceforth is one of steady progress towards a goal which gradually took definite shape in the ten years which followed his settling in London. The first step towards it was taken by the publication of 'Social Statics.' Many of his evenings were devoted to it during his first year in London. Great pains were taken with the style, and it was the end of 1850 before the book saw the light.

Before considering its contents more carefully it will be well, at the point now reached, to ask what the seven years just reviewed may be regarded as having added to Spencer's mental equipment and outlook, and what general characteristics of the man may be gleaned from his narrative. It is clear that his multifarious activities had given him a considerable knowledge of men and business affairs, while his studies and experiments had increased his acquaintance with physical science and natural history. Besides novels, he also read some of the books which were impressing his contemporaries, such as 'Sartor Resartus,' Emerson's 'Essays,' and Ruskin's 'Modern Painters.' The last-mentioned he seems to have valued chiefly because it gratified his spirit of dissent by daring to express unfavourable opinions about some of Raphael's works. There are several references of an antagonistic nature to Carlyle's doctrine of hero-worship in the 'Social Statics,' and Carlyle appears from time to time in the 'Autobiography' as the incorporation of retrogressive ideals. In one passage "some months in a dark dungeon on bread and water" are suggested as a cure for his anti-utilitarianism and his "ridiculous notion that happiness is of no consequence." But though unaffected by alien ideas, Spencer was not insensible to vigour and charm of style, and his reading at this time extended to the poets.

Shelley's 'Prometheus Unbound' he pronounces, in a letter of 1845, to be "the most beautiful thing I ever read by far," and he rates Shelley about that time as "by far the finest poet of his era." The mature philosopher is rather at a loss to explain this early enthusiasm, and can only surmise that the poem satisfied one of his organic needs, variety. He finds the same trait in connection with food. "Monotony of diet is not simply repugnant; it very soon produces indigestion." The reader will probably conclude more justly that the Spencer of the forties was more of a human being than the dyspeptic analyst of the 'Autobiography.' A letter to his intimate friend, Lott, in 1844, describing a journey through South Wales, reveals a vivacity of unsophisticated feeling which goes much farther to explain the phenomenon than the laboured hypothesis referred to.

As regards his philosophical equipment, it is to be remarked that there continues the same singular absence of the metaphysical, and even of the psychological interest. "All through my life," he says, "Locke's 'Essay' had been before me on my father's shelves, but I had never taken it down; or, at any rate, I have no recollection of having read a page of it." Mill's 'Logic' he glanced at when it came out, but did not carry the study far. When he came across a translation of Kant's 'Critique of Pure Reason' in a friend's house, he stumbled at the outset over the doctrine that time and space are subjective forms, and went no farther. "It has always been out of the question," he explains, "for me to go on reading a book the fundamental principles of which I entirely dissent from. Tacitly giving an author credit for consistency, I, without thinking much about the matter, take it for granted that if the fundamental principles are wrong, the rest cannot be right, and thereupon cease reading—being, I suspect, rather glad of an excuse for doing so." Acting on this highly dangerous principle, he tells us that whenever, in later years, he took up the 'Critique,' he similarly stopped short after rejecting its primary proposition. Spencer's interests during the period under review continued, in fact, to be those of physical science on the one hand and of socio-political theory on the other. But although he had no traffic with the philosophers, a certain amount of reflection on what may be called natural theology was inevitable as his belief in historical Christianity dropped from him. The older natural theology summed itself up in the doctrine that the world had its origin in the creative act of a personal God. A letter to his father in 1848 shows that Spencer had considered this theory and definitely set it aside as incapable of proof, taking up for himself a purely agnostic position.

"As regards 'the ultimate nature of things or origin of them,' my position is simply that I know nothing about it, and never can know anything about it, and must be content in my ignorance. I deny nothing and I affirm nothing, and to any one who says that the current theory *is not* true, I say just as I say to those who assert its truth—you have no evidence" (i. 346).

The turn given to the argument and the phraseology in which it is expressed anticipate very closely, as he claims, the doctrine set forth in 'First Principles' twelve years later. In truth, beyond the new name given to it in baptism by Huxley, there is nothing recondite in this easy method of shelving the question. It is the daily practice of millions. Besides, the cosmological problem isolated thus and treated as a quasi-scientific question ceases to have a properly religious interest. "Men have fought for the doctrine that God made the world," says

Mr Mallock, in his philosophical novel, "merely because they considered it essentially bound up with the doctrine that a God exists who has dealings with the human soul." It was because, with Spencer, the religious emotions were so little engaged that the agnostic position seemed to him so simple, and apparently satisfied him so completely.

The choice of a satisfactory title for his volume caused considerable difficulty, and the one eventually fixed upon led to misapprehensions of a kind to which Spencer was all his life peculiarly sensitive. The title he originally had in view, 'A System of Social and Political Morality,' comes much nearer a simple and intelligible description of the contents than the scientific metaphor which he afterwards pressed into his service: a friend, however, whom he consulted thought it too bald and threadbare. 'Demostatics,' a word used in the Introduction (but suppressed before publication) was the next idea. Spencer considered that it accurately described the subject-matter of the book, namely, the maintenance of social equilibrium through conformity to the law of equal freedom, and suggested at the same time the strictly scientific character of the treatment. But the publisher was decisive against this pedantic neologism, and the term 'Social Statics' was eventually determined on as expressing the same idea, though his uncle warned him that it would be taken by many people for social statistics. The sub-title in the original form, "a system of equity synthetically developed," is perhaps more accurately descriptive than that which finally appeared, "the conditions essential to human happiness specified, and the first of them developed," though the second has the advantage of indicating a relation between the new work and the general Utilitarian doctrine of contemporary English thought. The title,

'Social Statics,' if it was not productive of the confusion which his uncle feared, produced not unnaturally a widespread impression that the ideas promulgated in the book were inspired by the social philosophy of Comte, who had actually employed the same term for one of the divisions of his system. It is true that a perusal of the book would have disclosed fundamental differences between the two thinkers; but it was difficult for the ordinarily constituted man to conceive that any one should undertake a treatise on social philosophy without making himself acquainted with Comte's work, a knowledge of which, through Mill and others, had been spreading in England for ten years previously; still less that he should use a technical title of that thinker's coinage without intending to indicate some relationship between their views. But we have seen how, when he set about systematic reading for his book, Spencer consistently eschewed his predecessors in the same field; and, incredible as it may seem, we have no reason to doubt his assertion that he "then knew nothing more of Auguste Comte than that he was a French philosopher—did not even know that he had promulgated a system having a distinctive title, still less that one of its divisions was called 'Social Statics.' The misunderstanding thus originated continued to haunt and waylay Spencer through the greater part of his life, much to his annoyance, and was the occasion of emphatic and repeated disclaimers.

When we turn to the work itself, the source of its inspiration is found to be much nearer home. The conclusions, as we have seen, are, with very slight modifications, those of the 'Letters on the Proper Sphere of Government.' With the practical doctrines he remained entirely satisfied; it was with their theoretical basis that he was concerned. He desired, in accordance with the synthetic bent of his mind, to exhibit the various conclusions as so many applications of a single principle, from which, when formulated, they might be deductively derived. The principles of "the Spencer family," in short, have to be philosophised, and the principles of the Spencer family were an exceptionally clear and logical expression of the principles of the English political dissenters, and of contemporary Radicalism generally. Spencer began his systematic reading for the book in the year of the abolition of the corn laws. The philosophical Radicals had given place, in popular influence, to the Manchester school; but both were at one in their devotion to the principle of *laissez-faire.* By both the laws of political economy were interpreted, not in the modern scientific sense as statements of what would happen under certain given conditions — statements, therefore, necessarily abstract, and in no sense preceptive as to what ought to happen in the concrete,—but as ordinances of nature divinely instituted, with which it would be impiety as well as folly to interfere. Those who were not in the habit of speaking theistically shared the current optimism as to the beneficent operation of these great impersonal forces. The old Liberalism also, fresh from its campaign against privilege, still occupied the field with its purely negative ideal of freedom from restriction.

Such was the contemporary English world in which Spencer's political thinking grew to maturity; by temperament "radical all over," he absorbed the principles of political individualism and economic optimism so completely, that they assumed for him the guise of intuitions of the moral sense. When he proceeds to formulate the "true fundamental intuition which can be logically unfolded into a scientific" (or, as he elsewhere calls it, a purely synthetic) "morality," what we get is the famous doctrine of Natural Rights, deriving in England from John Locke, exported to France and receiving there world-wide expression from Rousseau and the Declarations, which embody "the principles of 1789," re-imported for English political use by Tom Paine and the earlier Radicals, and practically animating the Benthamite reformers, in spite of the fact that Bentham wrote a treatise on 'Anarchic Fallacies' to expose the French Declaration.[1] "The law of equal freedom," or "the liberty of each, limited alone by the like liberty of all," is the first law, says Spencer, and "we may almost say that the first law is the sole law" on which scientific morality and the organisation of society depend. Or, as he states it later in italics, "Every man has freedom to do all that he wills, provided he infringes not the equal freedom of any other man." He cites it himself in one place as the doctrine that "all men are naturally equal," and expressly refers, in illustrative vindication, to Locke's 'Treatise on Civil Government,' the Declaration of American Independence, "the late European revolutions and the preambles to the new constitutions that have sprung out of them," "the political agitations that have run a successful course within these few years," and even to "the maxim of the Complete Suffrage movement." This principle being laid down, it follows that government is a necessary evil; is, indeed, "essentially immoral" (p. 207). It is necessary because man, now compelled by the increase of population to live in the social state, retains the predatory instincts of his primitive life, and therefore does not uniformly respect the rights of others. But it is a transitional phase of human development — not essential but

[1] Cf. *supra*, p. 13.

incidental. Progress is in all cases towards less government; and, "as amongst the Bushmen we find a state antecedent to government, so may there be one in which it shall have become extinct." Indeed such extinction is inevitable, because the process of civilisation means the adaptation of man to his new conditions. Man possesses indefinite adaptability, and "humanity must in the end become completely adapted to its conditions."

> "Progress, therefore, is not an accident, but a necessity. Instead of civilisation being artificial, it is a part of nature; all of a piece with the development of the embryo or the unfolding of a flower. The modifications mankind have undergone, and are still undergoing, result from a law underlying the whole organic creation; and provided the human race continues, and the constitution of things remains the same, these modifications must end in completeness. As surely as the tree becomes bulky when it stands alone, and slender if one of a group; as surely as the same creature assumes the different forms of cart-horse and race-horse, according as its habits demand strength or speed, . . . so surely must the human faculties be moulded into complete fitness for the social state; so surely must the things we call evil and immorality disappear; so surely must man become perfect" (p. 65).

In the meantime, till this consummation is arrived at, the State has its function. It may be defined as "men voluntarily associated for mutual protection" (p. 275). There is "nothing to distinguish it in the abstract from any other incorporated society." Citizenship is "willingly assumed," and one of the indefeasible natural rights enumerated is "the right to ignore the State"—that is, to "secede from" it, "to relinquish its protection, and to refuse paying towards its support" (p. 250). Police protection (and, he now adds with a grudge, protection against external enemies) being the purpose for which the State is instituted, its duty must be rigorously limited to this function. When it seeks to "interfere" in any other way, whether it be by trying to regulate commerce or by maintaining a religious establishment, by instituting poor-laws or providing for national education, by imposing sanitation or maintaining the currency and the postal arrangements, it is transgressing its proper sphere and displaying, indeed (p. 295), "an absurd and even impious presumption" by taking into its own hands "matters that God seems to be mismanaging," and undertaking to set them right. Those in whom the power of self-restraint needs educating

"must be left to the discipline of nature, and allowed to bear the pains attendant on their own defect of character. The only cure for imprudence is the suffering which imprudence entails. . . . All interposing between humanity and the conditions of its existence—cushioning off consequences by poor-laws or the like—serves but to neutralise the remedy and prolong the evil. Let us never forget that the law is adaptation to circumstances, be they what they may" (p. 353).

So again:—

"Inconvenience, suffering, and death are the penalties attached by nature to ignorance as well as to incompetence—are also the means of remedying these. And whoso thinks he can mend matters by dissociating ignorance and its penalties, lays claim to more than divine wisdom and more than divine benevolence" (p. 378).

To guard ignorant men against the evils of their ignorance by protecting them, for example, against quack prescriptions, is "to divorce a cause and consequence which God has joined together." What a contrast there is, he exclaims, between the "futile contrivances of men and the admirable silent-working mechanisms of nature" (p. 355).

"Always towards perfection is the mighty movement—towards a complete development and a more unmixed good; subordinating in its universality all petty irregularities and fallings-back, as the curvature of the earth subordinates mountains and valleys. Even in the evils the student learns to recognise only a struggling beneficence. But above all he is struck with the inherent sufficingness of things, and with the complex simplicity of those principles by which every defect is being remedied—principles that show themselves alike in the self-adjustment of planetary perturbations and in the healing of a scratched finger, in the balancing of social systems and in the increased sensitiveness of a blind man's ear, in the adaptation of prices to produce and in the acclimatisation of a plant. Day by day he sees a further beauty, . . . contemplation thus perpetually discovering to him a higher harmony and cherishing in him a deeper faith. And now, in the midst of his admiration and his awe, the student shall suddenly see some flippant red-tapist get upon his legs and tell the world that he is going to put a patch upon nature. Here is a man who, in the presence of all the wonders that encompass him, dares to announce that he and certain of his colleagues have laid their heads together and found out a way to improve upon the divine arrangements. . . . These meddlers, these self-appointed nurses to the universe, have so little faith in the laws of things and so much faith in themselves that, were it possible, they would chain earth and sun together lest centripetal force should fail! Nothing but a parliament-made agency can be depended on. . . . Such, in essence, is the astounding creed of these creation-menders."[1]

"Astounding" is the word which most readers will be inclined to apply to these and many similar passages of Spencer's by reason both of their apparent heartlessness and of their colossal optimism. It will be observed how, along with the doctrines already referred to, Spencer reproduces in his argument the deification of nature's arrangements, which plays so great a part in eighteenth century thought. He talks freely of "the Creator's purpose" and "the divine idea" (which is, indeed, the title of one of his chapters), and, as we have seen, of the resistless march of progress carrying this idea to its

[1] 'Social Statics,' p. 293 (p. 323 in the reprint of 1868).

realisation. This deeply-rooted optimism, a relic of the "natural religion" of the preceding century, Spencer carries over into his later philosophy of evolution, after he has dropped the theistic setting; and though he broke it down at points, as he proceeded, by inconsequent admissions, he was unaware—and probably many of his readers are equally unaware — how much his original espousal of the theory was due to the working of this optimistic teleology, and how insensibly it influenced his reading of the evolutional process. Progress as a beneficent necessity, complete adaptation as the goal—these are the original inspiring thoughts, even although they be crossed in the end by the paralysing thought of "Dissolution," which reduces the cosmos to an aimless cycle of alternate building up and pulling down.

It is obviously impossible in the present context to criticise Spencer's political individualism. It has been pointed out times without number that the theory which he carries to its apotheosis is as unhistorical as it is unphilosophical. The pre-social unit with his natural rights never existed; the free individual is the goal of social evolution, not its starting-point. We can only note, therefore, that, however salutary Spencer's later protests may have been in his 'Man *versus* the State,' as a counterpoise to crudely conceived socialistic schemes, or as an invigorating discourse upon the virtues of self-help, his social theory in its totality is no more than a survival in the modern world. An organic theory of society and the State, derived more or less remotely from Hegel or from Comte, has definitely superseded the older individualism, though, as time goes on, incorporating more fully into itself the truths and ideals of the earlier view; for Hegel also, it may be remembered, defines the history of the world as "none other than the progress of the consciousness of freedom." Save for a few anarchists and the new individualists who range themselves under Nietzsche's banner,—individualists strangely unlike the old, whose profoundest belief is in the inequality of man and the right or duty of the stronger to subjugate and exploit his neighbour,—the conception of man as essentially social, and of the State as the organ of the general will, has so firmly established itself that Spencer's pamphlets during the last twenty years sounded like a belated echo, and he had the air, even to himself, of one crying in the wilderness. The remarkable thing is that while Spencer wrote a special essay on "the social organism" as far back as 1860, and greatly contributed to popularise the phrase, his own political thinking remained, to the end, dominated by the conceptions of an abstract and unhistoric individualism, an essentially pre-evolutional phase of thought.

The importance assigned to 'Social Statics,' and the space devoted to tracing the education and life-circumstances of which it was the outcome, are justified by Spencer's own statement in 1879 when he interrupted the regular course of his publications to write 'The Data of Ethics.' He has begun to fear, he says in the Preface to that book, that health may not permit him to reach 'The Principles of Ethics,' the last part of the task he had marked out for himself. "This last part of the task it is," he continues, "to which I regard all the preceding parts as subsidiary. Written as far back as 1842, my first essay, consisting of letters on 'The Proper Sphere of Government,' vaguely indicated what I conceived to be certain general principles of right and wrong in political conduct; and from that time onwards my ultimate purpose, lying behind all proximate purposes, has been that of finding for the principles of right and wrong in conduct at large a scientific basis." In similar terms a letter of the same date declares that "the whole system was at the outset, and has ever continued to be, a basis for a right rule of life, individual and social." Besides this estimate of the place which his ethical and political doctrine held in its author's scheme of thought, it has already been pointed out that the principles and assumptions which he elaborated in 1850 were of decisive influence in shaping his statement of the philosophy of evolution. A closer consideration of the steps by which his cosmic doctrine was reached yields proof of this assertion.

The chief interest of the decade between 1850 and 1860 lies in the gradual evolution in Spencer's mind of the idea of a system of philosophy. In the series of articles published during these years, supplemented by his comments in the 'Autobiography,' we can follow the stages of his thought with some minuteness. To these years belongs his intimacy with George Eliot and the formation of lasting friendships with Lewes, Huxley, and Tyndall. It was in a ramble with Lewes, in the autumn of 1851, that he first met the expression, "the physiological division of labour," which stamped firmly upon his mind the analogy between biological and social evolution, of which we already find traces in the 'Social Statics.' His friendship with Lewes also led him to read not only his friend's novels, but also his 'Biographical History of Philosophy,' from which he derived his first acquaintance with the general course of philosophical thought. "Up to that time," he says significantly, "questions of philosophy had not attracted my attention." And although, by his theory of benevolence and justice in 'Social Statics,' he has shown his aptitude for psychological reflection, psychology likewise (apart from some phrenological speculations) had remained outside his interests. "I had not, up to 1851, made the phenomena of mind a subject of deliberate study." The next step in the organisation of his ideas, and one to which Spencer consistently attributed decisive importance, was his coming across the formula in which Von Baer summed up the development through which every plant and animal passes — the change from homogeneity to heterogeneity. It obviously expresses in a more generalised form the aspect of organic growth already described by the economic metaphor of division of labour. Formulating the nature of the transformation in a purely structural instead of a functional way, and presenting, as Spencer says, "a more graphic image" of the change, it naturally suggested the transference of the conception to the inorganic world. But before this idea definitely took shape in his mind, Spencer's newly awakened psychological interest led him to extend the idea of development to the mental sphere. He had long before given in his adhesion to the Lamarckian doctrine of the transmutation of species, moved rather by a species of anti-supernatural instinct than by adequate evidence in support of it; and in 1852, in a short essay on 'The Development Hypothesis,' he had publicly professed his faith in the theory, basing it upon the cumulative effect of functionally produced modifications. In the 'Principles of Psychology' (which occupied him during 1854 and 1855) mind, animal and human, is treated in close connection with its bodily conditions; and the biological idea of adaptation is transferred to the mental sphere, progressive adaptation being defined as increasing adjustments of inner subjective relations to outer objective relations; while the correspondence between the two is described as advancing from the homogeneous to the heterogeneous, and as increasing in speciality and complexity. It is significant that the closing paragraph of the 'Psychology' emphatically repeats the belief of 'Social Statics' in the "beneficent necessity displayed in the progressive evolution of the correspondence between the organism and its environment." This correspondence "must become more and more complete"; "the life must become higher and the happiness greater." The admission of free-will, it is argued, would interrupt this "advance to a higher harmony." "There would be an arrest of that grand progression which is now bearing humanity onwards to perfection."

The same inspiration is revealed in the title of his next important piece of work, an essay on 'Progress, its Law and Cause,' which he agreed to write for 'The Westminster Review' in the autumn of 1854. This article, which states the law of evolution for the first time as a law of universal application, had its origin in the stir and enlargement of his ideas which accompanied the writing of the 'Psychology'; but, owing to the breakdown which followed the publication of that work, it did not appear till 1857. It may be regarded, he says, as "the initial instalment of the 'Synthetic Philosophy.'" Beginning with the nebular hypothesis, Spencer sweeps the law with a wealth of illustration through cosmic, geologic, organic, and social phenomena, and concludes, exactly in Von Baer's terminology, that, "from the remotest fact which science can fathom, up to the novelties of yesterday, that in which progress essentially consists is the transformation of the homogeneous into the heterogeneous." He next proceeds to ask whether the universality of the law does not imply a universal cause, and this cause he finds in what he calls the multiplication of effects. Every cause produces more than one effect, and hence "it is an inevitable corollary that through all time there has been an ever-increasing complication of things." "Should the nebular hypothesis ever be established, then it will become manifest that the universe at large, like every organism, was once homogeneous; that, as a whole, and in every detail, it has increasingly advanced towards greater heterogeneity." And "thus," he concludes on the old note, "progress is not an accident, not a thing within human control, but a beneficent necessity" ('Essays,' i. 52).

Scarcely had he finished this essay, however, before he seemed to discover a more ultimate cause of evolution in the instability of the homogeneous.

"The social parts of any homogeneous aggregation are necessarily exposed to different forces,—forces that differ either in kind or amount; and, as a corollary from the law of 'the conservation of force,' it follows that unlike changes will be produced in the parts thus dissimilarly acted upon." ('Essays,' i. 281.)

At the same time he took occasion to supplement his account of the evolutionary process by calling attention to certain features which had been overlooked in the previous essay. "As usual, Herbert, thinking only of one thing at a time," was a frequent reproach of his father's in his boyhood; and in his preoccupation with the advance towards greater heterogeneity he had overlooked or temporarily forgotten the fact that it is not an advance towards mere heterogeneity, but is characterised by what he here calls "subordinate integrations." In the living being, for example, the parts become consolidated into definite organs with distinct functions, which are at the same time closely united as members of one whole. And so we arrive at the definition of the law which appears in the first edition of 'First Principles' (1862):—

> "Evolution is a change from an indefinite, incoherent homogeneity to a definite coherent heterogeneity, through continuous differentiations and integrations" (p. 216).

The formula had not even yet, however, reached its final stage of elaboration. In 1864, while working at the 'Classification of the Sciences,' he awoke to the fact that, in making differentiation the primary trait, he had been, as it were, putting the cart before the horse. Aggregates of matter must first be formed before the growth of complexity in their structure can be profitably considered. Hence the primary phase of the process is the integration of matter, a process which necessarily implies a concomitant dissipation of motion. Accordingly, in 1867, 'First Principles' was largely recast for a second edition; and the evolution formula appeared in its final shape:—

> "Evolution is an integration of matter and concomitant dissipation of motion, during which the matter passes from an indefinite, incoherent homogeneity to a definite coherent heterogeneity, and during which the retained motion undergoes a parallel transformation."

For our present purpose, however, the subsequent elaboration of the formula is of subordinate interest; the important step was taken by Spencer in the two essays referred to above. This is shown by the fact that, within three months of the publication of the second, he had drafted the scheme of a system in which "the concrete sciences at large should have their various classes of facts presented in subordination to these universal principles." Commenting in the 'Autobiography' on the nature of the advance made, Spencer characterises it as a transition of the theory in his own mind from the inductive to the deductive stage.

"With this change from the empirical to the rational, the theorem passed into the region of physical science. It became now a question of causes and effects reduced to their simple forms—a question of molar and molecular forces and energies; a question of the never-ending redistribution of matter and motion considered under its most general aspects."

At the same time he adds—

"The indefinite idea of progress passed into the definite idea of evolution when there was recognised the essential nature of the change as a physically determined transformation conforming to ultimate laws of force." ('Autobiography,' ii. 12.)

Both these statements are true, though in both cases their implications are different from what Spencer imagined. By progressively generalising the statement of what happens in development so as to arrive at a "graphic image" of the process, Spencer has at length reduced it to a problem in mechanics. Now whatever happens may unquestionably be described as a phase in "the never-ending redistribution of matter and motion"; but it is quite another thing to suppose that, when we look at the process or the product in that abstract way, we have "recognised the essential nature of the change." On the contrary, that is the *least* we can say of it, the most abstract description we can give of it,—a description, moreover, which leaves out, as we shall see, all that we ordinarily understand by evolution. And that leads to Spencer's second statement regarding the substitution of the idea of evolution for that of progress. There seems no reason to doubt, from the whole history of the idea in Spencer's mind, and from his first mode of stating it, that the statement of evolution was originally intended to apply to the universe as a whole. "The universe at large," he had said, "like every organism, was once homogeneous; as a whole, and in every detail, it has unceasingly advanced towards greater heterogeneity." It was this conception of one vast cosmic process, irresistibly advancing towards a great consummation, which inspired his imagination,—a consummation which might not inaptly be styled, in language used by himself in 'Social Statics,' the realisation of a divine idea. In particular, this 'beneficent necessity' was carrying mankind onwards to the goal of a perfectly adjusted human life. But it soon became evident that, if the cosmic process be regarded simply as redistribution of matter and motion, the series of changes which we have described as Evolution is no more characteristic of it than the opposite series of changes which may be called Dissolution.

Accordingly, in 'First Principles,' this counter process is for the first time introduced, towards the close, in a chapter on equilibration, in which it was pointed out that, in every case, the process of evolution has its impassable limit. Spencer is now driven, accordingly, to relegate his goal, "the establishment of the greatest perfection and the most complete happiness," to the penultimate stage (that of what he calls "the moving equilibrium"), the last stage of all being that complete equilibration which, in the case of an organism, we call death. Unable, however, to acquiesce in "universal death" as the final goal, he finds refuge in the idea of "alternate eras of evolution and dissolution"—"an alternation of evolution and dissolution in the totality of things." But it is perfectly illegitimate to deal with "the totality of things" as a finite evolving object; and if it were possible, then no such resurrection as Spencer anticipates from the clash of systems would be possible, for there would be only *one* dead mass left. But, in point of fact, the two processes are always going on simultaneously; and, if we are to be quite strict, neither notion has any application to the ceaseless shiftings of the cosmic dust. One organism, society, or system is growing towards its perfection while another has entered upon the downward path. Moreover, when we speak of such individuals, and of their perfection and evolution, we are introducing conceptions which are quite irrelevant and quite unintelligible at the purely mechanical standpoint. Nor can the process of evolution, so regarded, be deduced from any laws of matter or energy known to physicists. The hopeless ambiguity of Spencer's law of the persistence of force, and of his use of physical conceptions generally, has often been criticised, but never so conclusively — one might almost say so remorselessly — exposed as in Professor Ward's 'Agnosticism and Naturalism.'

The projected interpretation of "the detailed phenomena of life and mind and society in terms of matter, motion, and force," and the consequent "development of science into an organised aggregate of direct and indirect deductions from the persistence of force," was thus, *ab initio*, foredoomed to failure. In the case of life, there is the belated but none the less significant and courageous confession of Spencer himself, in the chapter on "The Dynamic Element in Life," added to the revised edition of the 'Principles of Biology' in 1898. "We are obliged to confess," he says, "that life in its essence cannot be conceived in physico-chemical terms. The processes which go on in living things are incomprehensible as results of any physical actions known to us" (pp. 117, 120).

Of his own previous definition of life he does not hesitate to say that, while it gives due attention to the connections among the manifestations, "no attention has been paid to that which is manifested. Its value is comparable to that of a cheque on which no amount is written." We are forced, therefore, to conclude that "that which gives the substance to our idea of life is a certain unspecified principle of activity. The dynamic element in life is its essential element." A similar difficulty met him in the case of mind or consciousness, the specific nature of which was clearly irreducible to material terms. In this case, Spencer sought to evade the difficulty by falling back upon the modern principle of psycho-physical parallelism, but at the cost of importing into his system a dualism quite inconsistent with the promises held out in 'First Principles' of a deduction from the persistence of force. To note these inevitable failures implies no desire to vindicate a supposed miraculous creation of certain life-germs, as an appendix to the material world, at some given moment in the past. Creation in such a sense does not enter into science, and it forms no part of modern philosophy. What is meant is simply that, if we attempt to "interpret the phenomena of life and mind and society in terms of matter, motion, and force," instead of reaching, as Spencer contended, "the essential nature" of the phenomena, we leave that nature out altogether. And this he ultimately confessed.

It may seem a strange thing to say that the ideas of the apostle of evolution were, philosophically speaking, of a pre-evolutional type. But, after all, it is not more of a paradox than what so many commentators have demonstrated of Kant, that the author of the critical philosophy was still, on many points, in bondage to the dogmas of pre-critical thought. Spencer's idea of explaining all phenomena in terms of molar and molecular forces is akin to his treatment of religion; or rather, the latter is a special case of the general point of view. Religion is a phenomenon in which a historical development is demonstrable towards worthier conceptions and nobler feelings; but, although recognising this development, Spencer ends by finding the essence of religion in the acknowledgment of an unknowable power—a residuary belief which he finds common to all forms of the religious consciousness. To some extent, it may be said, Spencer emancipates himself from his own logic and seeks a law of development; but the tendency thus exemplified, to find "the essential nature" in rudimentary abstractions like matter and motion, or in some feature which remains the same through all the stages of a process, is really to thrust us always back upon a bare beginning or an identical element, and so, in effect, to deny the reality of evolution altogether. Spencer congratulated himself, as we have seen, upon the substitution of the *definite* idea of evolution for the indefinite idea of progress; but few self-congratulations have ever been more premature, and already, in the second edition of 'First Principles' (p. 286), there is a paragraph intimating that the term is "open to grave objections," and is only used, *faute de mieux*, because it is "now so widely recognised as signifying sundry of the most conspicuous varieties" of the process, that it would be impossible to substitute another word. What he professed to seek was "a word which has no teleological implications" ('Autob.,' i. 100). Perhaps he meant by that phrase adaptation by an external designer; in any case he failed to see that his own cosmic conception, at least up to its penultimate stage, was through and through teleological; and that, without a teleology of some sort, there can be no talk of development, but only of indifferent and meaningless change.

It was undoubtedly, as we have seen, the teleological implications of the process, especially in an ethical and social regard, which from the beginning cast their glamour over Spencer himself. As late as 1882, in a postscript to his speech in New York, he speaks of Nature as leading men unknowingly or in spite of themselves to fulfil her ends—"Nature being one of our expressions for the ultimate cause of things, and the end, remote when not proximate, being the highest form of human life." And only in the edition of 1900 was a sentence withdrawn from the 'First Principles' which stated that, after deducing from the persistence of force all the various characteristics of evolution, "we finally draw from it a warrant for the belief that evolution can end only in the establishment of the greatest perfection and the most complete happiness" (ed. 4, p. 517). He had explained in a controversial essay that the fittest who survive are not necessarily, or indeed most frequently, the best; yet as late as 1893, in the preface to the second volume of his 'Principles of Ethics,' while expressing his disappointment that in this part of the subject he has derived no direct aid from the general doctrine of evolution, he says that indirectly it sanctions certain modes of conduct by showing that they "fall within the lines of an evolving humanity, are conducive to a higher life, and are for this reason obligatory." So impossible is it to exorcise the teleological implications of the word, so meaningless would the word be without them.

And if Spencer himself was to the last unconsciously swayed by these implications, it was certainly, in part, to the comforting suggestions of the word that the theory owed its prestige in uncritical circles. Another factor which helps to explain the extraordinary vogue of

Spencer's philosophy was its coincidence in point of time with Darwin's discovery. But for the inductions by which biological evolution was established as a fact, it seems doubtful whether a speculative theory like that of Spencer's would have commanded, in scientific and general circles, the attention and acceptance which, as a matter of fact, it gained. Spencer became the philosopher of the new movement; and if many of the ardent fighters of its battles were probably in Darwin's case, who honestly confessed that he "did not even understand H. Spencer's general doctrine,"[1] they were equally ready to "suspect that hereafter he will be looked at as by far the greatest philosopher in England, perhaps equal to any that have lived."[2] And as the protagonists were men of distinguished ability, men to whose ideas the future belonged, Spencerianism became the creed to which every one naturally gravitated who desired to take part against obscurantism. Similar motives operated to spread his fame on the Continent, where the feud between "enlightenment" and "clericalism" is bitter and constant. Partly, also, continental thinkers who stood above such animosities (a historian like Höffding,[3] for example) were impressed by the fact that here at last was an English thinker who had given to the world a *Weltanschauung*—a complete system of philosophy; a philosophy also which realised their expectations by carrying out consistently the realistic traditions of English thought.

But these more or less adventitious aids are not sufficient to explain Spencer's reputation. It is more deeply based. Although his philosophical interpretation of the process was radically at fault, and although he has, of course, no property in the idea of evolution as such, still

[1] 'Life and Letters,' iii. 193. [2] Ibid., 120.

[3] 'Die Englische Philosophie,' p. 241.

his early and independent espousal of the idea, and his consistent advocacy of its universal extension at a time when such views were very far from being in the air, made him an intellectual force of great importance. So completely has the idea passed into the fibre of our thinking, that it is difficult for the men of the present generation to estimate the full extent of our debt to Spencer's work. And especially is this the case as the philosophical defects of his own imposing structure become more and more evident. The absence of the metaphysico-religious element in his constitution and his ignorance of preceding philosophy, both of which the 'Autobiography' so strikingly confirms, explain what a critic so fair and temperate as Henry Sidgwick was fain to call "the mazy inconsistency of his metaphysical results." Dominated by an exclusively physical imagination, he accepted as dogmas the practical assumptions of common-sense. Hence, when attacked by thinkers like Green and Professor Ward, although sensitive in points of detail, he completely failed to appreciate the fundamental defects or inconsistencies against which their criticisms were directed. But it was impossible for a mind so active as Spencer's, so fertile in hypotheses, and so full of apt illustration, to marshal the sciences of life and man under the guidance of a great idea without enriching them by a wealth of luminous suggestion. In the very context of the stricture quoted above Sidgwick speaks of "the originality of his treatment and leading generalisations, the sustained vigour of his scientific imagination, the patient, precise ingenuity with which he develops definite hypotheses where other thinkers offer loose suggestions."

What is here said of the 'Psychology' is no less true of the 'Biology' and of his important contributions to sociological theory. But besides such departmental work, it was much to hold aloft in an age of specialism the banner of completely unified knowledge; and this is, perhaps, after all, Spencer's chief claim to gratitude and remembrance. He brought home the idea of philosophic synthesis to a greater number of the Anglo-Saxon race than had ever conceived the idea before. His own synthesis, in the particular form he gave it, will necessarily crumble away. He speaks of it himself, indeed, at the close of 'First Principles' (ed. 1), modestly enough as a more or less rude attempt to accomplish a task which can be achieved only in the remote future, and by the combined efforts of many, which cannot be completely achieved even then. But the idea of knowledge as a coherent whole, worked out on purely natural (though not, therefore, naturalistic) principles—a whole in which all the facts of human experience should be included—was a great idea with which to familiarise the minds of his contemporaries. It is the living germ of philosophy itself.

REVIEWS

JONES'S PHILOSOPHY OF LOTZE.[1]

PROFESSOR JONES has gone very thoroughly to work upon Lotze, for this book — which runs to 375 pages — deals only with "the doctrine of thought," as set forth, for the most part, in his 'Logic,' and a second volume is promised which shall deal with Lotze's metaphysical doctrines. Even those who are most grateful to Lotze for his services to philosophy may be disposed to think that this is to rate his importance too highly; for, with all his acumen, Lotze is not a philosopher of the first rank. The unsystematic character of his mind forbids us to place him among the *dii majores* to whom commentaries are rightly dedicated. It is not, however, the sympathetic deference of a disciple which has induced Professor Jones to devote so much attention to Lotze's methods and conclusions. Lotze is used throughout as an object-lesson. The conclusion which the book seeks to establish is that "the main contribution of Lotze to philosophic thought, the only ultimate contribution, consists in deepening that Idealism which he sought to overthrow. He yields *a tergo*, and as an unwilling witness, an idealistic conception of the world" (Preface). The

[1] A Critical Account of the Philosophy of Lotze (The Doctrine of Thought). By Henry Jones, M.A., Professor of Moral Philosophy in the University of Glasgow. The following critical notice appeared in 'Mind,' October 1895.

purpose of the book is thus not only to disarm Lotze's criticism of Hegelian idealism by convicting him of inconsistencies, but also to re-inculcate Hegel's fundamental tenet. It may be doubted whether this is the best way of approaching either Lotze or Idealism; for it necessarily thrusts into the background the elements of truth underlying Lotze's criticism which gave it its vitality, and which Professor Jones seems now and again to acknowledge. On the other hand, the indirect method of approaching the idealistic position involves so much controversial detail that we do not get beyond a very general statement of the position itself. But as a living contribution to the philosophical problem as that is shaping itself at present in English-speaking countries, the volume possesses a distinct importance of its own, and it is doubtless in this light, rather than as a historical monograph upon Lotze, that the author would like his book to be regarded. Needless to say that Professor Jones brings critical insight to the destructive part of his work, and force and fervour to the constructive part which supplies the nerve of the whole. The whole book is vigorous and remarkably fresh, and the emphasis laid in the last chapter upon the "frankly realistic" nature of his own theory gives Professor Jones's presentation of Absolute Idealism a degree of originality which differentiates it from the ordinary versions of English Hegelianism that descend from Green.

The first chapter, which deals with "The Main Problem of Lotze's Philosophy," takes a general view of Lotze's historical position in relation to the main currents of thought during the century, and gives some account of his chief philosophical contentions, the motives which underlay them, and the schools or tendencies against which they were directed. It is so well done that the ordinary reader will regret that more of the like is not vouchsafed him; the remaining chapters plunge at once into "the doctrine of thought," and are sufficiently stiff reading. As Professor Jones points out in this chapter, it is as a critic of the two dominant tendencies of the century that Lotze possesses historical importance. He criticises, on the one hand, the Naturalism or Materialism which was so confidently propounded in the middle of the century as the philosophical outcome of science, and, on the other hand, the claims of "pure thought"—what he considered to be the exclusive intellectualism of dialectical idealism and its inadequate provision for the spiritual needs of the individual. To say, however, that Lotze "sets himself *against* the two great constructive movements of modern thought *on behalf of the contents of the ordinary* consciousness,"[1] is rather an unfair way of stating the case; and, indeed, Professor Jones admits that this "may seem to be a hard saying," and even that "taken absolutely it is not true." He supplies himself a more generous estimate when he says, a little farther on, that "Lotze has avoided the one-sided development of abstract views, placed himself at the point of collision of the primary interests of human life"; or again, "It is no small honour to Lotze that, in an age which was given over to abstract constructions of man and the world, he stood almost alone protesting against the rash haste which secured unity by sacrificing its content." In the light of these admissions, the original statement would be more correct if, for the words which Professor Jones italicises, we substitute others and read the sentence thus: Lotze set himself against the two great constructive movements of modern thought *on behalf of elements of experience which they alike neglect.* It is his

[1] The italics are in the original.

massive protest against the sacrifice of "man's inalienable and highest aspirations" (as he terms them in the 'Microcosmus'), combined with his skilful exposure of the weak places of systems that would override our deepest needs, to which he owes his honourable place in the history of nineteenth-century thought. By his undaunted reassertion of the fundamental truth of the view of the world implied in moral or spiritual experience, he re-inspired confidence in many who felt the consequences of Materialism and a deified Logic to be almost equally disastrous, but who had been intimidated by the assurance with which the system-makers promulgated their conclusions. And if, as the century draws to a close, there is a very general and growing recognition of the limitations of the scientific point of view, and if Absolute Idealism, on the other hand, in the person of Professor Jones and others, endeavours to dissociate itself from the abstractions of "Panlogismus," and acknowledges more freely the defects of many statements that have passed current,—this result is due in no small degree to Lotze's patient work between 1840 and 1880, a period of forty years during which he must often have seemed to himself and to others like the voice of one crying in the wilderness.

In point of fact, he has exercised a more pervasive influence than usually falls to the lot of any one who is not a thinker of first-rate originality and genius. No doubt Lotze has been enlisted as an ally, or rather adopted as a champion, by many representatives of what Professor Jones calls "the popular and theological consciousness," and it is not to be denied that the curiously unsystematic character of Lotze's mind, and his habit of balancing conflicting possibilities without indicating any definite conclusion, give him at times the air of falling back upon popular thought. But it has to be remembered that what Lotze means to defend is not the specific formulæ of any accepted creed or system, but only the ethical or spiritual convictions that underlie its dogmas, and of which perchance these dogmas may be a very imperfect expression. To put it even more generally, it is simply the spiritual view of the world for whose safety he is concerned. Similarly Lotze's revolt against Panlogism and his insistence on the part played by the feelings, both in the structure of reality and in our reconstructive estimate of it, has no doubt favoured the development of a type of theological thought which seeks to fence off the territory of religion from reason altogether, and thereby ingeniously evades an answer to the question of the metaphysical truth or untruth of the doctrines it teaches. But this divorce of the ethical or religious from the rational can hardly be considered part of Lotze's own programme. He has left on record in many passages his appreciation of the effort of speculative idealism, and if that idealism was really, as he says, in pursuit of "the supreme and not wholly unattainable goal of science," then there is no part of experience from which reason can be, as it were, warned off. But of course the historical consequences of a doctrine may always be fairly produced in evidence against it, and, so far, Professor Jones is quite within his rights in pointing out the dangers involved in Lotze's positions, or at least in his way of stating them.

But it is time to pass from these generalities to the precise thesis of Professor Jones's book. The points in Lotze's doctrine of thought on which Professor Jones lays most stress—and which he sets himself to controvert—are (1) the subjectivity of thought, and (2) its merely formal or instrumental function in our experience.

Under the first head, he refers to the numerous passages in which Lotze insists that while our thoughts are valid or true of things—correspond to things—they yet are not the things themselves. "The things themselves do not pass into knowledge; they only awaken in us ideas which are not things." "We may exalt the intelligence of more perfect beings above our own as high as we please; but so long as we desire to attach any rational meaning to it, it will never *be* the thing itself, but only an aggregate of ideas *about* the thing." To condemn or disparage knowledge on account of this necessary subjectivity is, however, according to Lotze, quite unjustifiable, unless we assume that the function of knowledge is not to know things but to be them. In a sense, Professor Jones admits the obvious truth of these considerations; but at the same time he intimates that Lotze's way of stating the case makes "the rift between thought and its objects final." But the two points mentioned above are too closely connected to be kept definitely separate in exposition, and the central part of the book, after the two introductory chapters, is devoted rather to the second—that is to say, to a critical analysis of Lotze's limitation of thought to a formal or instrumental function in our experience. Thought, according to Lotze, is, as Professor Jones puts it, "only a single part or element or faculty of mind, occupying a restricted place amongst several others, which co-operate with it in the production of the contents of our intelligent life" (p. 50). More particularly, thought is dependent upon sense and an "unconscious psychical mechanism" for its content. Again, the feelings and emotions are absolutely irreducible to thoughts or conceptions: so much so that, as Lotze says, "it is possible that even divine intelligence would find nothing in the conception of knowledge alone that should necessitate feeling to issue out of it." It is to feeling that we owe the consciousness of the worth which objects have for us. Feeling, as the source of our judgment of value, thus takes precedence of cognition, for the Good is a higher category than the True. Indeed it may be said that to feeling we owe the ideal of knowledge itself—the conception of an all-comprehensive and harmonious whole,—and feeling also awakens the impulse to seek it. Finally, thought yields only hypothetical necessity; absolute or unconditional necessity is given only in the immediate certainty of æsthetic and moral conviction. "It is not pure intelligence, whether we call it understanding or reason, that dictates to us those assumptions which we regard as inviolable; it is everywhere the whole mind, at once thinking, feeling, and passing moral judgments, which, out of the full completeness of its nature, produces in us those unspoken first principles to which our perception seeks to subordinate the content of experience." "The fact that there is truth at all cannot in itself be understood, and is only comprehensible in a world the whole nature of which depends upon the principle of the Good" ('Microcosmus,' Bk. ix. c. 5). Professor Jones summarises the position thus: "The conception that thought depends upon a foreign source for its data lies at the root of the whole attempt of Lotze to limit its powers. It leads him, in fact, to share the material of thought between feeling on the one side and sensation on the other. Feeling supplies it with the ideals which inspire and guide knowledge, and which express, although indefinitely, the harmonious totality of experience; and sensation supplies it with the material out of which is elaborated our world of sensuous objects" (p. 63). And he points out a parallelism in some respects between Lotze's Feeling and Kant's Reason, feeling being for

Lotze the source of our moral and religious ideals. But he considers the dualism of Lotze's doctrine more dangerous, inasmuch as it leads (or has led historically) to the subjugation of intelligence to feeling, to despair of philosophy and an appeal to faith and "the intuitions of the heart."

After this analysis of Lotze's doctrine, the third chapter proceeds to redargue the position so far as concerns the account given of the relation between perception and conception. Attention is called at the outset to some of Lotze's metaphors. Thought is "a tool," or, again, thinking is the path we take to the hill-top; it is the circuit we are compelled to make in consequence of the position of the human mind, not at the centre of things, but "somewhere in the extreme ramifications of reality." By thinking we succeed in reconstructing the real world; we do get our view from the hill-top. But "the act of thinking can claim only subjective significance. . . . All the processes which we go through in the forming of conceptions, in classification, in our logical constructions, are subjective processes of our thought, and not processes which take place in things." According to Lotze, however, these subjective processes do in the end enable us to reach an objective result, and Professor Jones describes his attitude as an attempt to "strike a middle path between the Scepticism which severs knowledge and reality and the Idealism which seemed to him to identify them." The remainder of the chapter is intended to prove the impossibility of such a *via media*.

The specific function of thought, according to Lotze, is "to reduce the coincidence of our ideas to coherence." It does this "by adding to the reproduction or severance of a connection in ideas the accessory notion of a ground for their coherence or non-coherence." It thus converts an associative into a reflective or rational experience. This leads Professor Jones to ask what is the nature of the relation which exists between the associative and the thinking form of consciousness. "Does thought *produce* the principles which give coherence to the contents of our experience, or does it only *discover* them in that experience? Is the original datum of thought a genuine manifold with no inherent connections, or is there in truth no such thing as a manifold, but only what *appears* to be a manifold, because the principles of unity within it are latent or merely implicit?" (p. 84). He finds Lotze's answer "ambiguous, if not inconsistent," and it may be said at once that he lays his hand here upon serious weaknesses in Lotze's statement. The last sixteen pages of this chapter form a very cogent piece of reasoning, as well as an admirable piece of philosophical writing. Professor Jones succeeds, I think, in showing that Lotze wavers between a representation of the datum "now as a mere meaningless state of consciousness, and now as a world of objects related in space and time." "According to one view, so much is supplied to thought that nothing is left to it except to 'sift' the rich content of perceptive experience and rearrange it, without adding anything to it except the reasons for its combinations. Thought, on this view, is formal and receptive, and its only work is that of reflection. It presents the old world over again, but in the new light of an ordering principle. According to the other view, it is only through the intervention of thought that there are either ideas or an intelligible world at all. It arrests the shifting panorama of subjective states of consciousness, objectifies and fixes them so as to give them meaning, and then relates them into a systematic world of knowledge. On this view, everything, except the absolutely meaningless subjective data, is due to the spontaneous activity of thought. In other words, thought, instead of being receptive and formal, is essentially constructive, the cause on account of which alone there can be either ideas or objects, or connections between them" (pp. 96, 97).

Now it is plain enough that Lotze is here working at a real problem; but every careful student of his 'Logic' must admit that in trying to articulate a theory of what actually happens, he involves himself in serious confusion. Professor Jones is, in my opinion, substantially right when he finds that the root of this confusion is "the assumption that the first datum of knowledge is the subjective state, or the change in consciousness consequent upon the varying stimuli arising from the outer world, and that the first act of thought is to objectify this subjective. His whole doctrine rests upon the psychological hypothesis that what we first *know*, indefinitely enough perhaps, is a subjective state, and that the first act of thought is to make this state in ourselves representative of an outward object. The subjective is projected, reified, posited, so as to become an object" (p. 105). As against this, Professor Jones successfully maintains that, just as we do not infer the existence of a seen object from physiological changes in our brain or nerves, but, on the contrary, infer these processes because we have first seen the object, so, although it is true that consciousness as a matter of fact must change in order that we may know the object which incited the change, that "does not prove that we first *know* the change in ourselves and then infer the object. On the contrary, the first in the order of events is again the last in the order of thought. . . . In the order of knowledge the objective comes first. . . . The reality first given to us indefinitely, opens out upon us into differences, and sunders into the primary distinctions of subjective and objective. But we are not entitled, on account of the fundamental character of this distinction, to forget or deny the unity of the reality in which the distinction takes place; nor is there any justification for fixing a complete gap between the subjective and the objective, and compelling thought in some unknowable way either to *objectify* the former or a part of it, or to leap blindly from one world into the other, from the sphere of mere subjective states to that of external facts corresponding to them. . . . If we begin with the purely subjective, we must end there. . . . Lotze himself nowhere explains this extraordinary process of seizing upon a mere change in consciousness, flinging it, or a part of it, into a sphere in which it can confront the self as a not-self, and endowing it with a quasi-independent existence. Nor is it explicable, . . . for in order to begin at all, we must already have an object" (pp. 105-113).

I think it can hardly be denied that Lotze's account of the objectification of the subjective as the first operation of thought, converting impressions into ideas, lays him open to this criticism, and is, in point of fact, fundamentally misleading. It is an attempt, in an account of knowledge, to get behind the fact of knowledge altogether, to explain how that which is not in any sense knowledge —"nothing but a state of consciousness, a mood of ourselves," a "mere internal movement," a "meaningless change in the state of the soul"—is transformed into knowledge, and comes to have significance or cognitive value for the subject in which it takes place. Now if thought is to objectify or in any way to deal with these subjective states, it must have some knowledge or awareness of them as such; and that implies the fact of knowledge as already existing. It is indeed obviously impossible for us to place ourselves outside of this fact and explain how knowledge of any sort is possible.

Nothing is more certain than that "the miracle of knowledge" has, from a logical and ultimate point of view, simply to be accepted. As Professor James puts it ('Psychology,' ii. 8): "In his dumb awakening to the consciousness of *something there*, a mere *this* as yet (or something for which even the term *this* would perhaps be too discriminative, and the intellectual acknowledgment of which would be better expressed by the bare interjection 'lo!') the infant encounters an object in which (though it be given in a pure sensation) all the categories of the understanding are contained. . . . Here the young knower meets and greets his world; and the miracle of knowledge bursts forth, as Voltaire says, as much in the infant's lowest sensation as in the highest achievement of a Newton's brain." From a physiological or psychological standpoint, we may, of course, say that the miracle bursts forth on the occasion of certain antecedent processes; but to ask *how* these processes give rise to the unique relation of knowledge is to involve ourselves in a hopeless hysteron proteron. To enquire how there is such a fact as knowledge at all, may indeed be said to be the ultimate form of the type of enquiry which Lotze so often indicates—the desire to know how being is made. To say that "thought" creates knowledge out of mental states unreferred, is a highly misleading way of saying that knowledge in the finite consciousness depends upon organic stimulus. Such "mental states" are the hypothetical result of the organic stimulus, interposed between that stimulus and the mental reaction in the shape of attention; but even psychology can say nothing of these hypothetical states beyond consigning them to the convenient receptacle of the sub-conscious. The desire to *explain* the actual passage from the organic to the conscious, to catch nature in the act, as it were,—half in and half out, as Dr Stirling somewhere puts it,—is probably at the root of theories of objectification like Lotze's, but the interposition of unreferred states does not really help to elucidate the transition, or to ease in any way the acceptance of the miracle of knowledge.

The consequence of this false start on Lotze's part is that at one time he talks as if the whole intelligible world were the work of thought, superinduced upon a meaningless datum; at another time he speaks of thought as a purely formal function, which receives from perception a world of objects in space and time, and which is limited to the reflective discovery of the grounds of the coherence of what is already associatively combined for it. These are the two views which Professor Jones signalised in the passage quoted above, and it is plain that they are the same two views which we find imperfectly reconciled in Kant's account of the synthesis of imagination. Lotze's "unconscious psychical mechanism," which prepares the data of sense for the advent of reflective thought, is just the "blind but indispensable function of the soul," which plays so important a part in the Kantian exposition. And it seems to me that Professor Jones's method with Lotze here may be instructively illustrated by the divergent views which commentators have taken of this part of the Kantian theory. According to one interpretation of Kant, objectivity, order, and connection are first introduced by the categories into the formless manifold of sense; the apperceptive unity consciously acting through these functions seems thus actually to *make* the world we know. This is the impression we carry away from much of Green's writing, and to this view, if I am not mistaken, Dr Caird's first commentary lent some countenance.

Dr Stirling's 'Text-book to Kant,' on the other hand, largely in a spirit of polemic against the subjectivity of this view, laid undivided stress upon the preparatory work of imagination, to the extent of apparently making the whole work of thought otiose, a "stamping" of connections already given. From this point of view he ended by characterising Kant's whole scheme of the categories as a laborious "superfetation." Dr Caird, in the second edition of his Commentary, gives a more discriminating account of Kant's real meaning by emphasising the words which Kant himself italicises, namely, that the synthesis of the imagination, although "blind" inasmuch as it does not bring the categories consciously into play, yet takes place *according to the categories.* The work of the reflective understanding is simply to bring to explicit consciousness the principles in which the associative or pre-rational consciousness has been unconsciously proceeding. Neither in Kant nor in Lotze, however, is this distinction between the associative and the rational consciousness drawn with sufficient clearness and breadth. I know no place where it is so satisfactorily worked out as by Professor Laurie in his 'Metaphysica Nova et Vetusta.' Professor Laurie employs the apt term Attuition or the attuent mind to designate the receptive consciousness of objects, and of the relations between objects, possessed by the higher animals or by a child before the emergence of active Reason in the strict sense of that term. Reason converts attuits or passive recepts into actively grasped percepts, and in its search for grounds transforms (some instances of) sequence into causal connections. In general, it makes possible the beginnings of science, the beginnings of our human knowledge of a stable system of things. It will not be denied that this pre-rational consciousness exists; and (although the life of reason in every case rises from it as a basis) the distinction between the two can hardly, it seems to me, be too sharply drawn. The two lives are on different planes, and there is no passage from the one to the other save by a leap. The presence of the reason-impulse means all the possibilities of science,—it means morality, art, and religion, and all the possibilities of human history; its absence means the absence of all these. But the attuent consciousness, although without the formative impulse of reason it does not possess the notion of objectivity and truth which gives rise to science, is very far from being limited to a succession of purely subjective states or atomic sensations. It receives images of objects which it distinguishes from one another, and some of which it comes to associate together. This Lotze sees clearly enough, and hence he attributes so much to sense and the unconscious mechanism, and apparently leaves so little for thought to do. Professor Jones is perhaps hardly just—or, let us say, hardly generous—to Lotze's intention here; his criticism somewhat resembles Dr Stirling's method with Kant. He beats Lotze up and down the field, thrusts him back upon his "meaningless changes in the state of the soul," quotes his acknowledgment that thought is necessary to objectify these, and then claims that he has surrendered his whole position and admitted the presence of thought in perception from the very first and throughout the whole process. Or if this is not granted, he insists that Lotze reduces thought to an otiose appendage of sense. The success which attends this method of criticism is due, as we have seen, to Lotze's blundering attempt to get behind knowledge altogether and describe how "impressions" are converted into "ideas." But if we disregard this and look at the facts as they are, we are bound to admit that the sensuous and associative stage does exist, and so does the rational. Lotze expresses the difference between the two by saying that in the latter thought has supervened, affirming and organising. This may not be an unexceptionable, but surely it is a fairly legitimate, way of stating the difference, seeing that Lotze always means by thought the reflective, consciously ratiocinative function, the logical understanding. It is the case that thought, so understood, adds nothing but its own form to the sense-matter presented to it, and that many of the connections which it establishes among sense-objects are merely reaffirmed or actively taken possession of. But, even so, the imposition of this form is surely all-important; it is the first condition of an intelligible world. And there are, besides, notions of reason which cannot be said to be *given* in sense at all, such as those of cause and end. Lotze signalises the first as constituting in an especial sense the form of reason, when he says that thought has to convert coincidence into coherence; sense only knows *b* after *a*, reason knows *b* through *a* or because of *a*.

Professor Jones makes it a general objection to Lotze that "the same series of processes seem to be repeated upon two different levels, once by feeling or experience and once by thought" (p. 93). But this is exactly what happens. Moreover, the reproach seems out of place in the mouth of one who professes a general allegiance to Hegel; for, according to Hegel, all advance is simply repetition of the same form at different stages. Professor Jones would probably reply that it is just because Lotze does *not* take the associative and the rational consciousness as different *stages* of the same life or the same world, that he finds his statement of the case objectionable. Indeed this is what he does say: "The world of sense and the world of thought correspond point by point [*i.e.*, in Lotze's account]; but Lotze does not try to furnish any reason for this correspondence and mutual adaptability. If he had supplied such a reason, the worlds of thought and sense would have become species in a universal, to use his language, or different stages in the evolution of a single principle of reason, to use the language of idealism." "We might expect the simple conclusion that because the higher is possible only if it is also in the lower, therefore it *is* in the lower, and the lower is only an elementary form of the higher" (pp. 99, 100). Now I am not concerned to defend Lotze's way of stating the case. I have already admitted and emphasised his grave initial error. I will go farther, and add that he frequently does seem to leave sense and thought side by side or over against one another as unrelated opposites. He treats the laws of thought—the conditions of the thinkable—as if they were written upon the sky of some abstract heaven, and had no inherent relation to reality. He repeatedly stops to give fresh expression to his astonishment that the world is responsible to thought at all, and not, *ab initio* and essentially, unthinkable. Such preposterous astonishment certainly seems to imply that the mutual adaptability is the result of a happy accident; and so far Lotze falls behind Kant, who also emphasised the mutual adaptation of sense and thought, but adduced it as evidence that the world has its origin in intelligence as regards its matter no less than as regards the formal categories. To speak as Lotze does is certainly, so far as language goes, to divorce reality from intelligence and to leave it standing as an "unknown external something," as "unknown things and processes," as "things themselves inaccessible to observation which we suppose to underlie our sensuous perception," as "an invisible something which we suppose to be outside us." These expressions, all culled from Lotze's 'Logic,' prove sufficiently that he commits what I agree with Professor Jones in considering the unpardonable philosophic sin—the assertion of the thing-in-itself as an unknown and unknowable kernel of reality. In the light of this sinister consequence, one can understand Professor Jones's jealousy of Lotze's procedure in delegating to sense and the psychical mechanism one after another of the functions of "thought." He seems to Professor Jones to hand over these functions to an essentially non-rational process and to leave thought with its occupation gone, an uncalled-for excrescence on the self-acting system of sense. This danger does lurk, we may admit, in Lotze's general habit of thought, but it does not necessarily attach to the distinction between the work of sense and association and the subsequent work of reflective thought. One may emphasise the work done by the attuent consciousness, and even speak of "thought" as a formal function which supervenes upon a ready-made world, without in the least intending to deny that the world of attuition is a preformation of reason in sense. Professor Laurie, for example, after making this distinction the pivot of his whole exposition, finds no difficulty in concluding "that the outer is not merely an x negating my self-consciousness, but that, on the contrary, it is Reason externalised, and that, as universal reason, it is one with the moments of my finite reason. . . . It would be a strange thing indeed if the energy of Reason seizing the external found that the one did not answer the other—that the datum of sense defeated the process of dialectic, that the plastic power of Reason encountered material which it failed to mould. It would be equally strange if the datum of sense failed to find its knower and interpreter, if it for ever remained what it appears to a dog or a horse ('Meta. Nova et Vetusta,' 2nd ed., pp. 213 and 227).

But while we may intelligibly speak thus of the external world as the externalisation of reason (seeing that the formal categories of reason are reflected in its structure), it must still be maintained that the way in which Hegelian idealists speak of "thought" is calculated to darken counsel. Thought, whether we wish it or not, is identified beyond recall with the intellect as such. Philosophers will never make "thought" do duty not only for thought but for sense, feeling, and will as well. Professor Jones himself admitted lately, in an article on Lotze published in the 'New World,' that "thought" is an inapt and unfortunate term as an expression of what the Idealists mean. Commenting on Lotze's opposition of experience or "the whole mind" to thought or thinking, he added: "This is a change of terminology which Idealists would not care to oppose. In fact, 'whole mind' or 'spirit' expresses their meaning less ambiguously than 'thought,' in so far as the former terms cannot be easily confused with the purely formal faculty of the logician." And he further spoke of "the idealistic identification of reality not with abstract thought but with spirit and its manifold activities." It is disappointing, therefore, to find him throughout this volume using Thought in the traditional Hegelian sense, which has been prolific of so much confusion. The outcome of this usage is the reduction of the world to a system of thought-relations, as we find it in Green's laborious and, after all, ineffectual, attempt to eliminate the function of sense in perception. Though we may be able to say nothing of sense as sense (and this lies in the nature of the case), the difference between perception and conception remains fundamental and irreducible. The one is immediate relation to, or experience of, reality; the second, though itself also, of course, a real experience, is, as compared with the first, a mediate relation, which may doubtless give a fuller and truer account of the real, but which depends for its whole meaning—and for its existence—upon the primary and vital relation of perception. Green is obliged to fall back surreptitiously upon the sense-data which he seems afraid openly to acknowledge. In various passages Professor Jones fully recognises the necessity of *two* factors—"sense" and "thought." "Sense by itself," he says, "gives as little as thought by itself. The whole problem lies in the nature of the relation between these two factors. No one now can well deny the need of either, and the difficulty which we have to meet is how to conceive of both so as to enable them to co-operate and produce the concrete fact of knowledge, in which form and content interpenetrate. . . . Hegel and his followers would find a unity beneath their differences, and regard that unity as best characterised by the term Thought or Spirit" (p. 300). Here he gives us, it is true, the alternative of "spirit," but in other passages he talks of "the Idealism which found nothing in the world except thought" (p. 99), of "the Hegelian view that thought is a constructive and concrete reality" (p. 287), of "the truth of Idealism which makes thought think thought" (p. 154). Now surely, if the living whole consists of thought *and* sense, it cannot but provoke misunderstanding to give to the whole the name of one of the factors. To say that thought thinks thought, that there is nothing in the world except thought, cannot but be taken as an attempt to evade acknowledgment of the facts of sense. Yet that acknowledgment finds its way into the statements of even the most uncompromising idealists.

Thought cannot get to work unless it has a "material" (p. 105), unless it has "elements of sense" to work upon (p. 104). It "seizes upon an indefinite reality and articulates it into system" (p. 359); but the articulation cannot proceed unless the reality is somehow given in order to be seized. Professor Jones also speaks quite freely at times of "the sensuous and the intelligible elements" of experience (p. 335), or, what is the same thing in other words, of "the content and forms of our experience" (p. 303). He speaks of conception as abstracting from "our sensibility," and in one place he says that what he has tried to show, as against Lotze, is that the "immediate forms of knowledge [perception, feeling, &c.] could not *supply thought with its necessary data* unless they were armed with all the powers of thought, *as well as with those which are peculiar to themselves*" (p. 325). He here admits that thought requires data, that these data are supplied by immediate forms of knowledge, and that these immediate forms of knowledge have powers peculiar to themselves.

But the form in which he clothes the admission enables us, I think, to understand what he and other idealists are really fighting for, under cover of an unfortunate terminology. He is contending for the inseparability, the mutual implication, of sense and thought, which seems to him to be threatened by the emphasis which Lotze and others lay upon the contribution of sense. Sense seems to him to be asserted as a source of data altogether alien to intelligence, and to be put forward as the sole depositary of reality; and this is either to play into the hands of a sensationalistic scepticism, or to evoke the spectre of a hopeless dualism. As against such a supposed position, Professor Jones contends, in words already quoted, for "the mutual implication of the content and forms of our experience." When Lotze says that "what is good and evil can as little be *thought* as what is blue and sweet," and asks whether the essence of love and hate can be exhausted in concepts, he retorts by asking "whether love and hate and blue and sweet can be given *without* thought." The answer, he says, is obvious; "sense, by itself, gives as little as thought by itself." To this way of stating the case I, for one, have no objection, and I cannot think that Lotze would have denied the position. So, again, in regard to the relation of thought and reality—which is another form of the same question,—what Professor Jones proves, and what he has doubtless really at heart, is the necessity of acknowledging *ab initio* what he calls in one place their "ontological affinity" (p. 334): "If the world is to reveal itself to man's thought, it must have ontological affinity to his thinking powers." Just as we must acknowledge the "correspondence and mutual adaptability" of sense and thought, or, in other words, the "ontological relation between the two elements of knowledge" (p. 329), so we must not treat the world as a reality independent of thought and unrelated to thought; for, in that case, it would of necessity remain to the end unknowable by thought. Here again I have nothing to object to, but why does Professor Jones go on to obliterate distinctions and reinvoke the old confusions by translating "ontological relation" into "ultimate identity" (p. 330), and speaking of sensation and perception not only as "essentially related to thought," but as "identical with" thought? Surely there may be necessary relation without identity; in fact, if there were identity, the relation would be impossible. Thought and reality are not the merely different, but neither are they the merely identical. Moreover,

Professor Jones's relapse into such phrases is inconsistent with what he says of the value of Lotze's criticism of the idealistic position.[1] And I should like to add that in insisting on relation, while denying identity, I am not actuated by a precisian anxiety about a word or phrase; for as soon as we speak of identity, the way is prepared for that sublimation of experience into the world of mere "thought" which Professor Jones condemns as strongly as any one. I find Professor Jones himself upon this dangerous inclined plane in his attempt to explain away the difference between perception and conception, or to maintain, at least, that the difference "is only a difference in degree of definiteness" (pp. 346 *et seq.*) "Redness," he says, "if we contrast it with colour, is a particular perception, but if we contrast it with its own shades of crimson, scarlet, and so on, it is a universal conception." But we are moving here altogether in a world of conceptions. Red is a concept whether we contrast it with colour in general or with its own shades; the percept red is always a particular shade of red, though we may not stop at the moment reflectively to particularise it. The concept crimson or scarlet itself does not reach the inexhaustible particularity of its own sense-presentation, as that is constituted by what Professor Jones calls the "aggressive relations of time and space and our sensible affections." These relations and affections may be "comparatively insignificant to the

[1] "Hegel, as against his predecessors, opposes mainly the tendency so to separate the real and ideal as to obscure or annul the principle which reveals itself in both of them: Lotze directs his main attack against what he conceived to be their immediate identification by Hegel. And it is this which, in my opinion, makes him so valuable as an expounder of Idealism, and helps us to know more clearly than Hegel's immediate successors what he meant by the principle of thought which he identified with the principle of reality" (p. 273).

true understanding of things," but it hardly becomes us to complain of their "aggressive" character, seeing that they are, as it were, the tissue in which the real world is given to us. I heartily agree with the contention that we must not regard perception as giving us the truth of reality once for all, and conception as leading us on a path of abstraction farther and farther away from the nature of things. Our conceptual account of the world, as formulated by the sciences, and ultimately by philosophy, is nearer the truth than the inadequate judgments of perception with which we start. In this sense, the process of knowledge is continuous; it is, as Professor Jones says, "a process of discovering distinctions within an indefinite subject" (p. 362), or the "articulating into system" of "an indefinite reality" (p. 359). But it is still true that conception has only a mediate relation to reality, while in perception there is an immediate relation. We cannot explain in what this direct experience consists, for that would be to make it mediate—would be, in fact, to dig up the roots of our own life. All we can say is that without this direct contact with reality, or rather this immediate presence of reality in us, there would be no subject within which to discover distinctions, no reality to articulate into conceptual system. The distinction, therefore, between perception and conception is not only "undeniable within its own limits"; it is primary and fundamental, and the attempt to minimise, if not to obliterate it, seems to me perhaps the most questionable and dangerous part of Professor Jones's book. In one sense, as explained above, it is true to say that reality, *i.e.*, the true account of reality, is reached only at the end of our scientific and philosophical analysis; but, in another sense, it is as true to say that reality is given in perception or, more generally, in immediate experience, and given there alone. Lotze may not sufficiently distinguish these two senses, but they are not in themselves inconsistent, as Professor Jones seems to think (p. 356).

I have left myself no space to comment upon the more detailed criticism of Lotze's logical doctrines; but for penetrative analysis the chapter on Lotze's theory of the Judgment (chap. iv.) is one of the best in the book. The laboriously artificial theory into which Lotze is led by his start from pure identity is successfully shown to reduce Judgment in the end to a useless tautology—except so far as Lotze supplements his original principle by that of Sufficient Reason, which is tantamount to the idea of a system of related elements. Professor Jones justly censures Lotze's characteristic method of patching up the defects of one principle by supplementing it by another. In this case, the second principle, which alone makes thought possible, is treated by Lotze as a fortunate accident (!), and the two are left standing inconsistently side by side. Chap. v. contains a very full exposition of Lotze's theory of Inference, which is submitted to criticism in chap. vi. "The symbol of inference is not mechanical connection but organic growth. It is the evolution of the contents of a single, though not a simple, idea; and evolution neither admits of anything new nor simply repeats itself." The fundamental function of thought consists "not in connecting the discrete but in differentiating a unity." This view is convincingly driven home throughout the chapter, which contains a luminous account of the actual reasoning process. Lotze's theory is found to be involved in contradiction because it starts from the opposite view, that the operation of thought consists in connecting the discrete. It is the same view which leads him, in his account of Judgment, to the verge of declaring that predication is either idle or impossible.

In his account of Inference, the same dominating idea is seen in his attempt to escape from this conclusion by passing from Subsumption to Substitution. Substitution, as Professor Jones observes, "is not inference at all. It is rather the result of a process of inference. The mathematician will not substitute $a+b+c$ for x, unless he has already ascertained that they are equivalent; and the process of inference lies in the discovery of that equivalence, after which the act of substitution may follow as a matter of course" (p. 242). It must be admitted, I think, that Lotze's account of inference is vitiated by the original sins of his theory of Judgment, but I am not sure that Professor Jones's account of the advance of knowledge is, at bottom, so different from Lotze's as he thinks. He blames Lotze for attributing all the processes that are effective in the growth of knowledge to "sense, perception, and faith" (p. 267)—"intuitive processes resting on material knowledge" (p. 254). But when he gives his own account—"thought has only one way of proving a truth, namely, that of showing that it is already contained in the premises. And it shows that it was already in the premises *by a more exhaustive investigation of them*" (p. 243)—Lotze might fairly ask whether this investigation is in strictness part of the *reasoning* process. Or, again, when he says speaking of mathematical calculation, "The inference is in no wise *based* upon mathematical considerations, but upon the material premises; and into these premises the investigator throws all the wealth of his previously acquired knowledge of nature. And the more discriminative his knowledge, or the more systematic, or the greater the degree in which he is able to focus the light of the whole world on the problem in hand, the greater his success in developing the indefinite system which is in the datum into an explicit system of necessarily relative elements. *It is consideration of the material which enables him to predict*, and to extend his universal law over cases not yet observed" (p. 262)—is this essentially at variance with Lotze's own statement, that "the discovery of a universal law is always a guess on the part of the imagination, made possible by a knowledge of facts"? The difference here would seem to be in the main one of terminology. Lotze, with his analytic habit of mind, represents as the co-operative result of a number of factors what Professor Jones describes as a single living process. And if we extend a similar lenience to Lotze's account of the relation of sense to thought—upon which Professor Jones returns at the beginning of this chapter on Inference,—might not a sympathetic expositor say that Lotze's prefiguring of the universals of thought in corresponding universals of sense might be plausibly interpreted as another way of saying that the real is ideal? And I cannot forbear pointing out in this connection that Professor Jones's repeated insistence here on the "constitutive" nature of thought as "producing" its "content" (p. 227) turns out on closer investigation to have a modified and much more modest meaning. It is constitutive of the content "in the sense that the particulars cannot exist except in their coherence" (p. 228). It thus "comprehends and penetrates its content," but it does not constitute or creatively give its sensuous matter. This is the same conclusion as we arrived at in dealing with this point more fully above.

I do not, however, put forward these suggestions as a complete justification of Lotze's procedure, still less with any intention to minimise the value of the searching examination to which that procedure has been subjected by Professor Jones. On the contrary, I think that that examination has laid bare serious defects in Lotze's statement, and that Professor Jones has, in the main, made good his assertion of two warring tendencies in Lotze's thought. Lotze is, at bottom and in his intention, it seems to me, at one with what we may agree to call the idealistic view of the universe. But he stood chronologically nearer to Hegel than we do. In his youth the Hegelian system was still a living theory, held by its adherents with a rigour and vigour of which, at this distance of time, we have little conception. To us now —even to those who are most inclined to call Hegel Master—his system has already become historical: it is simply the last great type of Idealism or Spiritual Monism. But we do not hesitate to criticise, or simply to drop, the asperities of the original statement, and to present what we consider the vital principle in a form moulded by our own controversies and adapted to our present needs. But when Lotze began to write, time had not yet softened the outlines of the theory, and thrown its details into the shade; and he may probably be accepted as a better authority than the present generation on its original lineaments. He stood forth, in any case, as the unsparing critic of "the dialectical idyll" and the too exclusive intellectualism of the Hegelian system; and the emphasis given in his writings to this critical note has led to his being (erroneously) regarded as fundamentally at variance with the principle of Idealism. Other characteristics of his work combined to strengthen this misconception. His mind is analytical and critical rather than constructive; and as it is his habit to begin by criticism of some popular conception or accepted theory, he seems to be always starting (to use his own metaphor) somewhere in the extreme ramifications of the subject. He seems never to weld his conclusions together from a central point of view. In a book like the 'Microcosmus,' which meanders through the whole region of the knowable, this want of unity of conception becomes no less than distressing to the philosophical reader. Fresh as his criticisms generally are, and instructive as his laborious analysis undoubtedly often is, his habit of balancing conflicting possibilities and then passing to another theme is as undeniably irritating and unsatisfactory. One cannot wonder if it produces upon many readers the impression that a solution of the difficulties has been abandoned, and that the result is simply a return to the *disjecta membra* of popular orthodoxy. And even the attempts at co-ordination which we find are apt to appear to the thinker of speculative and synthetic tendencies as the mechanical piecing together of elements reached by different methods and belonging to inconsistent theories of the world. I do not say that this impression is just, but it must be admitted that it is not without excuse. Hence I do not think that Lotze can claim a permanent place as a thinker with a system of his own. There is great danger that those who go to him in search of such a system without much previous philosophical training will miss the point of much of his finest work, and simply be strengthened in their antecedent prejudices and unphilosophical beliefs. But after all these liberal deductions, it remains true that, by his criticism of dogmatic materialism on the one hand and of dogmatic intellectualism on the other, he has been a most important factor in guiding contemporary thought towards truer conclusions; and the reader who is in some measure abreast of the tendencies of modern speculation will still find much in his writings that is incisive and memorable and convincingly reasoned.

I have not dwelt *seriatim* and separately with Professor

Jones's concluding chapters on "The Subjectivity of Thought" and "The Principle of Reality in Thought and its Processes." As they sum up and bring to a focus the principles on which the whole critical argument of the book depends, they have been frequently laid under contribution in the foregoing account. But reference should be made to the criticism of Lotze's fundamental and characteristic position, that "all our conclusions concerning the real world rest upon the immediate confidence or the faith which we repose in the universal validity of a certain postulate of thought which oversteps the limits of the special world of thought." "As regards the ultimate principles which we follow in this criticism of our thoughts," he says elsewhere, "it is quite true that we are left with nothing but the confidence of Reason in itself, or the certainty of belief in the general truth that there is a meaning in the world." Otherwise expressed, it is only the Good which has in itself the complete right to be; and this is recognised in a judgment or postulate of value, which carries us beyond the merely intellectual region into the domain of feeling. But Lotze nowhere says, as Professor Jones makes him say, that this judgment is possible "apart from and without the co-operating activity of thought." He only says that it would be impossible to a thought which was not coloured by feeling. The criticism here appears to me, therefore, hardly fair to Lotze, especially as Professor Jones seems unwilling to deny that the Good and the Real may be taken as identical, and metaphysics ultimately based upon ethics (p. 295). And when, in his concluding chapter (the robust realism of which I have already signalised), Professor Jones says that "the only way to reach reality at the end of the process is to take our departure from it" (p. 334); or, again, that Idealists "have made this conception of the systematic and rational coherence of reality their starting-point, in such a manner that they do not doubt, any more than men of science do, that the endeavour of thought will lead to truth, or that reality will yield its treasures to the inquiring intellect," and that hence they "return once more to the attitude of ordinary consciousness and of science, and commit their thinking to the guidance of fact"—may it not fairly be asked whether this "starting-point" is not itself of the nature of faith? Doubtless it is a necessary assumption, and one which the advance of knowledge, in particular the growing coherence of knowledge, tends more and more to confirm; but is it not ultimately a trust, a supreme hypothesis?

DEWEY'S STUDIES IN LOGICAL THEORY.[1]

THE pre-eminent obligation which the writers of this book express to Professor James, as well as the general trend of the doctrines they expound, connect the volume obviously with the philosophical attitude which calls itself Pragmatism, and which is so much in evidence at the present time. But it is not always easy to harmonise the utterances of the adherents of this creed, nor, in some cases, is it easy to know what precisely they intend by their principle. Hence it will be best in dealing with the book to limit the discussion to the positions actually advanced, or apparently accepted, by the writers, and, for the rest, to treat it as a serious and detailed discussion of logical doctrines in a new light, rather than as a "manifesto" in support of a new philosophical faith. In so doing, I believe we shall best consult the wishes of the editor and his contributors; for though they speak with the confidence of those who find themselves in possession of a fresh clue to old-standing difficulties, they speak without pretentiousness or undue contempt for the theories they claim to supersede. They

[1] Studies in Logical Theory. By John Dewey, with the co-operation of Members and Fellows of the Department of Philosophy of the University of Chicago. The University of Chicago Press, 1903. The following critical notice appeared in 'The Philosophical Review,' November 1904.

make no claim of finality or of systematic completeness. "The point of view," says the editor, referring to possible divergencies among the eight contributors to the volume, "is still (happily) developing, and showing no signs of becoming a closed system." The divergencies, however, so far as I can judge, are really remarkably slight, observable for the most part only in the greater emphasis or sweep with which one writer or another states principles or doctrines common to all. It is, indeed, most unusual to find a series of philosophical papers by different writers in which (without repetition or duplication) there is so much unity in the point of view and harmony in results. That this is so is a striking evidence of the moulding influence of Professor Dewey upon his pupils and coadjutors in the Chicago School of Philosophy. The unfamiliar phraseology in which the writers sometimes couch their meaning makes the volume far from easy reading at first, but there always *is* a meaning to be grasped; and, as a carefully thought-out contribution to the "live" thought of the day, the book reflects honour upon the university among whose publications it appears.

The chief points of agreement—and therefore the main contentions of the book—are concisely stated by the editor in his prefatory note; and as the statement may be regarded as in a sense official, it may profitably be set down here for reference. "All agree that judgment is the central function of knowing, and hence affords the central problem of logic; that since the act of knowing is intimately and indissolubly connected with the like yet diverse functions of affection, appreciation, and practice, it only distorts results reached to treat knowing as a self-enclosed and self-explanatory whole,—hence the intimate relations of logical theory with functional psychology; that since knowledge appears as a function within experience, and yet passes judgment upon both the processes and contents of other functions, its work and aim must be distinctively reconstructive or transformatory; that since Reality must be defined in terms of experience, judgment appears accordingly as the medium through which the consciously effected evolution of Reality goes on; that there is no reasonable standard of truth (or of success of the knowing function) in general, except upon the postulate that Reality is thus dynamic or self-evolving, and, in particular, through reference to the specific offices which knowing is called upon to perform in re-adjusting and expanding the means and ends of life." The obligation of the writers is further expressed "to those whose views are most sharply opposed. To Mill, Lotze, Bosanquet, and Bradley the writers then owe special indebtedness." The inclusion in a common category of thinkers so different in standpoint as those named strikes the reader at first with surprise, but its meaning and justification, from the point of view of the essayists, becomes apparent in the detailed criticism to which Professor Dewey subjects Lotze's theory of knowledge (in Essays 2, 3, and 4), and in Miss Thompson's critical analysis of Bosanquet's theory of judgment in the paper which follows. The opposition of what we may call the new view to that which the essayists regard as held in common by the authors mentioned, and substantially as the logical tradition of previous philosophers, is summarily expressed by Professor Dewey when he contrasts the "epistemological" with the "instrumental" type of logic.

This antithesis introduces us at once to the main thesis of the volume. Thought, it is urged, is not something "pure," "absolute," or by itself,—whose occupation is to mirror or represent an independently complete and self-existent world of reality; it is to be regarded as one function among others arising in the course of experience, and as having for its sole purpose the transformation, reconstruction, or reorganisation of experience. Now in such a statement it seems to me there is much to which we may cordially assent, though perhaps without regarding it as the exclusive discovery of the pragmatists; while there are other implications of the words which we should be compelled to regard as false, or at least as misleading, in the form stated. We may agree, for instance, in the emphatic condemnation of the representational view of knowledge which has so disastrously dominated modern philosophy. Professor Dewey and his fellow-essayists argue convincingly that the view of knowledge as copying or reproducing an independent reality inevitably issues in scepticism, because in the very mode of stating the question it opens a gulf between thought and reality which no subsequent effort is able to bridge. "In whatever form the 'copy' theory be stated," says Professor MacLennan, "the question inevitably arises, how we can compare our ideas with reality and thus know their truth. On this theory, what we possess is ever the copy; the reality is beyond. In other words, such a theory, logically carried out, leads to the breakdown of knowledge." Professor Dewey's exposure of the shifts to which Lotze is driven by his initial acceptance of this dualism is a masterly piece of analysis, running for a considerable part of the way on the same lines as Professor Jones's criticism in his 'Philosophy of Lotze.' The whole conception of "two fixed worlds" must undoubtedly be abandoned. As Professor Dewey excellently puts it in his opening pages: "Neither the plain man nor the scientific inquirer is aware, as he engages in his reflective activity, of any transition from one sphere of existence to another. He knows no two fixed worlds—reality on one side and mere subjective ideas on the other; he is aware of no gulf to cross. He assumes uninterrupted, free, and fluid passage from ordinary experience to abstract thinking, from thought to fact, from things to theories and back again. Observation passes into development of hypothesis; deductive methods pass to use in description of the particular; inference passes into action with no sense of difficulty save those found in the particular task in question. The fundamental assumption is *continuity* in and of experience. . . . Only the epistemological spectator is awaıe of the fact that the ordinary man and the scientific man in this free and easy intercourse are rashly assuming the right to glide over a cleft in the very structure of reality."

If epistemology is understood to imply belief in a cleft of this nature, then the sooner both the name and the thing are banished from philosophy the better. In this shape the supposed problem is inherited from Descartes's individualistic starting-point and the two-substance doctrine which he impressed on modern thought. But the isolation of the mind as a subjective sphere, intact and self-contained, *outside and over-against reality*, necessarily implies that reality is in a strict sense unknowable. Hence the scepticism and agnosticism which infect so many modern theories of knowledge. But reality is one: the knowing mind and its thought are themselves within the course of reality, parts of its process, immersed in the give-and-take of living experience. Whether we talk of reality or of experience does not seem greatly to matter if we are agreed that there is no real world except the world which reveals itself to us in our experience and of which we feel ourselves to be a moving part. Whatever term we use, the essence of our contention is the unity and continuity of the world. And if I read the signs of the intellectual world aright, this conviction has so penetrated recent philosophical thought that the long-drawn discussions as to the possibility and validity of knowledge which so keenly occupied the theorists of the seventeenth and eighteenth and much of the nineteenth century seem to revolve round a self-made difficulty, and have ceased to that extent to possess a vital interest for us. We may be vividly enough aware of the poverty of our knowledge both in extent and intent, but that there should be in knowledge an inherent incapacity to know at all is too topsy-turvy a notion to give us a moment's uneasiness.

This conviction of the unity of existence, I repeat, has so permeated the best thought of the time that it cannot be claimed by the pragmatists as an insight specifically their own; and it strikes one, therefore, with a sense of surprise to find Bosanquet's theory of judgment selected for critical analysis as typical of the old representational view. There are certainly phrases in Mr Bradley's work which might seem to leave us, contrary to the author's intention, with an unknowable Reality lurking behind the world of ideas which we predicate of it. But Professor Bosanquet, one would have thought, had taught more persuasively than any other living writer the unity of experience and the fallacy of all dualistic conceptions. And perhaps it is really because he so nearly approaches what they consider the true position that the Chicago logicians have undertaken to show to what extent the old leaven still works in him and makes him fall short of the perfect truth. On turning to the essay in question, I cannot help thinking that Miss Thompson lays undue stress on expressions which are perfectly legitimate, and indeed unavoidable, in any theory which recognises objectivity in knowledge at all. After all, there is a nature of things to which our ideas have to adapt themselves, if it would be well with us; and in this sense the real world is certainly independent of our ideas, and unmodified by what we think about it. Why, according to the pragmatists themselves, it is the difficulty of coping with a "situation" which is the evoking cause of thought. Such a "situation" is the very type of an independent world, whose precise nature we have to learn with more or less expenditure of labour, if we are successfully to extricate ourselves from our difficulty. The primary function of knowledge, in such a case, is to represent the situation accurately, in order to find a way out of it. But if such phrases are at once innocent and inevitable in the mouth of a pragmatist, they cannot in themselves fairly be held to convict Professor Bosanquet of dualism.

But the main objection of the critic seems to be to Bosanquet's description of knowledge as a system of judgments about reality—reality being ultimately given for each individual "in present sensuous perception and in the immediate feeling of my own sentient existence that goes with it." This position (which, again, I hold to be beyond dispute) is, I submit, entirely transformed when it is paraphrased as "the mere assurance that somewhere *behind the curtain of sensuous perception* reality exists" (p. 92). This is a version of the critic's preconception rather than of the author's natural meaning. Similarly Professor Bosanquet may be venturing on slippery ground when he permits himself to speak of the individual's "point of contact with reality as such," and (still more so) when he describes the immediate subject as "the point at which the actual world impinges on my consciousness." But it is a far cry from such lapses of expression to speaking of Bosanquet's real world as "that against which we have bumped." The first of the two phrases would not indeed, I think, in the context of Bosanquet's theory, suggest any suspicion of the old dualism, except to one morbidly on the outlook for symptoms of that virus. An alternative phrase of Professor Bosanquet is that the real world *is present* in perception; and while such phrases imply that there is more of the world, and more in the world, than is apprehended by us at the moment, they cast no doubt upon the actuality of the apprehension. Indeed, I cannot see how this immediate apprehension of reality differs from "the immediate experiences," or the unreflective "ways of living," which the essayists everywhere assume as the matrix out of which reflective or logical thinking develops, and into which it resolves itself again. And when Green's criticism upon the logic of Locke and Hume—namely, that "the more thinking we do the less we know about the real world"—is applied to Bosanquet's theory, and the result is said to be avoided only "by a pure act of faith," it is surely as open to Professor Bosanquet as to his critic to reply that the results of thinking validate themselves by the harmony or system which they introduce into our experience. All thinking starts in faith, and is justified by its works. If that is pragmatism, then we may all set up as pragmatists. But the badge of pragmatism, in the ordinary sense attached to the term, is the utilitarian estimate of knowledge as everywhere ultimately a means to practical activity of the biological and economic order. And in regard to this estimate I cannot do better than quote a few sentences from Professor Bosanquet's Inaugural Address at St Andrews, in which he aptly traces the pragmatist contention to the very same obsolete view of knowledge which his critic here attempts to fasten upon him. After referring to the "debasement of the conception of knowledge which followed from the separation between world and individual, characteristic of the modern mind," he proceeds: "In this whole conception, that Cognition is something secondary, it seems to me that we have a mingling of obsolete logic and meaningless spatial metaphor. The entire fabric is annihilated when we realise a single point. Knowledge is not a reproduction of an outside world, but an endeavour to realise our nature by the construction of a harmonious experience. The truth of Cognition is not its correspondence to something else, but its degree of individuality in itself. In a word, Cognition is one great aspect of the life of the soul, in so far as it is lived apart from the struggle against matter. I have not repeated the ancient doctrine that it forms by itself the essence of morality and religion; but genuinely to understand how this doctrine fails to be true, is a problem which modern popular philosophy has never approached at all. Certainly it is true that in Cognition our nature affirms itself after a completer type than in the Volition of everyday life."[1]

The eloquent vindication of *Theoria* in the Aristotelian sense, of which these sentences form part, raises the whole question whether the pragmatists' view of knowledge is not due to the limitations which they themselves put upon the term. The writers in this volume insist upon the "derivative and secondary," the "intermediate and instrumental character" of thought; and by thought they agree in meaning "reflective thought," or reasoning. Thought, in this sense, as Professor Dewey puts it in his opening sentences, "comes after something and out of something and for the sake

[1] On the Practical Value of Modern Philosophy, p. 14.

of something." "Thinking is a kind of activity which we perform at specific need, just as at other need we engage in other sorts of activity: as converse with a friend; draw a plan of a house; take a walk; eat a dinner; purchase a suit of clothes; &c., &c." This view of thought as a specific function within experience is fundamental with all the writers, and they use a variety of terms to express the other phases of experience with which they contrast it. Thought is said to arise out of "unreflective antecedents," which are sometimes described as "ways of living"; and when the thinking process has been successfully carried through, it "allows us to proceed with more direct modes of experiencing." Its aim, indeed, is "the resumption of an interrupted experience." Experience, with or without some adjective, is thus the term on which the writers most generally fall back. Reality is described by Professor Dewey as "the drama of evolving experience," a "world of continuous experiencing." Conflict in the contents of our "experiences" makes them "assume conscious objectification. They cease to be ways of living, and become distinct objects of observation and consideration." Objects thus "only gradually emerge from their life-matrix." "The object as known" is accordingly, we are told, "not the same as the object as apprehended in other possible modes of being conscious of it" (p. 251). When even the conclusion or the completed judgment — the insight at which we arrive—is emphatically denied to be a judgment at all (p. 122), it becomes plain that the terms thought and knowledge are being used exclusively of the psychological process of solving a difficulty or arriving at a conclusion on some matter about which we are in doubt. Judgment is therefore described as essentially dynamic, "developmental," "transitive in effect and purport." That is to say, it exists, as it were, only momentarily in the passage from one mode of activity to another; as soon as a "re-adjustment" is effected, "experience" flows on. "There is always antecedent to thought," says Professor Dewey, "an experience of some subject-matter of the physical or social world, or organised intellectual world, whose parts are actively at war with each other,—so much so that they threaten to disrupt the entire experience, which accordingly for its own maintenance requires deliberate re-definition and re-relation of its tensional parts. This is the re-constructive process termed thinking; the re-constructive situation, with its parts in tension and in such movement toward each other as tends to a unified experience, is the thought situation" (pp. 39, 40). He calls it elsewhere "the particular functional situation termed the reflective" (p. 18).

But in proportion as we narrow in this way the application of the term "thought" by emphasising its "intermediate" character and its double dependence,—"its dependence upon unreflective experience for existence and upon a consequent experience for the test of final validity,"—it is plain that debate as to the exclusively practical reference of thought becomes inept; the question as to this particular mode of experience being settled by definition, and everything turning, as to the general question, on the nature of those antecedent and subsequent modes of experience which admittedly include so much of our conscious life. For by the antecedents of thought is not to be understood a pre-rational or merely animal consciousness, but the general course of our lives, so far as it flows on smoothly without working itself up into those express efforts of purposive attention which constitute a "thought-crisis." The antecedents are, in short, as Professor Dewey puts it, "our universe of life and love, of appreciation and struggle." And each crisis, in turn, has for its result a unified or harmonised experience which, as we have seen, is the test of its validity. "The test of thought," says Professor Dewey, "is the harmony or unity of experience actually effected. In that sense the test of reality is beyond thought as thought, just as, at the other limit, thought originates out of a situation which is not reflectional in character." Those experiences beyond thought as thought—"pauses of satisfaction," to employ a phrase of Professor Royce's adopted by Professor Moore in the last essay—are obviously the end for which the thought-process, in the sense defined, exists. But to regard them in turn as merely practical or instrumental is gratuitously to fall into the snare of the infinite regress; while to speak of them as volitional or active states is true only in the sense that all our states are energisings of the conscious self. The satisfaction may be gained in the theoretic insight of the man of science and the philosopher, or in the æsthetic contemplation of a landscape or a picture, as well as in the smoother working of some practical activity in the ordinary sense of that word. This is borne out by the acknowledgment, at the close of the long essay on "Valuation as a Logical Process," that "the æsthetic experience would appear to be essentially post-judgmental and appreciative. . . . As an immediate appreciation it has no logical function, and on our principles must be denied the name of value. . . . It may have its origin in past processes of the reflective valuational type. Nevertheless, viewed in the light of its actual present character and status in experience, the æsthetic must be excluded from the sphere of values." Without commenting on this arbitrary inversion of terms, which refuses the title of value to what might more reasonably be taken as the typical instance of an experience possessing independent value, it is sufficient to note that, on this showing, the whole realm of æsthetic experience, as post-judgmental and extra-logical, is excluded by the writers of this volume from what they mean by thought. Now the insight and the glow of art, of knowledge as such, or of religious vision, certainly display what we may call the static character of intuition, rather than the features of what one of the essayists aptly labels "the doubt-inquiry process" of discursive thinking. But intelligence, reason, or thought in the highest sense, is of the very essence of such states,—is indeed the basis of their possibility,—for art, science, and religion are the triple differentia of the human from the merely animal consciousness. And, in spite of "our reigning biological categories," it is in the vision of truth and of beauty and of a perfect Good that man realises a satisfaction which, though it may be transient in his individual experience, he recognises as not merely instrumental but an end-in-itself,—the satisfaction of his specific nature.

It is the more to be regretted, therefore, that these Studies throw no light on the nature of those non-reflective experiences which apparently include so much more of our life, and which are certainly so much more valuable than the function of thought in the narrower sense in which it is differentiated from them. Professor Dewey recognises the existence of the problem, but he passes from it. "The nature of the organisation and value that the antecedent conditions of the thought-function possess is too large a question here to enter upon in detail." It may be hoped that in another place he will undertake "the wholesale at large consideration of thought" which he says that he is here "striving to avoid." He draws a distinction in the opening essay between logic in the narrower sense, as the theory of "the particular functional situation termed the reflective," and "the logic of experience, logic taken in its wider sense." "In its generic form," he says, the latter "deals with this question: How does one type of functional situation and attitude pass out of and into another; for example, the technological or utilitarian into the æsthetic, the æsthetic into the religious, the religious into the scientific, and this into the socio-ethical, and so on?" Such an investigation, involving, as it necessarily would, an analysis of the attitudes in question, could not fail to prove instructive in Professor Dewey's hands. Its result would be, I think, to limit and qualify the pragmatist position in such a way as to deprive it of much of its paradox and novelty, without robbing it of the truth and interest which it undoubtedly possesses.

In the narrower sphere of logic just indicated,—in logic proper, apart from epistemological or metaphysical issues of a general nature,—the discussions of the present volume are markedly fresh and suggestive; and it need not be denied that they owe these qualities in no small degree to the stimulus which the writers derive from their general point of view, and to the systematic way in which they utilise for the purposes of logic the results of functional psychology. Professor Dewey's incisive criticism of Lotze has already been mentioned. Special reference might perhaps be made to his criticism of Lotze's metaphors of the scaffolding, which is taken down when the building is completed, and of the path to the viewpoint at the mountain-top. Such a view of our thinking procedure, he contends, makes thought a tool in the external sense or a merely formal activity. The work of erecting should not be set over against the completed building as a mere means to an end; "it *is* the end taken in process or historically. . . . The outcome of thought is the thinking activity carried on to its own completion; the activity, on the other hand, is the outcome taken anywhere short of its own realisation and thereby still going on. . . . Thinking as a merely formal activity, exercised upon certain sensations or images of objects, sets forth an absolutely meaningless proposition. The psychological identification of thinking with the process of association is much nearer the truth. It is, indeed, on the way to the truth. We need only to recognise that association is of contents or matters or meanings, not of ideas as bare existences or events; and that the type of association we call thinking differs from the associations of casual fancy and reverie in an element of control by reference to an end which determines fitness, and thus the selection of the associates, to apprehend how completely thinking is a reconstructive movement of actual contents of experience in relation to each other, and for the sake of a redintegration of a conflicting experience" (pp. 79, 80).

Miss Thompson's analysis of "every live judgment," as involving a situation in part determined and taken for granted and in part questioned, is very ably stated. In the doubt-inquiry process of the judgment, the subject represents what is given or taken for granted in each case; while the predicate is that part of the total expression which is taken as doubtful or tentative. As soon as the doubt arrives, there is always present some sort of tentative solution; and if the subject may be described as fact or real, the predicate is for the time being ideal. The opposition of fact and idea thus becomes a relative opposition within the total process of experience, and one which is continually being resolved. As Miss Thompson puts it: "All judgment is in its earliest stages a question, but a question is never *mere* question. There are always present some suggestions of an answer, which makes the process really a disjunctive judgment. A question might be defined as a disjunctive judgment in which one member of the disjunction is expressed and the others implied. If the process goes on to take the form of affirmation or negation, one of the suggested answers is selected. . . . The question as to whether a judgment turns out to be negative or positive is a question of whether the stress of interest happens to fall on the selected or on the rejected portions of the original disjunction. Every determination of a subject through a predicate includes both." The same point is well put by Professor Dewey in his introductory essay in connection with the growth of science and the passage of mere hypothesis into accepted theory; and the idea is instructively worked out in Dr Ashley's essay on "The Nature of Hypothesis," to which Professor Dewey contributes an interesting comparison of Mill and Whewell. The whole discussion is eminently fresh, and seems to me an illuminative contribution to logical theory, though I do not believe that the interpretation given is bound up so closely with "the practical and biological criterion of fact" as some of the writers seem to suppose.

Dr Gore's treatment of the relation of the image to the symbolic idea (which may, as one of the essayists puts it, become a mere index-sign) is one of the most convincing parts of the book. The idea as working symbol connects itself, he contends, with the final stage in thinking, when the content of the image has become so familiar that it acts as a direct, or, so to speak, automatic stimulus. "We are working along lines of habitual activity so familiar that we can work almost in the dark. We need no elaborate imagery. Guided only by the waving of a signal flag or by the shifting gleam of a semaphore, we thread our way swiftly through the maze of tracks worn smooth by use and habit. But suppose a new line of habit is to be constructed. No signal flags or semaphores will suffice. A detailed survey of the proposed route must be had, and here is where imagery with a rich and varied yet flexible sensuous content, growing out of previous surveys, may function in projecting and anticipating the new set of conditions, and thus become the stimulus of a new line of habit, of a new and more far-reaching meaning. As this new line of habit, of meaning, gets into working order with the rest of the system, imagery tends normally to decline again to the *rôle* of signal flags and semaphores" (pp. 198, 199). Some mention should also be made of Dr Stuart's analysis of the process of ethical deliberation as consisting essentially in the action and reaction of the previously accepted moral standard and the new mode of conduct contemplated (pp. 196-202). But it would obviously be impossible in a notice like the present to enumerate all the points of interest in the volume. The specimens given may suffice to suggest how much stimulus and instruction it provides for all genuine students of logic.

M'TAGGART'S SOME DOGMAS OF RELIGION.[1]

MR M'TAGGART'S last volume is written in the clear, crisp style to which he has accustomed his readers, and in substance it may be described as the negative complement of his own constructive theory, expounded in 'Hegelian Cosmology.' The real drift of the argument can hardly be understood without reference to the earlier volume, and in what I have to say I will endeavour to connect the two books. Mr M'Taggart begins by defining what he means by "dogma" and "religion." By "dogma" he means any proposition which has metaphysical significance, and a religious dogma is one whose acceptance or rejection by any person would alter his religious position. He considers various definitions of religion, including the suggestion that religion is identical with morality; but he rightly contends that the two names denote separate things, and should therefore be kept distinct. Arnold's definition of religion as "morality touched by emotion" is commented upon The defect of that definition is, that it does not indicate the source of the emotion. Religion, says Mr M'Taggart,

[1] Some Dogmas of Religion. By John M'Taggart Ellis M'Taggart, Doctor in Letters, Fellow and Lecturer of Trinity College in Cambridge, author of 'Studies in Hegelian Dialectic' and 'Studies in Hegelian Cosmology.' London: Edwin Arnold, 1906. The following critical notice appeared in 'The Hibbert Journal,' October 1906.

may best be described as "an emotion resting on the conviction of a harmony between ourselves and the universe at large"; and some belief in such a fundamental harmony between our ideals and the nature of things has always been implied, he contends, in religion. Religion is conceived in common usage as "something which brings with it rest and peace and happiness."

This view of the relation of religion to morality seems to me fundamentally sound, and is substantially identical with the position formulated by Höffding in his 'Philosophy of Religion,' that "the characteristic axiom of religion is the conservation of value — the conviction that no value perishes out of the world." Religion would certainly seem to imply such a belief. Ethics, or morality as such, only tells us what the "good" is. It does not tell us how far the good is realised, or is capable of realisation. That depends on our view of the nature of the universe as a whole. But, as Mr M'Taggart says, a view of the universe as a whole is a metaphysical belief or a dogma. In this large and ultimate sense, therefore, dogma is essential to religion. Our beliefs on metaphysical subjects are, accordingly, far from being as unpractical as many people suppose. They may be of supreme importance for the determination of our attitude towards reality in general and towards our own lives in particular. "It will depend on those beliefs," says Mr M'Taggart in a fine passage, "whether we shall consider the universe as determined by forces completely out of relation with the good, or whether, on the contrary, we may trust that the dearest ideals and aspirations of our own nature are realised, and far more than realised, in the ultimate reality. It will depend on them whether we can regard the troubles of the present and the uncertainties of the future with the feelings of a mouse towards a cat, or of a child towards its father. It will depend on them whether we look on our pleasures as episodes which will soon pass, or on our sorrows as delusions which will soon be dispelled. It will depend on them whether our lives seem to us worth living only as desperate efforts to make the best of an incurably bad business, or as the passage to a happiness that it has not entered into our hearts to conceive. It will depend on them whether we regard ourselves as temporary aggregations of atoms or as God incarnate. . . . These questions are not devoid of practical importance. It is common to speak of metaphysical problems as abstract and unpractical. In reality, all other questions are abstract as compared with these, and most, as compared with these, are unpractical."

But how is dogma to be established? In other words, how are such metaphysical convictions to be justified? In his second chapter Mr M'Taggart considers various attempts at justification. Dogmas are sometimes supported by the assertion that they do not rest on arguments at all, and cannot therefore be shaken by them. They rest on the immediate conviction of the believer. "If the person who holds a belief in this manner," says Mr M'Taggart caustically, "mentions the fact to me as a reason why I should not waste his time in trying to upset it, he is acting in a perfectly reasonable manner. And it is also strictly relevant to mention it if he is writing an autobiography, for it may be an important fact in his life. Also it is relevant as a contribution to statistics. It shows that one more person has this particular conviction in this particular way. But it is not relevant if it is put forward for any other motive. Above all, it is absolutely irrelevant if it is put forward as a reason to induce other people to believe the same dogma." Dismissing this view, therefore, he proceeds to consider the argument that a dogma must be true because it is held by all, or by most people. If it were really held by all, it would be superfluous to spend time in proving it. This argument must therefore mean no more than that the belief is, or has been, very general. But the opinion of the majority has very often been proved wrong in the past; and besides, the appearance of a decisive majority for a particular dogma is often gained by first excluding certain nations on the ground of their asserted inferiority. This test of truth, therefore, cannot be applied with consistency or safety. Nor can the truth of a religious dogma be proved by miracles. Finally, there is the argument from consequences. If a particular dogma is not true, this argument runs, the universe would be intolerably bad, and therefore the doctrine must be true. Put in this way, however, the argument evidently begs the very point in question; for what reason have we at this point to assert that the universe is not very evil? Moreover, in arguing from our desires and aspirations to their fulfilment, men too often ignore the races to which they do not belong, and also leave out of account those of their own race whose desires are different from their own. Such arguments are generally put forward in favour of the orthodox ideas of a particular time and place. This is notably the case, for example, with the doctrine of immortality. And if it is argued that any dogma which would paralyse our activity cannot be true, we may ask whether there is really any dogma the belief in whose truth would paralyse action. "It would be absurd to act, no doubt, if action made no difference in any result which was of value. But neither materialism nor any other dogma which has ever been maintained could lead to this conclusion. We may not survive the death of our bodies, and the race may be destined to endure for only a few brief millions of years; but meanwhile the race has not yet ceased to exist, and here we are, particular individuals, and while we are here, whatever the future may be, it is better that we should be full than hungry, better that we should work than steal, better that we should read Robert Browning than that we should read Robert Montgomery." As a last resort, an appeal is often made to faith in matters of dogma on account of the limitation of our knowledge. Of the limitation of our knowledge Mr M'Taggart is as profoundly convinced as Hume, but, as he neatly puts it, "it is somewhat remarkable that our want of knowledge on any subject should be put forward as a reason for coming to a particular conclusion on that subject."

So far as these arguments are concerned, therefore, Mr M'Taggart's result is entirely negative. He next proceeds to discuss in detail the three dogmas of God, freedom, and immortality, which are usually considered to form the substance of religious belief. He begins with the question of human immortality, arguing, in the first place, that the presumption against immortality, produced in many people by supposed results of physical science, should be discarded. Science is concerned solely with uniformities in the routine of our perceptions. Physical science can have nothing to say, for example, on the question of the independent existence of matter, which is only one theory about the causes of our sensations, and a theory which, on examination, is found to be involved in inconsistency. The "self," therefore, cannot be treated as an activity of the body. Its conscious existence is, on the contrary, a primary reality. On lines which recall Berkeley and Lotze, Mr M'Taggart thus leads up to the theory of monadistic idealism which he had already advocated in his 'Hegelian Cosmology,' and, as in that book, he again proceeds to connect the belief in immortality with the belief in pre-existence. "The present attitude of most Western thinkers to the doctrine of pre-existence," he says, "is curious. Of the many who regard our life, after the death of our bodies, as certain or probable, scarcely one regards our life before the birth of those bodies as a possibility which deserves discussion; and yet it was taught by Buddha and by Plato, and it is usually associated with the belief in immortality in the Far East. Why should men who are so anxious to-day to prove that we shall live after this life is ended, regard the hypothesis that we have already survived the end of a life as one which is beneath consideration?" Mr M'Taggart himself believes that any evidence which will prove immortality will also prove pre-existence.

The ethical argument that immortality is demanded by the claims of the moral personality, and that such a belief is required if we are to vindicate the goodness of God or the moral order of the universe, Mr M'Taggart dismisses on the general ground that the nature of reality is obviously not incompatible with the existence of *some* evil, and therefore we cannot hope for an *a priori* proof that any particular evil is too bad to be consistent with the nature of the universe. We are forced back, therefore, he says, "on the purely metaphysical arguments." These, as partially disclosed here and more fully developed in 'Hegelian Cosmology,' turn out to be based on abstract considerations as to the nature of substance. They are, indeed, curiously pre-Kantian in character, and it is strange to find so profound a student of Hegel using substance throughout as the ultimate category in speaking both of the self and of God. The perdurability of substance naturally refers just as much to the past as to the future. Substance, indeed, is conceived as that which can neither be created nor destroyed. Mr M'Taggart believes accordingly that our present existence has been preceded by a plurality of lives, and will be followed in like manner by a plurality of future lives. The obvious objection to this theory is the fact that we retain no memory of those previous lives, and Mr M'Taggart, it is to be noted, does not imply that in the lives to come we shall have any memory of our present existence. "An existence that is cut up into separate lives, in none of which memory extends to a previous life, may be thought to have no practical value." He labours hard to prove that this is not so, his most important argument being that though the actual experiences are forgotten, their results in the training of mind and character may be carried forward into the next life, so that the man will be wiser and better in the second life because of what has happened in the first. He will, as it were, have a better start; he will build in the new life upon the foundations laid in the old. This sounds, however, more plausible than it really is, and depends upon the ambiguity of the word "person." "In spite of the loss of memory," says Mr M'Taggart, "it is the same person who lives in the successive lives." Now, as Mr Bradley has forcibly recalled to us, it is exceedingly difficult to determine precisely what we mean by personal identity and what its limits are. Obviously, within the present life, countless items of our experience lapse from conscious memory and survive only as aptitudes, dispositions, and tendencies. But they play their part in training the mind and tempering the character. Our personality is not exhausted, therefore, by the individual experiences we can consciously recall. Still, although much may persist only in this sub-conscious fashion, it seems clear that a continuity of conscious memory within certain limits is involved in the ordinary notion of personality, so that a complete break of such continuity (and this is supposed to occur between one life and another) would make the assertion of personal identity in the two lives unmeaning. Locke is arguing, therefore, on right lines when he emphasises in his well-known chapter "that personal identity consists not in the identity of substance, but in the identity of consciousness."

I cannot help feeling that throughout the discussion Mr M'Taggart substitutes for the living and concrete unity of self-consciousness, as manifested in experience, the numerical unity of a soul-substance or indestructible soul-atom on which the personal unity of experience is supposed to depend, or in which it is somehow housed. This soul-substance forms, as it were, the vehicle by which the mental and moral qualities acquired by an individual in the course of a single life are transmitted to the next incarnation to be his working capital and the starting-point, possibly, of further advance. The two lives are thus continuous in the sense that both have the same metaphysical substrate, and the identity of substance manifests itself, on Mr M'Taggart's theory, in identity or continuity of attributes. But even so, it is surely paradoxical, or rather simply misleading, to speak of this continuity as "personal identity," and to say that in spite of the loss of memory it is "the same person who lives in the successive lives." The identity that exists is the identity of an object for an onlooker; it does not exist for any one of the successive incarnations. Each self is the realised unity of its own separate life, and if the new life is not consciously knit to the old, it is unmeaning to speak of the new individual as the same self. Mr M'Taggart argues that the loss of memory need not render immortality valueless, because the present life has value, although, admittedly, it carries no memories beyond itself. Why, then, he says, should not future lives have value, although in the same way without memory beyond themselves? "In that case a man will be better off for his immortality, since it will give him an unlimited amount of valuable existence, instead of a limited amount. And a man who believed that he had this immortality would have a more desirable expectation of the future than if he did not believe it." Certainly the future lives, when they come, have the same chance as this life of being valuable to the persons who have to live them, and as the lives go on for ever, there will thus be "an unlimited amount of valuable existence"; but there is to me a savour of mockery in the saying that the "man" is better off because the prospect gives "him" an unlimited, instead of a limited, amount of valuable existence. Mr M'Taggart himself is candid enough to add that "if a man should say that he takes no more interest in his own fate, after memory of his present life had gone, than he would take in the fate of some unknown person," he does not see how he could be shown to be in the wrong. "*His own* fate" is so far a question-begging description of the facts, since it implies the truth of Mr M'Taggart's theory of what constitutes identity. He puts the case more fairly in 'Hegelian Cosmology' when he says: "Suppose a man could be assured that in a short time he would lose for ever all memory of the past, would he consider this to be annihilation, and take no more interest in *the person of a similar character* who would occupy his old body than he would in any stranger?" In both connections Mr M'Taggart expresses his own conviction that most men would regard the fortunes of this hypothetical individual with an interest at least analogous to that which they take in their own conscious survival. That is a question which could only be determined by statistics, and I will at least record my adhesion to the opposite view. I am not here arguing in defence of an immortality accompanied by memory. I can vividly appreciate the stimulus of the Positivist view that all the good of every life becomes the enduring possession of the race; or, on more homely ground, I can understand a man working for his family or his country without giving a thought to his personal continuance. But I fail to understand what special interest a man can take in the unknown series of those who are to inherit his soul-substance, any more than in the equally unknown series of those who had the usufruct of it before him. Nor can I see how what I should describe as the non-personal immortality of such individual substances, should "make any difference to our attitude towards reality in general and towards our own lives in particular."

I think, however, that I see in what consists for Mr M'Taggart the attraction of the belief, considered not with reference to the particular person who is misleadingly described as immortal, but as a general theory of the nature of existence. It is because it seems to guarantee an idealistic theory of the universe. Mr M'Taggart holds, and in this I agree with him, that value resides only in the experience of conscious beings. Such values are realised (it may be, progressively realised) in the present life of the human race upon the earth; but if these values are realised only in perishing individuals, in perishing civilisations or races,—if our solar system, for example, is after a given time to pass away, leaving behind it no result beyond a certain increase in the temperature of surrounding space,—there is an aimlessness in this ceaseless process of building up and pulling down which is at variance with our moral ideas, and seems to contradict the belief that spiritual values constitute the ultimate facts of existence. In order to save the situation, therefore, Mr M'Taggart argues that reality consists, in ultimate terms, of a definite number of eternal "selves" or monads, which appear over and over again in the time series, and serve as the media in which the cumulative results of experience in the time-process are preserved. These spiritual entities flower, as it were, in successive lives. They constitute the "fundamental differentiations of the Absolute," which is, in fact, only a name for the "assembly of spirits" formed by these "finite individuals, each of which finds his character and individuality in his relations to the rest, and in his perception that they are of the same nature with himself." Such a "city of God" has been recognised by various thinkers as the highest form of the spiritual ideal, but the attempt to give precision to the idea by converting it into the doctrine of a definitely determined number of eternal self-existent substances seems to me to obscure the true meaning of personality and to exemplify the kind of metaphysical speculation from which Kant, and still more Hegel, was supposed to have set us free.

The other dogmas above referred to—the existence of God and the freedom of the will—are treated by Mr M'Taggart in a more exclusively negative sense. Not only does he set himself to demolish the ordinary arguments by which they are supported, but he holds that on metaphysical grounds they can be shown to be untrue. The discussion of free-will seems to me below Mr M'Taggart's usual level of freshness and incisiveness. He attacks a "freedom of indetermination" for which I do not think any champion would enter the lists. What upholder of freedom, for example, would accept the statement that "according to the indeterminist theory our choice between motives is not determined by anything at all"? And when Mr M'Taggart says that "on the determinist hypothesis an omnipotent God could have prevented all sin by creating us with better natures and in more favourable surroundings," and that "he cannot see what extraordinary value lies in the incompleteness of the determination of the will, which should counterbalance all the sin, and the consequent unhappiness caused by the misuse of that will," the answer is that creatures so turned out would not be moral beings at all. They would be things, and not persons. Mr M'Taggart's own arguments treat the question entirely on the plane of efficient causality, on which motives are regarded as external forces impinging upon a given "nature"—that is to say, an inherited or implanted disposition. But such schematic representation remains entirely outside the realities of the moral consciousness. In the fundamentals of ethical theory, however unfortunately he may sometimes have expressed himself, Kant's insight is unerring, and the basis of all ethical discussion is just the difference between a person and a thing. A being who can only act under the idea of freedom is really free in the sense required by ethics. It is the judgment of the moral agent upon his own action which can alone tell us the real nature of the act, however justifiably the psychologist, the historian, or the social reformer may deal with it from another point of view. I believe that a more sympathetic study of the great master in ethics would have made Mr M'Taggart's chapter on "Free Will" more adequate to its theme.

Belief in immortality and belief in God usually go

together. Indeed, the tendency of modern thought is rather to make the conviction of immortality dependent on the doctrine of God. But for Mr M'Taggart the one doctrine excludes the other. The eternity of finite selves in the sense explained above negates for him the supposition that the Absolute is a self or person. "It would be difficult," he has told us in his 'Hegelian Cosmology,' "to find a proof of our own immortality which did not place God in the position of a community rather than a person." In the present volume, Mr M'Taggart begins his discussion of the question by distinguishing God from the Absolute. The two terms are generally used, he allows, as synonymous; but the God of Spinoza, for example, is not personal, whereas personality seems inseparable from the ordinary idea of God. "By God," says Mr M'Taggart, "I mean a being who is personal, supreme, and good;" and the definition may be taken as coinciding, so far as it goes, with ordinary usage. By most men the attribute "supreme" is probably taken to imply that God is the Creator or Author of the universe; but in Mr M'Taggart's view it is not necessary for a belief in God that God should be conceived either as omnipotent or as creative, provided the belief is retained in a being who is personal, supreme, and good. He himself, indeed, denies the existence of God, if understood as a being omnipotent and creative, but he is willing to admit the possibility of a non-omnipotent God, whom he styles "the director of the universe," "a person of appreciable importance when measured against the whole universe," "one who fights for the good and who may be victorious." The only reason why we should not believe in the existence of such a God, he says, with a dash of cynicism, is that there is no reason why we should believe in it.

He first attacks the doctrine of an omnipotent and

creative God. The cosmological argument from the necessity for a first cause, he points out, is powerless. If we suppose that God exists in time, "then we have a substance which has persisted through an infinite past time." But if one substance can so exist without being caused, why not others? If God did not need a creator, why should "a man" or "a pebble" require one? On the other hand, if God's nature is timeless, then it is incapable of change, and the creation of the universe at a particular moment cannot, therefore, be explained from the nature of God. If we pass to the argument from design, Kant has already told us that it can prove, at most, the existence of an architect or designer, not that of an omnipotent creator. If it proved the existence of a God at all, says Mr M'Taggart, it would also offer a positive disproof of his omnipotence. He next proceeds to argue that the existence of evil in the world is incompatible with the belief in an omnipotent being who is also good. He repudiates with not unnatural warmth the theory of Pascal and Mansel that goodness in God may mean something quite different from what is called goodness in men. He refers to Mill's famous saying in this connection as "words which form one of the turning-points in the religious development of the world." This is, surely, somewhat exaggerated language, and in view of this high estimate of the sentiment, it strikes one as quaint when Mr M'Taggart goes on to criticise the prudence of Mill's resolve. It might be wiser after all, he suggests, to compound with such a God-monster than to risk the extremes of his malignity. It must be said that the discussion in this chapter is, on the whole, rather profitless, because Mr M'Taggart insists on taking omnipotence as implying the power to make contradictions true. It may be undesirable to use the word at all, but as those whom he is attacking never assert omnipotence in the sense of ability to override intellectual and moral necessities, the polemic is rather in the air. It is no pertinent answer, for example, to the argument that the evil in the universe is the result of free will, to say that "a God who cannot create a universe in which all men have free will and which is at the same time free from all evil is not an omnipotent God, since there is one thing which he cannot do."

Mr M'Taggart passes next to consider the alternative of a creative God who is not omnipotent, referring in this connection to Dr Rashdall's essay in the volume 'Personal Idealism.' If God is creative, he argues, nothing exists unless He decides to create it—unless, that is, He prefers its existence to its non-existence. We cannot, therefore, in strictness, speak of God's will as *thwarted* by the existence of evil, for He willed the universe as a whole with the evil in it. Such a being, he concludes, could not be a God in the sense in which we have agreed to understand the word, because he would not be good. Here again, however, there seems to be implied in Mr M'Taggart's argument the same interpretation of creative power as we found in the case of omnipotence. He understands by it power to compass moral, if not intellectual, impossibilities. The contention of those against whom Mr M'Taggart is arguing would be that moral goodness, or indeed the existence of a moral agent or a personality at all, is impossible without the risk (without the practical certainty, we may say) of the occurrence of evil volitions. But it does not follow from this, they would maintain, that evil is not repugnant in itself to the author of the universe. The discussion of the third possibility, that of a non-omnipotent God who is not regarded as creator but as one person among others, though indefinitely more powerful, leads to the less negative, but somewhat equivocal, result already indicated. To be frank, one sees no reason why this mythical "person of appreciable importance" should be dignified with the august name of God; and as a description of Mr M'Taggart's own conclusions the blunt expression in 'Hegelian Cosmology' seems preferable, "the Absolute is not God, and in consequence there is no God."

The concluding chapter considers the negative result of the whole discussion in its bearing on human happiness. The existence of an omnipotent creator, it is argued, would give us no reason to expect any goodness in the universe which we should not have expected otherwise. The existence of a non-omnipotent God would give us "no appreciable help towards a cheerful view of the universe," seeing that it leaves us uncertain how much God may be able to do. On the other hand, "it is quite possible without a belief in God to maintain that the nature of reality is such as to *ensure* the predominance of good. There might be a God and yet the universe might be, on the whole, bad. There might be no God and yet the universe might be, on the whole, good." The only way, therefore, of arriving at any certainty on this point "would be by the establishment of a complete system of metaphysics." Mr M'Taggart evidently refers here to his own theory as sketched in 'Hegelian Cosmology.'

In spite of its acuteness, and in spite of the flashes of deep feeling which redeem much that is merely clever, the book leaves me with a distinct impression of unreality. I may be to some extent disqualified as a critic. When one does not believe in a creator *ab extra*, whether omnipotent or non-omnipotent, and when the conception of a finite director of the universe strikes one as frankly fantastic, it is perhaps difficult to appreciate a laborious discussion of these alternatives. But if Mr M'Taggart was going to discuss religious dogmas to any purpose, he should have spent his time upon the view which is only mentioned in passing, that "God is the sole reality." Neither religion nor philosophy can seriously entertain any other alternative. In many cases this view has led to a denial of the personality of the divine; but even Martineau, personalist of the personalists, speaks of God as "the soul of all souls." The preliminary difficulty, therefore, which Mr M'Taggart alleges, of conceiving "how one person could be part of another," is of a nature which suggests a reconsideration of the conception of personality rather than the omission of a thorough discussion of the only vital theory of God and man. If I may say so without offence, Mr M'Taggart's treatment of the dogmas he discusses seems to deprive them of their primary reference to the needs and utterances of the religious consciousness. The doctrines seem, if I may so express myself, to become finitised and mechanised. I have already indicated my view of the doctrine of eternal soul-substances. Similarly, in the case of God, it is surely not the existence of "a substance which has persisted through an infinite past time" that we are concerned about, or even the existence of another person to love. When Mr M'Taggart speaks of the love of God as "something entirely distinct from reverence and admiration and gratitude — a feeling of one person for another, which is not unworthy to bear the same name as the feeling of friend for friend," I feel somehow that Spinoza's description of the *amor intellectualis Dei* and Kant's austere warning against importing the notion of "pathologische Neigung" into the practical love of God are at bottom more religious, and become the situation better. What does the existence of God, or the personality of God, mean for the religious thinker save the intense conviction of the rationality and the righteousness of the universe? And is it not strange to say, as Mr M'Taggart does, of faith in God (p. 69), that "it will only give us light on *one particular dogma*, that the world is wisely and righteously governed"? Surely this is the sum and substance of all religious faith and of all philosophical construction. Does it not carry with it the ultimate answer in regard to immortality as in regard to every other question? As Carlyle puts it in one of the pathetic outbursts of the 'Autobiography': "Perhaps we *shall* all meet Yonder, and the tears be wiped from all eyes. One thing is no Perhaps; surely we *shall* all meet, *if* it be the will of the Maker of us. If it be not His will, then is it not better so?"

REPRINTS

PHILOSOPHY OF RELIGION IN KANT AND HEGEL.[1]

INTRODUCTORY.

PHILOSOPHY, as metaphysic, is occupied in determining with increasing accuracy the definitions and the mutual relations of the three great objects of thought—God, the World, and Man. Religion, in its current acceptation, implies a certain theory of the nature of at least two of these—God and man—and their relation to one another. Philosophy and religion are, therefore, and have always been, most intimately connected. From another point of view, again, religion, considered as a subjective manifestation, is so universal a mark of human culture, when it advances above the lowest stages, that it cannot be left unnoticed by any philosophy which pretends to give an exhaustive account of man and his relation to the system of which he forms a part. Every epoch of culture has derived its specific form and colour from its relation to certain religious ideas: difference of civilisation means, in the main, difference of religious training. In these circumstances, it is perhaps not too much to say that the capacity of a

[1] As explained in the Preface, the chapters which follow were written in 1881, and appeared in the following year as the second part of a volume on 'The Development from Kant to Hegel.'

philosophy to find room for religion in its scheme of things becomes no unfair gauge of the adequacy or inadequacy of the system in question.

In Christian times the relations of philosophy and religion have been mainly determined by the attitude of reason towards the churchly doctrine of revelation. Three relations of the human reason to the things of God are possible.

(1) It may be said that the content of theology is matter communicated by God in an extraordinary fashion —truths otherwise unattainable, and on which it is beyond the competency of reason to sit in judgment. We have thus two spheres arbitrarily separated. As regards their mutual relation, theology is at first supreme and law-giving; reason, as the handmaiden of faith, is occupied solely in applying the premises which it receives from the hand of theology. These are the Middle Ages, the Ages of Faith. Then we have the relation of indifference, typically represented by a man like Bacon. When Bacon, in his circumnavigation of the intellectual globe, comes to *theologia sacra*, he steers clear of the subject with the remark: "If we proceed to treat of it, we must leave the bark of human reason and pass into the ship of the Church." Divinity, he says elsewhere, "is founded upon the *placets* of God." "In such there can be no use of absolute reason. We see it familiarly in games of wit, as chess or the like. The draughts and first laws of the game are positive . . . and not examinable by reason." The position is, in words, the same as that of the Middle Ages, but it is formulated in a different interest: the irreverent comparison is significant of the secular spirit that characterised Bacon and, in a measure, the whole Elizabethan generation. But the relation of indifference, or of mock subservience (as it

is found in Bayle), is necessarily transient: it merely marks the end of the period of unnatural separation. In the long-run reason claims the whole man. It is in virtue of his reason that he is the subject of a revelation; and he is continually being asked to exercise his reason upon parts of the revelation, even by those who most strenuously maintain the severance of the two spheres. It is only because there is a certain reason and fitness in the conceptions of revealed religion that he has ever made them his own, and that he continues to use them and to find in them some kind of meaning and edification. The external relation of reason to religious truth cannot, therefore, continue; nor can the encroachments of reason be stemmed by temporary distinctions between the *un*natural and the *super*natural.

(2) A natural movement of revulsion carries reason into assuming an extreme or purely negative attitude towards revealed religion, such as we find exemplified in the current of thought which prevailed during the eighteenth century. The dry light of the understanding has here usurped all the ground to itself; and the explanation of the rise of positive religions is sought in the hypothesis of deceit, ambition, and priestcraft. Religion is identified with morality *plus* an intellectual adherence to certain dogmas of current philosophy—the existence of God and the immortality of the soul—which are dignified with the title of Natural Religion. But it was impossible that this dry rationalism should survive the moving of the deeper springs of feeling that marked the close of the century. The first revival of a sense of historic probability showed the untenable nature of a hypothesis which derived man's greatest onward impulse from a hotbed of corruption and deceit. But to overcome the abstract opposition of reason and revelation, a philosophy

was needed which should give a wider scope to reason and a more inward meaning to revelation.

(3) This is the third position, as occupied by the best thinkers of the nineteenth century. It cannot be attained without the abandonment of the mechanical philosophy and the unhistorical criticism of the preceding age. So long as the Deistic view of God and of His relations to the world and history held the field, a revelation necessarily meant simply an interference *ab extra* with the established order of things. Deism does not perceive that by separating God from the world and man it really makes Him finite, by setting up alongside of Him a sphere to which His relations are transient and accidental. The philosopher to whom the individual self and the sensible world form the first reality gradually comes to think of this otiose Deity as a more or less ornamental appendage to the scheme of things. In France the century ended in Atheism, and in cosmopolitan circles in England and Germany the belief in God had become little more than a form of words. But if Individualism is provably untenable, all this will be changed. If man himself be inexplicable, save as sharing in the wider life of a universal reason, and if the process of history be realised (in an intimate sense, and not with a mere formal acknowledgment) as the exponent of a divine purpose, then revelation denotes no longer an interference with the natural course of that development, but becomes the normal method of expressing the relation of the immanent spirit of God to the children of men at great crises of their fate. The relation is never broken, the inspiration is never withdrawn, but there are times at which its nearness is more particularly felt. To these the religious sense of mankind, not without a true instinct, tends to restrict the term revelation

and such a turning-point is, for us, the advent of Christianity.

It was Lessing who first flung this fertile idea into the soil of modern thought, where it was destined soon to bear fruit an hundredfold. In spite of his own imperfect statement (in the 'Education of the Human Race' and elsewhere), he may be said to have founded the Philosophy of Religion in the sense in which it is now understood. Lessing and Kant stand together in Germany, closing the old age and opening the new. Every epoch-making mind has two sides. Like Janus, it looks two ways: one face is turned to the past, the other to the future. No one can read Kant intelligently without perceiving two tendencies that strive for the mastery. In Lessing the conflict between the old and the new is still more painful, and communicates an element of unrest to his whole life. When he is brought in contact with the manuscripts of Reimarus, the unmitigated representative of the eighteenth century, he is driven by a kind of revulsion to elaborate grounds for the defence of the idea of revelation, and even of certain dogmas of the Christian faith. But it was after all a *tour de force;* and when he was left alone, without the stimulus of opposition, he was apt to become once more a man of the Enlightenment like those around him. But he never attained their self-complacency. In his lifetime he gained only the distrust of both parties; now we can sympathise with his struggles, and recognise in him the pioneer of a new time. This indication of his position and influence must be enough in a sketch like the present, which does not aim at going beyond the limits fixed by the two names Kant and Hegel. We pass, therefore, without further preface, to consider the treatment which religion receives at the hands of Kant.

CHAPTER I.

THE KANTIAN PHILOSOPHY OF RELIGION.

The foundations of Kant's philosophy are laid in his ethics. It is only in connection with his ethical theory, therefore, that his Philosophy of Religion can be understood. The immediate consciousness of the moral law introduces us to a world of realities, from which, according to Kant, the categories and forms of our own thought exclude us in the sensible sphere. It is quite possible to accept the gist of Kant's position here, and at the same time to hold that we know all the reality of the sensible world that there is to know. There is no need to adopt Kant's mystification about things in themselves, as different from the things that are known; but he is right in saying that the world of sense is not noumenal, if by noumenon be understood the notion of that which can be an end-in-itself. The sensible world is essentially phenomenon; it exists for reason and as a means to rational consciousness. If it were possible to think of Nature out of that reference, it would be seen to be destitute of anything that could fairly be deemed to confer permanent value upon it. Its forms might flit for ever across the inane, without the suggestion of any end which they were there to realise, and which reason must pronounce as worthy, in its own self, of being realised. Without such an end-in-itself, existence is, literally, to the speculative mind a vain show. Philosophy may be intelligibly defined, from this point of view, as the search for the supreme end, which shall serve, as it were, to *justify* existence—something in the contemplation of which a rational being may find complete and permanent satisfaction, and to the advancement of which he may unquestioningly subordinate his individual efforts. The phenomenalness of the sensible world may be taken to mean simply that it does not supply to reason such an end. All the forms of its life are ends only in a relative sense; they have their true end outside of themselves. It is evident that, in this sense, there can be no more than one noumenon. The notion of end-in-itself implies that whatever is so designated receives its title because all other ends, relatively so-called, hold their significance in fee from it, and because there is nothing beyond itself with which it can be compared, or to which it can be subordinated. The idea of a plurality of ends-in-themselves may, at most, be employed, with a certain laxity, as indicating the variety of aims which are reduced to unity in the one central conception. Nor can there be any doubt where this one noumenon is to be found: reason or the rational being alone does not require to go outside of itself to seek its end. If it did, we should be embarked upon a hopeless *progressus in infinitum*, and must despair of any answer to the question, What is good in itself—what is *the* good? But reason is self-centred, and fixes its own end. Even in such a *progressus* the objects of pursuit would be, to all eternity, such as reason dictated to itself as worthy of attainment. Sooner or later the acknowledgment is forced from us that reason must itself be dominant in all its ends, and that it is impossible to cast off this sway. For reason, in other words the supreme end, of which all the rest are only specific determinations, must be the realisation of its own nature. Reason, therefore, or the rational being, as rational, is the sole noumenon or end-in-itself.

This may be described, without misrepresentation, as the permanent result of the Kantian Ethics; and it is essentially, from another side, the same as the result of the Critique of Knowledge. Just as the source of the categories cannot be brought under the categories, so the source of all ends cannot of itself be subordinated to any of the ends it sets up. The pure Ego cannot be compassed by any of its lower forms; "it must be thought through itself, and all other things through it." So here the ultimate, satisfying good of reason must be reason itself. In both cases the subject is recognised as raised above the sphere of things—as determining, not determined. Man bears in his own person the last principle of explanation, whether in a theoretical or in a practical regard. The value of Kant's result, however, depends on the interpretation put upon reason, and on the relation in which reason is supposed to stand to the worlds of knowledge and action. The fruitfulness of the principle is impaired, in Kant's own system, by the purely formal or abstract way in which it is taken. This makes it impossible for him to deduce either a real world or a concrete system of duties. In the Pure Reason the unity of apperception remains a form into which matter is poured from another source: in ethics, similarly, the result must be an imperative that commands nothing in particular, unless reason is seen to have creatively specified itself in the historical life and institutions of the world.

Kant's ethical position, however, must be put in a clearer light to be properly understood. "An intelligence," he says, "has this prerogative over all other beings, that he fixes his end for himself."[1] Nature is governed by mechanical, chemical, and biological laws, which it fulfils without knowing them. The animal has its ends fixed for it by recurring instinct, and, of itself, it does not move out of the beaten circle of these natural impulses. The mark of a rational being is that it is raised above the government of a succession of impulses. Intelligence consists in the power of realising mentally a general law or principle, and will is the power of determining action accordingly. By the possession of these twin faculties, man is differentiated from the brute. Will, freedom, personality in its most intimate sense, are all contained in the initial self-determination. It introduces us, in short, to the knowledge of good and evil, and makes us the subjects of another legislation, quite different from the natural. Intelligence has not been given to man merely to enable him to satisfy his animal desires more copiously and exquisitely: happiness is, in fact, far more effectually secured under the guidance of instinct than under that of reason. The possession of reason intimates another and a higher purpose to be realised in human life. With the transference of the reins from the hands of nature to our own, comes also the responsibility for the course of the driving. A beast fulfils its instincts, and is blameless; man, enlightened by consciousness, often abuses them. It is of the essence of reason to generate the conception of "ought." Morality is founded on this unique conception; and a moral or an immoral life becomes at once possible, according as we do, or do not, make its "objective law" the subjective law or determinator of

[1] "Die vernünftige Natur" is Kant's phrase here. 'Werke,' iv. 285. The references throughout are to Hartenstein's edition of 1867.

our will. The relation between the law which reason lays down, and our subjective freedom to follow the law or to swerve from it, is the subject-matter of morality; the idea of obligation which the relation contains, is formulated by Kant in the Categorical Imperative.[1]

In accordance with his usual custom, Kant proceeds to consider how such a command is possible—whence it derives its indisputable authority. He finds the explanation in a view of reason such as has been already indicated. The law is binding upon all rational beings, because it is reason's own law. The aspect of the law as a command—expressing necessitation—is due to the fact that we are not purely rational. We have a sensitive nature, and are swayed by sensitive determinants; hence our will is not holy, or in perfect conformity to the law. Nevertheless, it is not a foreign yoke that is imposed upon us; we are subject to our own legislation. Man as noumenon, or purely rational being, gives the law; man as phenomenon receives it. This is the principle of the Autonomy of the Will, by which Kant may be said to have solved the question of obligation. As long as the authority imposing the law is separated from the consciousness to which it appeals, its right to command may be called in question. The law must be such in its conception that every man may be, as it were, thrust back on himself, so as to recognise in it his own law.

[1] It is important to remark that the Categorical Imperative is simply the scientific formulation of the universal recognition, in some shape or other, of an "ought" and an "ought-not"; to which is added, in the Kantian Ethics, an account of the conditions under which alone such a universally binding command is possible. The history of the evolution of the conception of right, with its meaning always gaining in purity and complexity, is, therefore, quite beside the question investigated by Kant. The possibility of the occurrence of a moral action, and, consequently, the possibility of Ethics as a science, depends on the existence of such a notion, whether the form it assumes be adequate or not.

The moral *Sollen* is his necessary *Wollen* as member of an intelligible world,—that is, as a will capable of abstracting from the particular determinants of sense. The notion of such an absolute law is plainly, from another side, the same notion as that of an absolute End by which all action must be conditioned. The authority of the law springs, on this view, from the fact that it enjoins the realisation of what we recognise as our permanent and essential self. The position is, in ethics, the same as that of the self-conditionedness of thought in speculation. The End which intelligence fixes for itself cannot be, Kant says, a material end to be achieved; for in that case the will would be determined by something beyond itself. It must be an independent end (ein selbstständiger Zweck); and "this can be nothing else than the Subject of all ends itself."[1] Or, as he says elsewhere, "humanity, as objective End, ought to form, as law, the supreme limiting condition of all subjective ends."[2]

Such, then, is the foundation, and probably the most valuable part, of Kant's ethical construction. The Categorical Imperative, or the pure form of universally obligatory law, is "the sole fact of pure reason."[3] The *rationale* of the possibility of such a command is found in the idea of reason or the rational will as self-legislative, and so laying down a law which every rational being must recognise. In the 'Groundwork of the Metaphysic of Ethics,' Kant talks of deducing from this single Imperative "all the imperatives of duty." It cannot be said, however, that he has succeeded in con-

[1] 'Werke,' iv. 285. In the idea of a good will we must abstract, he says, "von allem zu bewirkenden Zwecke."

[2] Ibid., iv. 279.

[3] Ibid., v. 33, "das einzige Factum der reinen Vernunft."

necting his scheme of duties with his central principle. If he had paid more attention to the idea of reason as End, and so the source of the matter as well as the form of its action, it might have been possible to bring the particular and the universal more effectively together. But this would have meant virtually that reconsideration of the nature of the universal Self and its relations to the world which we everywhere miss in Kant, and which even in his ethical scheme remains fragmentary. The disjunction of the universal Self from the phenomenal world—in this instance, from the historical world of institutions and customs—is the source of the formalism which succeeding critics have so copiously blamed in the Kantian Ethics. The notion of End remains for Kant strictly convertible with the pure form of law. Hence he describes it, in the passages quoted above, as "limiting" condition—as an End which "must be thought negatively, that is, counter to which we must not act." This is quite of a piece with his unsatisfactory method of exemplifying his formula by taking up particular laws empirically, and testing them by comparison with its limiting condition. An absolute End, however, cannot be reached by abstracting from all real ends; it can be got at only by showing all real ends to be included in one conception. And if the notion of a universal or noumenal Self is to acquire positive content, it must not be separated from the reason that is in the world. Apart from the definite forms of that development, the Self is no more than an abstract point of unity. It was the impossibility of finding a real End in his abstract notion of the rational Self that made Kant round off his ethical system with a conception of the *summum bonum* which is essentially Eudæmonistic in character.

It was through the implications of the Categorical Imperative that Kant reached the completed theory of the world, which he found denied him in the theoretical reason. These implications are what he called the Postulates of the Practical Reason; and they correspond to the three Ideas which he designates in the 'Critique of Pure Reason' as the proper object of metaphysical inquiry—God, Freedom, and Immortality. The noumenal, and therefore unending, existence of the soul; the possibility of a reconciliation between the idea of free causation and the completely determined series of conditions demanded by reason in accounting for a phenomenon; and the reality of the idea of God,—are the questions treated by Kant in the Dialectic under the heads of Psychology, Cosmology, and Theology respectively. In the field of pure reason, the Idea of the Ego as noumenal unity, and the Idea of God as "the supreme and necessary unity on which all empirical reality is based," are simply points of view (Gesichtspunkte) by which reason introduces unity of system into its experiences. They are "regulative principles" or "formal rules" in the process of organising experience: we proceed *as if* all the phenomena of the internal sense were unified in one unchanging subject, and *as if* all phenomena, subjective and objective, were grounded in "one all-embracing Being as their supreme and all-sufficient cause." Similarly, we proceed in Cosmology according to the regulative Idea of the World as an infinite series of necessary causation; but the possibility is still left open of the existence of an intelligible or noumenal freedom alongside of this phenomenal determination, should such a conception be imperatively demanded on other grounds. The demand comes from the side of Ethics. Freedom, Immortality, and the Existence of God are involved, Kant maintains, in the unconditional Imperative of the moral law. They are the conditions requisite for the observance of its command; and they lose, therefore,—at least, so far as the practical reason is concerned,—their merely regulative character. They become objects of rational belief (Vernunftglaube). It is true that, just because the Postulates are reached on ethical grounds, they are not to be treated as theoretical dogmata. "Moral theology," he says, "is only of immanent use, namely, with reference to the fulfilment of our destiny here in the world." Indeed, to treat the Postulates as scientific facts would be to try to defeat the very object of reason in leaving us in this comparative twilight: it would make a disinterested moral will impossible. But none the less does this "moral belief" or "moral certainty" represent Kant's definite notion of the intelligible unity of the world.

The first of the Postulates to be deduced is that of Freedom. It is treated, indeed, by Kant less as a Postulate than as a fact: he calls it the one Idea of Pure Reason whose object is a fact to be reckoned among *scibilia*.[1] It is immediately deducible from the primary fact of the moral law. The Imperative is an absolute "Thou shalt"; and, in such a case, if the command is not to be quite meaningless, "We can, because we ought." Morality and Freedom thus reciprocally condition one another: the moral law is the *ratio cognoscendi* of Freedom, while Freedom is the *ratio essendi*, or the condition of the possibility, of the moral law. Hence, in spite of the inevitable determination of every event in the phenomenal sphere by antecedent events, Kant maintains the perfect freedom of the will, in each case of action, to choose between obedience and disobedience to the law.

[1] 'Werke,' v. 483.

Phenomenal antecedents can furnish no excuse for disobedience, for time does not enter into the conception of the immediate relation which exists between the will and the moral law. Though all a man's past actions have been bad, yet every fresh act of volition is an absolutely new beginning, in which he has a perfectly free choice between good and evil. He is conscious that he might have annulled the whole evil past, and acted morally, even while the actual immoral action which results is seen to flow with strict necessity from his phenomenal character, as revealed in his previous actions.[1]

[1] It is no part of my present purpose to trace the difficulties in which Kant's conception of Freedom involves him. By way of explaining the last statement, Kant says: "A rational being may rightly say of every illegal act he perpetrates that he could have left it undone, although, as phenomenon, it is sufficiently determined by the past, and so far infallibly necessary; for the act, with all the past that determines it, belongs to a single phenomenal character with which he endows himself (einem einzigen Phänomen seines Charakters, den er sich selbst verschafft), and by force of which he imputes to himself, as a cause independent of every sensuous determinant, the causality of those phenomena." Similarly Kant speaks of the empirical character as the "sensuous schema" of the intelligible. It seems from such passages as if, in each individual action, the agent were simply reaffirming the original act by which he took that intelligible character to himself. This is how the matter appears when it is thought out by Schelling. Freedom is placed in an original "timeless" act, which contains the seeds of all determination in itself. The letter of Kant leads directly to such a theory, as well as to the further application of the same idea by Schopenhauer to his doctrine of a blind or unconscious Will. Taken as science, Kant's theory of intelligible freedom seems to me untenable. There is no such separation between the phenomenal and the noumenal as he supposes, and if man is not free phenomenally, he is not free at all. In separating the *man* from his "character"—intelligible or phenomenal—an unwarrantable abstraction is involved: Kant seems to be in quest of the phantasmal freedom which is supposed to consist in the absence of determination by motives. The error of the Determinists from which this idea is the recoil involves an equal abstraction of the man from his thoughts, and interprets the relation between the two as an instance of the mechanical causality which exists between two things in nature. The point to be grasped in the con-

The second Postulate is the Immortality of the Soul. The law demands complete conformity with itself: it is to be the sole determinator of the will. In a being sensitive as well as rational, this conformity is never more than partial. Nevertheless, whatever the Imperative demands must be possible: if a holy will is not possible in humanity as a present achievement, it must be realisable under the form of an infinite progress or continual approximation to the idea of holiness. In this way the ethical Imperative guarantees to us an immortality in which to work out its behest. But the mere subjection of the will to the form of law represents only one side of our nature. Man has a phenomenal or sensitive nature, which cannot and ought not to be wholly left out of account. Subject to the supreme condition of conformity to the moral law—worthiness—man, as a sensitive being, asks for Happiness, and figures to himself the *summum bonum* as the combination of Virtue with Happiness. Now the moral law simply commands the sacrifice of all subjective desires or inclinations when duty calls; it does not provide for the making good to the individual of the possible, and even probable, loss of happiness which he may sustain. There is thus a breach between the consciousness of moral integrity and the happiness which consists in the satisfaction of ineradicable and harmless subjective desires. The consciousness of rectitude is in itself bare: it is only by a figure of speech that the

troversy is that a man and his motives are one, and that consequently he is in every instance self-determined. In reference to the Kantian position, it may be said that, inasmuch as the moral law is a permanent motive recognisable as his "proper self," a rational being must in every act acknowledge his "responsibility" to follow after, if haply he may attain to, this idea of his destiny. The presence of this moral ideal in man as man, and its infinitely regenerative power in breaking the yoke of the past, are all the facts that I can see to be contained in Kant's statements.

possession of the *mens conscia sibi recti* can be identified with perfect happiness. Worthiness to be happy is, of course, in an ethical legislation, the first requisite; but the perfect moral world for whose realisation man works, and in whose ultimate existence he believes, is one in which Happiness shall be the necessary consequence of moral desert.[1] This proportionality, however, is not realised in the present state of separation between the ethical will of the individual and the sway of mechanical causality in nature. The causal determination of nature by our will is regulated, as to the measure of its success, "not by the moral disposition of the will, but by the knowledge of the laws of nature and the physical power of using them in furtherance of our aims.[2] The ultimate equation of the two sides, which reason in its practical function declares to be a "moral necessity," is impossible without presupposing the existence of God as an Author of nature, whose causality is regulated by a regard to the moral disposition of His creatures. This, then, is the third and final Postulate, which completes the edifice of Kant's Ethical Theology. In other words, the idea of a perfect ethical legislation, which is contained in the Categorical Imperative, carries with it the idea of an ultimate harmony between the sensible sphere and the practical ends of reason. The moral law, though in itself without promise of Happiness, imposes upon us the realisation of this highest good as "the last object of all conduct." But the actual attainment of this object or end is impossible without the independent existence of

[1] Happiness (Glückseligkeit), it may be noted, is defined by Kant as "the satisfaction of all our inclinations (Neigungen): extensively, as regards their multiplicity; intensively, as regards their degree; and protensively, as regards their duration."—'Werke,' iii. 532.

[2] Ibid., v. 119.

the idea in God as the union of moral perfection with perfect blessedness. God, as "the highest original Good," is to Kant the cause of the ultimate adjustment of perfect happiness to perfect virtue in the world, and so the necessary condition of the *summum bonum.*[1]

Erdmann points out that all the three 'Critiques' close with Ethico-theology, or the system of rational belief contained in the Postulates of the moral reason. It is Kant's substitute for the Rational Theology or dogmatic metaphysic of the schools which he demolished. It is in the last analysis a system of ethical teleology, and it represents, as already remarked, Kant's final notion of the unity and government of the world. Criticism may be deferred till after consideration of the Kantian Philosophy of Religion, which stands in the most intimate connection with the ethical scheme just developed.

Kant has not left us to gather his Philosophy of Religion inferentially from stray references. He has expounded his view of the necessary content of true religion in a separate work, which, from the place it occupies in the development of the German *Religionsphilosophie,* has a fair claim to rank in importance alongside of the three 'Critiques.' This is the 'Religion within the Limits of Mere Reason.'[2] The exposition of

[1] Kant distinguishes between the existence of God as the highest "independent" or "original" Good—and the *summum bonum* as "the highest possible Good in a world," or "the deduced highest Good." Cf. 'Werke,' iii. 535, v. 135, 138. Speculatively, the distinction may be said to be, in one aspect, the same as that already drawn between the Idea as real and the same Idea as a process of realisation in time. But the two are not connected in this intimate way by Kant. God is simply cause, and, as such, remains a pure abstraction or *deus ex machina.*

[2] 'Die Religion innerhalb der Grenzen der blossen Vernunft.' 'Werke,' vi. 95-301.

the doctrines of true or absolute religion necessarily implies an account of the relation in which the different positive religions of the world stand to this pure religious truth. Kant's view of the function of positive religion, and his interpretation, in this connection, of the leading Christian doctrines, form, indeed, the most interesting and important part of the book. The language in which he expresses his ethico-religious positions is moulded throughout by a reference to the scheme of doctrines which the Christian Church has founded upon its sacred writings.

In the Preface, Kant indicates the relation which he conceives to exist between religion and morality. Morality, he says, leads necessarily to religion, the point of contact between the two being the notion of the *summum bonum,* and of the moral Ruler who realises it. We have seen that the End must not determine the will. Nevertheless, there can be no ethical action without the notion of some result flowing from our rectitude; and in a completed theory of the issues of life, such as religion uniformly professes to give, the notion of the End or final cause of all things necessarily comes to the front.[1] The content of philosophical theology and of ethics is, in fact, the same; but the latter deals with the ethical consciousness as such, and its foundation in the Categorical Imperative; the former—religion, as intellectually formulated in philosophical theology—presupposes this consciousness, and concentrates its attention on the metaphysical implications of morality, as the practical

[1] This ethical Idea is here called broadly the "Endzweck aller Dinge," and Kant presents it as the only means of combining the reference to End, which is the basis of freedom, with a teleological view of Nature. It is characteristic of Kant that, two pages farther on, he treats the necessity of the Idea as a species of condescension to the "unavoidable limitations of man and his faculty of practical reason."

reason reveals them in its Postulates. However, in spite of this difference of attitude, the whole aim of "religion proper," according to Kant, is moral or practical, and this must never be lost sight of in expounding it. We know nothing of the nature of God, for example, except so far as His attributes (and His actions) bear upon our conduct. Kant's religion, therefore, is his ethic writ large; but it is morality from the point of view, not so much of the individual consciousness, as of the divine ethical system of which the individual recognises himself to be a part. This recognition, with all that it may be found to imply, constitutes the distinctive mark of the religious, as opposed to the purely ethical, consciousness; so that Kant's theory of religion is often summed up—correctly, perhaps, but somewhat baldly—in the statement that religion is the recognition and discharge of duty as the will of God.

The *first* section of the book places Kant at once in striking opposition to the easy-going optimism characteristic of the eighteenth century, and of the general movement known as the Illumination or Enlightenment. It is entitled—"Of the indwelling of the evil principle side by side with the good, or on the radical evil in human nature." Kant begins by balancing against one another two opposing theories of human nature and history. The first asserts that the world lies in wickedness, and is going from bad to worse; the second—which he calls the "heroic"—sees in the course of history a continuous amelioration, due to the natural development of the healthy instinct of humanity. Kant proposes to mediate between these conflicting hypotheses by showing that man is by nature partly good and partly bad. First, he explains what he means by his terms. A man's moral quality depends, as Aristotle can tell us, not on the quality of his actions taken in themselves, but on the nature of the intentions which may be reasonably inferred from the actions. In the Kantian phraseology, a man is bad when the maxims according to which he guides his conduct are bad. Now the cause of evil, if the man is to be responsible for it (and responsibility belongs to the very notion of moral evil), must lie in the man himself. In saying that a man is bad *by nature*, therefore, there can be no talk of shifting the blame from man's own shoulders, and laying it upon some inevitable bias. In discussing moral questions we never leave the ground of freedom. The cause of the evil must lie in the free adoption of a fundamental maxim or principle of volition. The ground or motive of such a choice remains of course inexplicable, for we cannot go behind a free act. But the point to be borne in mind is, that the bias, if it should be proved to exist, must be first communicated to the will by an act of freedom. At the same time, if the adoption of a certain maxim as an underlying principle of ethical choice is found to be a universal characteristic of mankind, the ground of the adoption of this maxim—and, with it, the good or evil that it may contain—may fairly be said to be innate in human nature. It is innate in the sense that the will must be conceived to have given itself this bias before any opportunity arises for employing its freedom within experience. This "first subjective ground" may, therefore, be called by the more familiar term "disposition" (Gesinnung); and, though itself freely adopted, it must plainly have determining influence upon the whole series of our actions in time.

Should the disposition of humanity as such, therefore, exhibit a "propensity to evil" (Hang zum Bösen), that propensity would deserve to be called natural, even though it must be held to consist, as has been explained, and as Kant repeats, simply "in the subjective ground of the possibility of deviation from the maxims of the moral law." The deflection of the will from the law must be due to the fact that the will has taken to itself another maxim, which runs directly counter to the primary maxim of implicit obedience; and this causes a permanent incapacity to make the moral law the consistent maxim of conduct,—an incapacity which may fitly be called, Kant says, in the phraseology of Scripture, "the evil heart." Now the adoption of this evil heart has been described as our own act; yet it has been as emphatically declared to precede all acts. The word "act," therefore, must be taken here in two different senses; and Kant proceeds to explain that the origin of the propensity to evil, as the formal condition of all the immoral acts of experience, must be an "intelligible act, cognisable only through reason without any condition of time." It is just as impossible to assign a cause for this corruption of the supreme maxim of volition, as for any fundamental property of our nature; but it may fairly be called, again in the language of the Church, an act of original sin (*peccatum originarium*). The question of the origin of evil in the human heart is manifestly not a question of origin in time: time has nothing to do with the notion of the will or of a moral change. It is, indeed, a contradiction in terms to seek for the cause in time of a free action, in the same way as search is made for the cause of an event in nature. The cause of an ethical change must be ethical, and must lie, accordingly, simply and solely in the will itself. The question is confined, therefore, to the rational origin (Vernunftursprung) of the morally bad. That is to say, the existence of evil is taken simply as a fact, without any reference to time; and what is sought is the rational bond necessary for the thought-connection of this state of the human will with the normal (and therefore logically prior) state of complete conformity to the moral law. Ethically, the passage from the one state to the other, as taking place within the will, must necessarily appear as an immediate transition. Man is viewed as passing directly from a state of innocence to the commission of a morally bad action; and, from the ethical standpoint, every instance of the morally bad is such a lapse. The moral law judges every action as an *original* use of freedom, and finds no excuse for a man in the evil of his past, even though it may have become to him, as we say, a second nature. This "intelligible" departure from the perfect law is represented in Scripture as the Fall of man. As a strictly ethical fact, it is independent of considerations of time. It may be conceived as taking place in every immoral act; or, as universally characteristic of humanity, it may be conceived as taking place once for all. "In Adam all have sinned." The account in Genesis, when stripped of its narrative form, agrees, according to Kant, in all particulars with the ethical analysis. Even in the detail of the serpent, as a spirit tempting humanity to sin, we may see expressed the ultimate inexplicability of the origin of evil in a creature whose original nature is good.

Kant thus, in mediating between the two views of human nature mentioned at the outset, asserts the existence of a radical evil in man. The presence of evil consists in the fact that man, though conscious of an obligatory law, has yet adopted as maxim of conduct the occasional deviation from the same. Its ground is not to be sought in the sensitive nature of man and the natural impulses of which that is the root. These have in themselves no direct connection with evil, and we are, moreover, not responsible for their existence in us.[1] Nor can it be found in a corruption of the ethically legislative reason. Such a corruption would reduce man to a completely devilish condition. No man, however, can completely throw off allegiance to the moral law: it belongs to his essence, and refuses to be silenced. The solution of the problem of evil must be sought in the relation between the rational and the sensitive nature of man. The moral law would rule absolutely in his conduct, were it not that the sensitive nature (in itself harmless) supplies him with other and non-moral incitements to action. The evil heart consists in the reversal of the ethical order of precedence which subsists between these two classes of motives. The man who subordinates the pure motive of ethical obedience to "the motives of inclination"—which may be grouped under the general name of Happiness—is, in his intelligible character, bad, even though his empirical character, as it appears in his actions, may be blameless. The tacit adoption of a maxim of occasional deviation from the law in the interest of personal desires, is the root of all evil. "This evil is radical, because it corrupts the ground of all maxims. Moreover, as natural propensity, it cannot be eradicated; for that could only be done by means of good maxims, and inasmuch as the supreme subjective ground of all maxims is *ex hypothesi* corrupt, their adoption becomes impossible."[2]

"Nevertheless," Kant continues, "it must be possible

[1] It is not with flesh and blood, as Kant says, that we have to fight, but against principalities and powers; that is, according to his exegesis, against the unseen might of a maxim that infects all our willing.

[2] 'Werke,' vi. 131.

to gain the mastery over it, seeing that it is found in man as a freely acting being." This is the question which next emerges. How is a man who is thus by nature evil to make himself good? Whatever a man is morally, or is to become, must be his own work; yet how can a corrupt tree bring forth good fruit? It is something that passes our power of comprehension; but it must be possible, for the moral law commands its performance. The tree, happily, is not wholly corrupt; otherwise the task would be impossible. The moral law remains with us, and the susceptibility to ethical ideas which it implies is indestructible. What has to be done is to restore the law to the place of supremacy among motives of action which rightfully belongs to it. But the restoration, as we have seen, cannot be effected by any gradual process of amelioration. The supreme subjective ground of all maxims must be changed, or, in other words, the man must be renewed in the spirit of his mind. The passage from corruption to purity of moral maxim implies a revolution as radical as that of the original act of sin: by a single unalterable resolve, the man must undo what was then done. The subject who has effected this revolution within himself is ethically a new creature, and is accepted before God from that moment as good and well-pleasing in His sight. The change is likened in Scripture to a change of heart or a new birth. From such a point moral education must set out; for all possibility of progress lies in the fundamental, if often only half-acknowledged, principle of action which is then adopted. It is vain to enforce upon a man the performance of special duties so long as he is not, as it were, born again: the ground slips like sand from under our feet. Insight into the possibility of this restoration is no more attainable here than in any other case where the moral imperative seems to conflict with the determination of events by their antecedents. But that does not affect its real possibility. The principle of the natural depravity of the human will is not to be used dogmatically, so as to exclude the possibility of a regeneration. Its ethical function is simply to forewarn us that all is not right as things stand—that the state of nature, though it may often appear very harmless, is yet, from the point of view of ethics, bad. A dogmatic assertion of the futility of effort would, on the contrary, nip the moral life in the bud. In any case, even though the change of heart should be impossible without "higher co-operation," all true religion teaches that only he who has done all that is in his power—he who has not buried his talent—will be the subject of this divine grace. "It is not necessary, therefore, for any one to know what God does for his salvation; it *is* essential for him to know what he himself has to do, in order to become worthy of this assistance."

The struggle between the original good in man, as represented by the moral law, and his present evil disposition, forms the subject of the *second* section of the book. Kant entitles it "Of the struggle of the good principle with the evil for the dominion over man." The Christian Scriptures represent "this intelligible moral relation" of two principles in man as persons or powers outside of him, contending for the exclusive sovereignty over him. The evil spirit appears, in virtue of the Fall, as the prince of this world. But in the midst of the kingdom of darkness, the Jewish theocracy stood as a memorial of "the indefeasible right of the first proprietor." Among the Jewish people, in the fulness of time, appeared a Person who, according to the belief of his followers, announced himself as true man, and yet, at the same time, as one whose original innocence was unaffected by the compact which the rest of mankind had made, in the person of its first forefather, with the evil principle. "The prince of this world . . . hath nothing in me." By a resolute resistance to temptation, he declared war to the death against the evil principle and all its works. In its physical aspect, the strife could not end otherwise than in the death of him who thus attacked a kingdom in arms. But his death is itself the culminating "presentment of the good principle,—that is, of humanity in its moral perfection, as example for the imitation of every one." The kingdom of darkness exists still, but its power was broken by the example of that death. "To them that believe in his name"—that is, Kant interprets, to those who, upborne by his example, realise in themselves the same triumph over the assaults of evil—the transgressions of the past have no longer any terror. A new life has begun within them, and the fetters of the old have been struck off. Power has been given them to become the sons of God.

According to Kant, we have only to strip this account of its "mystic husk" in order to recognise in it an ethical content valid and obligatory for all time. It remains, then, to see his interpretation of its "spirit and rational meaning." In the first place, without any disparagement of its possible historical truth, the narrative form disappears, as such, in a statement of moral relations. "The good principle did not descend merely at a certain time, but from the origin of the human race it has descended from heaven in invisible fashion upon humanity." Of this the presence of a perfectly holy moral ideal in man alongside of his sensitive nature is sufficient proof. Humanity—or, more widely, rational existence—in its moral perfection, Kant here declares without reservation to be the only thing that can make a world the object of the divine decree and the End of creation. This Idea of a perfect humanity was in the beginning with God, and through it, or for the sake of its realisation, all things were made that were made. It is, in short, the only begotten Son in whom God is well pleased. To this ideal and prototype of humanity it is our duty to raise ourselves; and for this the Idea itself gives us strength, being present within us, as if it had descended from heaven. There is no objection to saying that the ideal is necessarily personified by us in a man, such as is represented in the Gospel history; but, in a practical regard, the reality of the Idea is independent of its exemplification. The prototype of an example must always be sought in our own reason. "Its presence there," Kant adds, "is in itself sufficiently incomprehensible, without supposing it hypostatised besides in a particular man." At the same time, such a divinely-minded Teacher, if he did appear, would be able to speak of himself with truth, as if the ideal of the good were actually manifested by him; for he would speak, in such expressions, only of the spirit which ruled his actions. It is of the "mind" which was in Christ Jesus, and which ought also to be in us, that account must be taken. The spirit of such a life—that is to say, ideal humanity, whether realised in a definite individual or not—is a complete satisfaction, in the eyes of supreme justice, for all men at all times and in all worlds. By identifying ourselves with this perfect mind, we put away our old heart and purify the ground of our maxims. It is true the law says: "Be ye perfect as your Father in heaven is perfect," and the distance that separates us from conformity to the perfect will of God is infinite; so that, in act, this ideal righteousness remains unattainable. But the morally purified disposition, as the germ from which all good is to develop itself, is accepted in lieu of the deed by God, who is the searcher of hearts, and who views the infinite progress of the moral life at once as a completed whole. The righteousness of the perfect Man is imputed to us, and covers our shortcomings.

The reconciliation of this with the principles of divine justice presents certain difficulties, however, which lead Kant to go into the theory in greater detail. The new heart is accepted before God as the earnest of an unresting progress in good, which He is pleased to regard as equivalent to that perfect righteousness to which, in his heart, the man clings. But even though the man contracts no new debts after his change of heart, yet, from the point of view of justice, the old remain unpaid. In avoiding offence for the future he does no more than his duty, and the doing of his duty to all eternity will yield no surplus of merit to weigh against the sins of his former life. The evil heart or disposition which he has cast off contained in itself, like a corrupt fountain, an infinity of transgressions, and calls, therefore, for an infinite punishment. The debt of sin, too, is the most personal of all obligations, and must in every case be paid by the sinner himself. Yet one who has laid hold on the good in the way described cannot be the subject of the wrath of God. How is this punishment to be borne by the man, consistently with the complete forgiveness of sin which accompanies repentance and the new heart? The answer is found by Kant in an analysis of the notion of the moral change that has taken place. The fundamental principle of the man's action, it must be noted, is changed, so that he is actually, in an ethical sense, *a new man*. Though he is physically the same person, yet, in the eye of a divine Judge, he is another.

In the language of Scripture, the change consists in putting off the old man and his deeds and putting on the new. The sacrifice which this implies—crucifying the flesh—and the sufferings which are the inevitable lot of humanity in this life (and which the old man might fitly have regarded, from the religious point of view, as the punishment of his disobedience) are cheerfully assumed and borne by the new man, not unwillingly as the wrath of an angry God, but in a spirit of perfect obedience. The pure mind of the Son of God present within him bears, as his substitute, the penalty of his past sins, redeems him by suffering and death, and finally appears as his advocate before the Judge. Or, if the idea be personified, it may be said that the Son of God himself does all this. The only difference between the two forms of expression is, that when we adopt the personified form, the death which the new man dies daily appears as a death suffered once for all by the representative of mankind. In this way, then, the claims of justice are satisfied, for the substitutionary office undertaken by the new man is something over and above the mere punctual discharge of his duty. At the same time, it is by an act of grace that this merit is reckoned to our account, inasmuch as the ideal of a morally perfect humanity exists in us as yet only as a set purpose of heart.

This imperfect, or merely germinal, character of the good within him need not, however, disturb unduly the man who has undergone this saving change. He must not permit himself to be tormented by a continual fear of backsliding; he must preserve the due mean between over-confidence and a cowardly distrust of the sincerity of his repentance. His steadfastness and continuous progress in the past form his only standard for judging of the probabilities of the future. The man, therefore, who can say, on an honest review of his actions, that his repentance has stood proof, sees before him the prospect of an endless future of the same happy progress. On the contrary, he who has always fallen back into evil, or sunk from bad to worse, has the outlook into an equally endless future of wretchedness. The attraction of the one view—Heaven—gives calmness and strength to the former; the horror of the other view—Hell—serves to rouse the conscience of the latter to stem the evil, so far as that may yet be.[1] Certainty of the unchangeable nature of our disposition is not possible to man, nor would it, if attainable, be morally beneficial; but a good and pure disposition begets a confidence in its own permanency, and acts thus as a Paraclete or comforter when our stumblings might cause us grave anxiety.

The first two sections of the book thus contain a statement of the main doctrines of ethical religion, together with an identification of this creed with the leading dogmas of Calvinistic Christianity. Kant's method is, first, to evolve the ethical position, and then, by means

[1] Kant emphasises here, it will be observed, the ethical advantages of the popular conception of an eternal state of happiness or misery in another life. On the other hand, he points out, in a long note, the disadvantages of the same conception when taught dogmatically. It is the same with the doctrine that the reckoning of each man's deeds is closed inexorably at the end of the present life. The doctrine, he says, is one of evident practical utility. It is eminently calculated to impress on men the importance of present repentance and welldoing. But the assertion of its dogmatic truth is just as little within the province of human reason as in the former case. "In short," he concludes, "if we limited our judgment to regulative principles of practical application, instead of extending it to constitutive principles of the knowledge of supersensible objects, it would stand better in very many particulars with human wisdom; and a supposed knowledge of what we at bottom know nothing about would not breed a groundless and too curious reasoning, plausible for a time, but becoming in the end prejudicial to morality." See 'Werke,' vi. 164-166.

of an allegorical interpretation of the Christian records, to exhibit its radical identity with this or the other doctrine of the Church. It hardly needs to be pointed out, however, that his statement of ethical truth would never have assumed the form it does in this book but for the fact that he found this scheme of doctrine already elaborated and, so to speak, in possession of the field. This is particularly obvious in regard to the laborious attempt, just considered, to give an ethical interpretation of the doctrines of Substitution and the Perseverance of the Saints. Throughout, it may be said, the real start is made from the dogma, which is then allegorised, with more or less success, into an ethical truth. The whole constitutes an attempt to extract a moral and purely rational meaning from a generally accepted interpretation of the Christian documents.[1] This, as will presently appear, is of the essence of Kant's position towards a positive religion which is received by us as a heritage from the past. The two remaining sections of the book

[1] In addition to the doctrines already involved in the preceding account, it may be well, for the sake of completeness, to state Kant's interpretation of the Trinity. The doctrine represents for him the union of holiness, benevolence, and justice in the Divine nature; and the contemplation of God in this triple capacity (as lawgiver, governor, and judge) is useful, he contends, in a moral view, as forcing us always to consider any one attribute as limited and conditioned by the others. It prevents us from regarding Him either as an earthly despot, ruling according to His mere good pleasure, or as a Being weakly indulgent to entreaty that has not its basis in moral reformation. The service we render Him is thus cleared of the anthropomorphic elements that so readily cling to it. Kant compares this triplicity in the notion of God with the separation of the legislative, executive, and judicial functions in the notion of the State. This circumstance seems to him to account for the occurrence of the idea in so many religions. It ought to be added, however, that hints towards a more vital notion of the Trinity are contained in what has been already said of the Idea of humanity as the true Son of God.

are devoted to defining the relation of positive and publicly established creeds to the moral faith, or, more particularly, the function of the former in the service of the latter.

The *third* section passes from consideration of the moral conflict within the individual to the definitive triumph of the good principle, which cannot be realised except in an ethical community, in which the purpose of the individual shall no longer be undermined, as at present, by the influence of his fellows. Such a commonwealth, all the members of which are governed by the same laws of virtue, is, in its very idea, universal and all-embracing: its foundation would be "the foundation of a Kingdom of God upon earth."[1] Its necessity is obvious. The isolation and cross-purposes of the ethical "state of nature" permit individuals, even with the best intentions, to act as if they were "instruments of evil"; it is the duty, therefore, of every one to abandon that state, and become a member of an ethical community. Inasmuch as this union is necessary for the complete triumph of the good, it is incumbent upon every one who aims at that triumph in himself and others. This idea of an ethical commonwealth is identical with the idea of "a people of God," by whom the laws of virtue are viewed as proceeding from a Lawgiver who is perfect holiness, and who searches the hearts of His subjects, so that the inmost secrets of their disposition are open before Him. The foundation of a kingdom of God is a work which, as a matter of fact, can be achieved by God alone. Nevertheless, man must not remain inactive: on the

[1] Hence the title of the third section: "The victory of the good principle over the evil, and the foundation of a Kingdom of God upon earth."

contrary, here, as in all ethical matters, "he must proceed as if everything depended on himself."

The idea of a people of God takes in man's hands the form of a Church. The Church, as it owes its foundation to man, may be called the visible Church, to distinguish it from the invisible universal Church, or the ideal union of all upright men in a morally governed universe. The only possible foundation of a universal Church (and, in its idea, every Church is universal) is the pure faith (der reine Religionsglaube), which has been already expounded. Those doctrines alone whose content is purely rational, and which are in no way dependent on historical facts, can command universal assent. But the natural need of mankind for something on which they can lay hold with their senses —some fact of experience which may serve, in a manner, as a voucher for the ideas of reason — has effectually prevented them, as history testifies, from ever founding a Church on this purely ethical belief. It is not easy to convince men that constancy in a morally good life is all that God asks from them, and that, in the performance of their duties to themselves and others, they are "constantly in the service of God." They persist in regarding God after the manner of an earthly monarch, who has need of honour and marks of submission from his subjects. There emerges, accordingly, the idea of a religion of ritual observance or a *cultus* (eine gottesdienstliche Religion). Morally indifferent actions are exalted even above the performance of duty, because they are supposed to be done *for* God. We invariably find, therefore, alongside of the moral code, a set of statutory or positive commands, which, as well as the former, are supposed to emanate from the divine will. The commandments of morality are discoverable by every man in his own reason, and they constitute for humanity as such the perfect and sufficient worship of God. It cannot be denied, however, that the addition of a set of statutory commands seems to be a necessity for man as a member of an ethical community; and these imply the form of a revelation — that is, of a historical belief, which, in contradistinction to a purely rational faith, may be called the belief of the Church (Kirchenglaube). The safest depository of this extra-belief, as it may be called, is found by experience to be a sacred book. But, in some form or other, a *Kirchenglaube* is found invariably, as if by an ordinance of nature, preceding the pure *Religionsglaube*. In the process of breaking in mankind to an ethical commonwealth, the one serves as the vehicle for the introduction and propagation of the other.

This being, then, one of the facts to which we must accommodate ourselves,[1] the question arises, What is the proper attitude of reason towards the Church's claim to be the depositary of a special revelation? Kant answers this question with the full measure of Critical caution. He indicates as his own position that of pure Rationalism, as opposed to Naturalism on the one hand and Supernaturalism on the other. The pure Rationalist does not, like the Naturalist, deny the possibility of a revelation; he is ready even to admit that a revelation may have been necessary for the introduction of the true religion. But he does not consider a belief in this supernatural origin and its accompaniments to be an essential part of saving faith, as the Supernaturalist does. The question

There is a ring of semi-ludicrous resignation about the copious array of particles in which Kant reconciles himself to the inevitable: "Wenn es nun also einmal nicht zu ändern steht, u.s.w."

of origin is thus shelved, as a transcendent inquiry which is beyond the scope of the critical reason, but which is at the same time of no practical moment. A religion must be judged, in the end, not by its origin, but by its content: its capacity to become a universal religion depends on the identity of its content with the moral faith which reason reveals. It is part of Kant's aim in this book, as we have seen, to exhibit this identity in the case of Christianity. In this connection he introduces a distinction which seems almost to contain a reference to Lessing's leading thought in the 'Education of the Human Race.' A religion, he says, which, objectively, or in respect of its content, is a natural religion, may yet, subjectively, or in the mode of its first appearance, be called a revelation. Where the religion is of such a nature that men might have arrived at it, and ought to have arrived at it, of their own accord by the mere use of their reason, but yet, if left to themselves, would not have reached it so early or so generally,—there, and in this specific sense, the term revelation cannot be objected to.[1] With this suggestion Kant leaves the matter, and we are at liberty to infer, if we like, that this was his personal view of the origin of Christianity: it is evident that he considers the subjective revealedness of a religion a question of little importance, when the religion is once there, and recognised as a natural or rational faith.

So far as a religion is objectively a revelation—that is, so far as it contains contingent or non-rational matter—it is, in Kant's view, temporal and local, and destined to pass away. The value of such positive creeds is not to be depreciated. They serve as vehicles for the ideas of true religion, and they are not to be rudely or thought-

[1] 'Werke,' vi. 254.

lessly attacked.[1] On the contrary, it is our bounden duty to utilise whatever historical *Kirchenglaube* we find in general acceptance around us. The "empirical belief," however, must be interpreted throughout in a practical or ethical sense. The theoretical part of the Church's creed has no interest for us, except so far as it aids us in realising our duty as the divine will, and in performing it as such. This is the supreme canon of interpretation: "All scripture is profitable for doctrine, for reproof, for correction, for instruction in righteousness." The interpretation may often appear forced, as regards the text of the revelation; nay, it may often really be so. But the interpreter is not, therefore, to be reckoned dishonest, as long as he does not pretend that the moral sense which he attaches to the symbols of the popular belief or its sacred books is the original sense in which they were intended by their authors.[2] Alongside of this interpretation in the interests of reason, the "learned" or historical interpretation may of course assert its place, as necessary for the systematising of the belief of the Church as a definite organisation within certain limits of time and space. But the historical belief is "dead in itself"; it is only by the comparative ease with which a revelation lends itself to an ethical exegesis that it justifies its claims to a divine origin. Historical belief is, in fact, in every case merely a leading-string to bring us to pure religion, and ought to be employed with the

[1] As Kant says in a note elsewhere: "All deserve the same respect, so far as their forms are attempts of poor mortals to body forth to themselves the Kingdom of God upon earth; but all deserve the same blame, when they take the form in which they represent this idea for the thing itself." —'Werke,' vi. 274, n.

[2] Kant refers approvingly, in this connection, to the philosophic allegorising of the pagan myths in later antiquity; which forms, indeed, an apt parallel to some of his interpretations of Biblical dogmas.

consciousness that it is nothing more. That Church is a true church whose creed contains the principle of continual approximation to this pure belief, so as to enable us eventually to dispense with the leading-string.

There are two articles of a "saving faith," Kant proceeds, resuming in effect what he had said in the first two sections. These are the belief in a satisfaction due for sin and the belief in the possibility of finding acceptance with God by perseverance in the good life. Kant again points out that a belief in satisfaction or substitution (in the sense already explained) is necessary only for the theoretical explanation of salvation; whereas the unconditioned command attached to the second article makes the improvement of a man's life the supreme principle of a saving faith. But so far as belief, in the case of the first article, is fixed simply on the idea of a perfect humanity, it is itself ethical; and the two articles represent "one and the same practical idea," in which the standard of holy living is contemplated from two opposite sides. But the same cannot be said if the article be taken to mean an empirical belief in the historical appearance of the ethical ideal in a definite individual. In this form, the idea is closely connected with the non-moral notions of expiation which are to be found in all religions. "But in the God-man," Kant says, "it is not what the senses apprehend, or what can be known of him through experience, but the prototype which lies in our reason, that is properly the object of saving faith." It is a necessary consequence of our natural development, he concludes, that religion should be gradually severed "from all empirical grounds of determination, from all statutes which rest on history, and which provisionally, by means of a *Kirchenglaube*, unite men for the furtherance of the good. So at last pure rational religion will reign universally, 'that God may be all in all.' . . . The leading-string of sacred tradition which did good service in its day becomes gradually no longer necessary, and is felt at last as a fetter, when humanity arrives at manhood. 'When I was a child, I understood as a child; but when I became a man, I put away childish things.'"[1]

In considering this process as exemplified in the historic religions of the world, Kant restricts his view to Christianity. He is apparently unable to trace any uniformity of development in the other faiths of mankind. In particular, it is worth noting that he emphatically denies to Judaism any connection with the Christian Church. The political and positive aspect of Jewish religion, the national exclusiveness which found expression in it, and the want of reference to the immortality of the soul, combine to make Kant do less than justice to the religious elements which the Hebrews undoubtedly possessed. The trouble which the first teachers of Christianity took to connect the new belief with historical Judaism, he considers to be a natural expedient on the part of men anxious to spread their principles among a prejudiced and exclusive race, but as in itself proving nothing. Of the actual history of Christianity Kant takes a very gloomy view. Its origin is obscure, for it is passed over without mention by the "learned public" of that day: we do not know, therefore, the effect of its doctrines upon the life of its early professors. But its later history, as exemplified in the Eastern and Western Empires, in the Crusades, and in the ambitious intrigues of the Popes, "might well justify the exclamation—*Tantum religio potuit suadere malorum!*" Such a fate was not to be escaped, so far as Christianity was founded

[1] 'Werke,' vi. 219.

on a historical belief; but, in spite of this miscarriage, "the true first intention" of its institution was evidently "the introduction of a pure religious belief, about which there could be no conflicting opinions." If asked what period in the whole known history of the Church is the best, Kant says he has no hesitation in answering—the present. The universal Church is already bursting the bonds of special doctrine in which it has been confined. As evidence in support of his opinion, Kant instances the general spread of a spirit of modesty and tolerance towards the claims of revealed religion, together with a firm conviction that in ethics lies the core of the whole matter. In the universal acknowledgment of these principles consists the coming of the Kingdom of God, which, in the sacred records, is represented chiliastically as the end of the world. But the universal Church will not come with violence and revolution: it will be the result of gradual reform and of ripe reflection. "The kingdom of God cometh not with observation." Empirically we cannot see to the end of this development,[1] but intellectually we must regard ourselves as already citizens of such a kingdom. "Behold, the Kingdom of God is within you."

The *fourth* section, "Of service and spurious service under the dominion of the good principle, or of religion and priestcraft," is more of the nature of an Appendix; and most of what is important in it has been already anticipated. Kant's object is to contrast the pure service of God, which consists in a moral life, with the spurious

[1] Indeed, in a note at another place Kant treats the idea of a universal Church as an Idea of reason, which can never be realised, but which is indispensable as a "practical regulative principle." Every Church, like every kingdom, strives after universal dominion; but always when it seems in a fair way to make good its pretensions, a principle of dissolution shows itself, which breaks it up anew into different sects.

notions of service that are the natural growth of a statutory system. He maintains the essential identity of Christianity with the moral religion; and, by a somewhat copious reference to the teachings of Christ in the Gospels, he has little difficulty in showing their exclusive reference to purity of heart and life. Even where the form of expression is accommodated to the traditions of Judaism, there shines through, according to Kant, "a doctrine of religion universally intelligible and universally convincing." But the "episodic means of recommendation" employed by Christ and the first teachers of His religion have been exalted by theologians into essential articles of faith, just "as if every Christian were to be a Jew, whose Messiah has come." By so doing, the doctors of the Church do their best to defeat the intention of the Founder of the religion, by imparting to it a statutory character. A religion so conceived is the natural soil in which false ideas of the service due to God spring up. Spurious service consists essentially in the notion of winning the divine favour by other means than by uprightness of moral will. Whether it be sacrifices, or castigations and pilgrimages that we lay on ourselves, or ceremonies, solemn festivals, even public games (as in Greece and Rome), the idea is the same: something is done specially for God, by way of proving our entire submission to His will, and inducing Him to look with a kindly eye upon His servants. Usually the more useless the action, the more efficacious is it supposed to be. The secret motive of such service is the hope of influencing to our advantage the unseen power that directs the destiny of man. In all its phases, therefore, it is Fetichism. The man supposes himself to influence God, and so employs Him as a means to produce an effect in the world. In opposition to this, true religion teaches that we have nothing to do but to cultivate a dutiful disposition. To such a disposition all things that are lacking in its righteousness will be added by Supreme Wisdom *in some way*—it matters not how. Everything, in short, depends on the order in which the two ideas of morality and the service of God are taken. We must begin with virtue, and end with the conception of our duty as a continual service of God by obedience to His will. Otherwise we make God himself an idol.

CHAPTER II.

CRITICISM OF THE KANTIAN STANDPOINT AND TRANSITION TO HEGEL.

There are two points in which Kant's treatment of religion differs from that of the *Aufklärung*—viz., in its recognition of the important function of positive creeds in leading men towards the true faith, and in its repudiation of the easy-going Optimism which is repugnant to the very genius of religion. The *Aufklärung* was profoundly unhistorical in its spirit, and was content, for the most part, to consider the genesis of positive religion as sufficiently accounted for by priestcraft and deceit. The doctrines, symbols, and sacred books of the historical faith appear to it, therefore, in a merely obstructive light. They are weeds which have to be pulled up; and when the ground is cleared, the doctrines of natural or of rational religion will have free course. Man is man all the world over: history cannot change the essential character of his reason; and reason reveals to him, by its natural light, the existence of God and the immortality of the soul. Any addition to this creed is superstition, and fires the iconoclastic zeal of the century. The attitude of the *Aufklärung* towards historical religion, or, what for it is the same thing, historical Christianity, is thus one of assault: it is purely negative. Kant's Philosophy of Religion, defective as it may be in many ways, represents a break with this spirit, and the dawn of something like a historical sense.

To begin with, the mechanical view of religion, as a contrivance of priests and lawgivers, is definitely given up. Positive or statutory religion is recognised as the leading-string which guides the race towards the realisation of the Kingdom of God. The leading-string is acknowledged to be necessary, if humanity is to attain this end; and a necessary means may fairly be regarded as of divine appointment. This implies an entire change of tone in the criticism of historical systems. They are no longer subjective delusions to be rudely brushed away: they are the steps on which the human spirit has mounted to its present elevation. They may express the pure religion imperfectly, and with much admixture of error; but the ladder which has served the childhood of thought, and which, it may be, still serves many of our fellow-men, is not there simply to be kicked contemptuously aside. Destructive criticism finds no favour with Kant. It is not that he himself holds to the literal sense of the Church's doctrines: on the contrary, it is pretty plain that his personal conclusions on these points were not very different from those of the *Aufklärung* generally. But the prevalent style of negative criticism (as exemplified, for instance, in the Wolfenbüttel Fragments), with its delight in demolishing miracles and laying bare discrepancies in the Biblical narratives, seemed to him to place altogether too much stress on the historical. Kant's whole aim was to separate what he conceived to be the true and eternal content of Christianity from the "husk" of circumstance in which those truths were first presented to the world. His own canon of interpretation is, as has been seen, exclusively ethical; and all questions of the original sense or historical accuracy of the sacred writings are simply left on one side. "We must not dispute unnecessarily over the historical weight to be attached to anything, if (whatever construction be put upon it) it contributes nothing towards making us better men. . . . Historical knowledge, which has no such universally valid inward reference, belongs to the ἀδιάφορα, concerning which each may believe what he finds to be for his own edification."[1] He speaks with something like contempt of the mode of dealing with Scripture which gets from it nothing more than an "unfruitful enlargement of our historical knowledge"; and in the same breath he places the truths of religion above historical proof. There is no point, indeed, on which Kant is more explicit than that, when we are once in possession of true religion and of the rational grounds on which it is based, it can be nowise fruitful to dispute the Biblical narratives and the popular interpretation of them. He applies this especially to the case of miracles, which constitute the *crux* of ordinary rationalism. The Christian miracles, for instance, may all be true, he says, as well as the miracle of inspiration, which guarantees the account of them. "We may let them all rest on their merits, and even continue to reverence the husk which has served to publish and to spread such a doctrine; but the credentials of the doctrine rest on a document preserved ineffaceably in every

[1] 'Werke,' vi. 137, note.

soul, and requiring no miracles to attest it."[1] This theoretical possibility of the miraculous, however, has nothing to do with religion, as we now understand it. Religion is degraded by being made to rest on such evidence; and practically, he adds somewhat ironically, the belief is harmless, for rational men never allow for the possible recurrence of such phenomena in the business relations of life. But, just because the historical is so unimportant in his eyes, Kant deprecates useless or wanton attacks upon the contents of the sacred books. "It is the most rational and equitable course, in the case of a book which is once for all there, to continue to use it as the foundation of instruction in the Church."[2] It is understood, of course, that in doing so we labour to bring out its really religious side, and endeavour to let the adventitious matter fall, as much as may be, out of sight. This attitude, we shall see, is shared by Hegel, who defends his position on very similar grounds.

The other point on which Kant parts company from the eighteenth century is his renunciation of the Optimistic view of life and of human nature. This brings him at once much nearer to a distinctively religious standpoint. It is a commonplace to say that the element of religion is not light-hearted satisfaction with the present, and a belief that all is going well. It is the need of some explanation for the cruel riddles of destiny that drives men to religion; and though its issue, as a celebration of the victorious purpose of God, is necessarily optimistic, yet the pain and the wrong of the present are an essential element. The root of religion may even be said to be a consciousness of present sin and misery. The human consciousness, as Kant remarks, seems instinctively to connect suffering with sin. When mis-

[1] 'Werke,' vi. 181. [2] Ibid., 231.

fortune comes upon him, man forthwith, as if by an impulse of nature, examines himself to see by what offence he has deserved the chastisement. Religion takes its rise in the consciousness of sin which is the result of this introspection. For the savage is sure to discover some neglect or transgression which has laid him open to the anger of his god, and his next step is to devise some method of atoning for his guilt. The mental analysis of the savage may be at fault, and his expiation immoral; yet the notions which his conduct involves are the germ of religion. Religion always goes within for its explanation, and the unsophisticated voice of the religious consciousness is invariably a cry of infinite unworthiness. Man is forced to acknowledge the justice of his punishment, and to admit that he has no right even to the measure of happiness and wellbeing he enjoys. The notion of "sin," which is peculiar to religion, contains more than that of wrong-doing. Wrong-doing is external and legal in its application, or, if the expression be allowable, it is a *finite* notion. Each action is viewed separately, and compared with an external standard. But religion, because it moves entirely in an inward or spiritual sphere, recognises no such separation. Action—even a single action—is the expression of the whole character. There can, therefore, be no measurement of guilt: the man sees only an infinite alienation of his whole being from holiness, and there comes the despairing question—How, then, can man be justified before God? The consciousness of sin, in other words, is the consciousness of the need of a reconciliation or atonement. These twin notions of sin and reconciliation are at the root of all that is distinctively religious. But both ideas were in abeyance in the eighteenth century, and, as a necessary consequence, there was a failure to fathom the religious consciousness and its manifestations in the historical religions of mankind. The eighteenth century was convinced that man was on the whole good; and its God was a species of *bon Dieu*, who could not find it in his heart to be an exacting master. Hence the significance of Kant's emphatic assertion that man is by nature not good, but that, on the contrary, there is a radical taint in the human will.

Nevertheless, it is impossible to regard Kant's treatment as wholly satisfactory, whether as regards the cause of evil or as regards the *rationale* which he offers of the nature of redemption. There is a wire-drawnness in his interpretation of the dogmas of the Church which is the result, in part, of a tendency, constitutional in Kant, to carry out his scheme too much into detail; in part, of the peculiarly elaborate and juridically conceived theory of Christian doctrine, which he assumed as his basis of operations. Hence, though there can be no doubt of the ingeniousness of the ethical interpretation, this, rather than its soundness, is apt to be the quality which most impresses the reader. Of course, to have any value at all, the interpretation of religion must be ethical; but the unconvincingness of Kant's theory is due to the separation of ethics from metaphysics. Hence the ethical problem appears as a problem of the individual alone, and to be worked out by the individual himself; and the consequence is that Kant hardly seems to regard his own construction as vital, and occasionally shows a tendency to cast it all to the winds, and to return with a fling to the simple moral command. In these respects, the Hegelian Philosophy of Religion, though essentially based upon the Kantian, has manifest advantages over it. It possesses the background of metaphysic, which seems essential to religion. Hegel's 'Religionsphilosophie' may even be said to be, in a sense, the centre of its author's thinking.

On the cardinal point of original sin, it must be admitted, I think, that Kant's theory of an "intelligible act," as the explanation of the origin of evil, is both mystical and unintelligible. It is useless to speak of the act as timeless, for the word "act," and the notion of evil as originating, are not thinkable by us except in terms of time. To a certain extent, however, Kant's language here may perhaps be viewed as an accommodation to the narrative form in which the Church presents the necessary implication of evil in the human consciousness. In describing himself as seeking, not the origin in time, but the *Vernunfturspruna*, of evil, he seems to indicate that he is showing, not how a creature, supposed to be originally good, passed into evil, but how evil is essentially bound up with the notion of the human will. This is borne out by a comparison of the theory of the Fall given in this book with a suggestive interpretation of the Mosaic story in a small treatise belonging to the year 1786, entitled 'Probable Beginning of Human History.'[1] The loss of Paradise is there interpreted as the transition from mere animality to humanity—"from the go-cart of instinct to the guidance of reason." The career of rational progress which was then begun is "for the race a progress from worse to better, but it is not the same for the individual. Before reason awoke, there was neither command nor prohibition, and therefore no transgression. But when reason began its work, and, weak as it was, came into conflict with the whole strength of the animal nature, evils, and —what is worse—when reason became more cultivated,

[1] "Muthmasslicher Anfang der Menschengeschichte,"—'Werke,' iv. 312-329.

vices, could not but arise, which were unknown to the state of ignorance. The state of ignorance was a state of innocence. . . . The history of Nature, therefore, begins with good, because it is the work of God; the history of Freedom begins with evil, because it is the work of man. For the individual, who, in the exercise of his freedom, looks only to himself, the change meant loss; but for Nature, whose aims are for the race, it was gain." The Fall from a state of animal innocence is thus at the same time the condition of the possibility of a life of rational freedom; and as humanity in this capacity is the only thing of "worth" in the world—or, to repeat Kant's phrase, the only possible object of the divine decree,—the Fall appears as a necessary part of that purpose, and as an advance upon the foregoing stage. Nevertheless, it consists essentially in the assertion of self, and in the setting up of ends other than those which Nature seems to have with the animal creature. It is viewed accordingly, in each case, as being, in the most intimate sense, a free or personal action. It must also inevitably appear as a transgression, for the first form of freedom is arbitrary selfishness. Consequently responsibility and the consciousness of evil are inseparably bound together, the one being possible only through the other.

Whether we choose to identify the "intelligible act" with such a transition from instinct to reason or not, the fact that Kant is formulating is simply this inevitable implication of evil in the moral consciousness. The fact is, after all, what we must stand by; for an actual genesis of reason and morality out of instinct is just as impossible to construct as a supposed intelligible act. The man (or animal) must have been morally accountable before the primal act, it may be argued, if he is to recognise himself as responsible for it afterwards, and so on *ad infinitum*. Consciousness cannot be treated in any of its phases as something which comes into being. The idea of an absolute beginning, in short, has no place in philosophy, because philosophy does not deal with a series of events: it deals with the notions which these events imply, and is content with showing how one notion is connected with another and with all others. The point in question here is the relation of the consciousness of evil to morality, and to the whole structure of human progress. The relation of reason to sense may certainly constitute the basis of morality, whether the inconceivable transition from a merely natural to a rational life was ever actually made or not. In Hegel we find substantially the same view as in the 'Muthmasslicher Anfang,' combined with the same curious allegorisation of the Biblical story. Hegel is at pains to show that the breach of the merely natural harmony carries with it the promise of a higher reconciliation in reason. By the conception of such a reconciliation as involved in the divine purpose, that is to say, philosophically, as eternally complete in God, he is able, without resorting to Kant's artificial doctrine of substitution, to put a more vital meaning into the leading tenet of historical Christianity.

Kant's whole theory of religion suffers from the limitations of his Critical standpoint. The central idea in religion, to which all others return, is the idea of God; and it is just here that the breakdown of Criticism becomes most apparent in the hands of its author. It must be remembered that, in spite of the ample materials which Kant supplies for the construction of a new theology, he never got fairly outside of the old-fashioned mechanical construction of Deism. God is, according to this conception, a Being by himself, to whom no necessary relations attach; but He is supposed, by an exercise of "will," to have "created" the world, and, with it, finite intelligences. The manner or the meaning of this creation is not explained, and so its assertion becomes simply a word. That is to say, reason, in its search for the causes of individual things, extends its range, and ends by asking for the cause of the collective fabric of things. As a temporary satisfaction, this causation is thrown back upon a Being postulated *in hunc effectum*, and called, in virtue of his function, the Great First Cause. The designations of Supreme Being, or Absolute Being, give no additional information as to his nature; and the inferential knowledge which Deism professes to have of its God will always be found to dwindle down to the bare assertion that he exists. It is against the possibility of proving the existence of such a deistic God that Kant does battle in the Pure Reason; and, in that regard, his arguments and those of others must be acknowledged to be conclusive—though only in that regard. Take, for example, his famous illustration of the hundred dollars. I may have an idea of a hundred dollars, but my pocket may be empty enough for all that. In like manner, Kant argues, I may have an idea of God, but that is far from proving, as the supporters of the Ontological argument would have us believe, the objective existence of a Being corresponding to my idea. Clearly, Kant's reasoning depends for its validity on the measure of analogy between God and the hundred dollars. If God is a Being or thing as separable from me as the hundred dollars are, then certainly there is no passage from idea to reality. Deism puts God at a distance in this way; and Deism, therefore, succumbs to Kant's illustration. But if God cannot be, in any sense, a thing or object, then the idea of God may very well be at the same time His real existence. If the idea of God is inseparable from consciousness as such—is, in fact, the perfect rational synthesis of which every consciousness is, and recognises itself to be, the potential form,—then this existence "in thought" seems to give all the reality that can be asked for. Unless, indeed, we are determined to materialise God into an object of our present or future senses, this is the only existence of which we can speak. If this idea be substituted for the deistic conception, it will be found that the utterly bare and self-contradictory notion of a First Cause must be exchanged for that of a final cause or End. In other words, it is absurd to seek a *cause* of the universe as a whole. The universe exists, —that is all we can say about it. But though a cause cannot be assigned, there is a sense in which a *reason* may. This will be found in the Idea, should this be discoverable, which the universe realises. The Idea is then the purpose or *raison d'être*, or simply the "meaning," of the universe. For the word purpose must not be held to imply a separation of the Idea (as in a scheming intellect) from its actual realisation.

This notion of the Divine existence, however, can hardly be said to have been definitely formulated in Kant's time, and accordingly it does not affect the course of his reasoning. In the sphere of Pure Reason, God remains, according to Kant, unknowable and unprovable. But Kant did not leave things so; for the existence of God is, as has been seen, a Postulate of the Practical Reason. What is more, it is postulated precisely in the old deistic sense. It is true, there is the saving clause, that what is reached on ethical grounds has, so far as we are concerned, only an ethical content, and is to be employed solely in an ethical interest. And for Fichte, accordingly, the notion became at once synonymous with that of the moral order of the universe. But by Kant the moral order is conceived, in the spirit of the baldest Individualism, as the final adjustment of happiness and virtue; and God becomes purely a *Deus ex machina* to effect this combination. The indignity of the position is obvious, for He is treated in the scheme primarily as a means towards the happiness of the particular individual. Once there, He is clothed, of course, with the qualities of moral Lawgiver; but the motive of His introduction at all is the one just indicated. The law and its authority are sufficiently explained, Kant admits, by the notion of the noumenal Self, and so the knowledge of duty as the will of God seems, in the Kantian scheme, a somewhat superfluous duplication of what we already possess. The noumenal and self-legislative Self is, indeed, when properly conceived, identical with the will of God, and leaves no room for any extraneous Deity. But the thoroughly mechanical idea of such a Power weighing happiness against virtue cannot be charmed out of the letter of Kant's theory. This has been the stumbling-block which has caused many to reject his Ethics *in toto*, and to identify the true Kant exclusively with the Critical scepticism of the intellectual theory. This, however, it has been already pointed out, is a mistake. Kant was not unfaithful to his method in the moral sphere: it is his method itself which is defective. It may be readily admitted that the great excellence of the Critical standpoint is, that it explodes the pretended knowledge of transcendent realities in which Dogmatic metaphysic had dabbled. But the weakness of Kantianism, in the hands of its author, is that the ghost of transcendent reality is not laid: it cannot be seen, but it is supposed still to stalk on the other side of knowledge. The temptation to transcendent speculation cannot be perfectly removed, except by a philosophy which is able to view experience as a whole, and to see realised in the synthesis of the actual the true sense of the objects which such speculation overleaps itself to reach. What is known, in a broad sense, as Hegelianism, is at least an attempt at such a complete and rounded philosophy; and in it the dualisms which vex us in Kant disappear. The ideas of God and man are still so far mutually exclusive for Kant, that what is done by man in history appears to be necessarily done without God. What is done by God, on the contrary,—as, for example, a revelation,—appears like a hand from behind the clouds thrust suddenly into the web of human affairs. Hence the antithesis between Naturalism and Supernaturalism, and the *non liquet*, which is the last dictum of the Critical reason. Hegelianism abolishes the antithesis, by conceiving the whole process of history as the work of God, and a growing revelation of His nature and purpose. It remains now to sketch very shortly, more by way of indication than of exhaustive exposition, some of the leading features of the Philosophy of Religion, as they appear from such a standpoint.

CHAPTER III.

THE HEGELIAN PHILOSOPHY OF RELIGION.

The metaphysical position of Hegel may be summarily distinguished from that of Kant, by saying that in the later philosophy thought is recognised as absolute or self-conditioning—as the unity, in other words, within which all oppositions are only relative. Thought is, therefore, the source of all the distinctions which make up the knowable universe—even of the distinction between the individual self and the objective world to which it is related. Thought itself becomes the object of philosophy, and the search for something "real," beyond and apart from thought, is definitely abandoned. The business of philosophy is henceforth the explication of the distinctions which belong to the nature of thought, and this is otherwise definable for Hegel as "the explication of God."

Philosophy thus becomes identical in its object with religion; for the constant aim of religion is to determine the nature of God, and His purpose in the individual and in the world. It is impossible to deny this metaphysical character to religion, and to present it simply as a set of empirical rules for conduct. "From the beginning of the world down to the present day," says Fichte, "religion, whatever form it may have assumed, has been essentially metaphysic." In other words, it is the need of a final synthesis, which both philosophy and religion strive to satisfy,—the one predominantly on the side of the intellect, the other predominantly on the side of the heart and life. Religion is never content till it apprehend the working whereby God is able to subdue all things unto Himself. After a more or less sufficient probing of the imperfection and wrong in the world, it will invariably be found putting forward some conception or theory, as the solution of the contradictions that baffle us from day to day. The conception may, or it may not, be adequate to the difficulties of the case,—that is according to circumstances. But it is the presence of this conception that imparts to religion the joy and confidence which are lacking in morality as such. Religion has been defined in our own day as "morality touched by emotion." The definition, as applied by its author, is both suggestive and beautiful; but it is still necessary to inquire into the source of the emotion. This, I think, is always derived from a certain view of the world as a whole,—that is to say, more or less articulately, from a metaphysical conception. It is the subject's identification of himself with a divine world-order, that is the perennial source of the religious emotion which lifts him who experiences it above the lets and hindrances of time. Without this, he is an atom struggling in vain with the evil of his own nature, and possibly, too, with the misery of surrounding circumstances. If he is to be successful in the struggle, he must be persuaded that he is not alone, or, in the language of religion, that God is for him, and that nothing, therefore, can be ultimately against him. The triumph that he only anticipates in himself and others he must conceive as secure of fulfilment—in fact, as already fulfilled in the eternal purpose of God. The peace which this conviction imparts is itself, in a sense, the realisation of that triumph in the individual,—his present reconciliation with God. It is also the most powerful dynamic that can be supplied to morality.

Kant himself was not able to eliminate the metaphysical side of religion entirely, though he considers it necessary only for "the theoretical explanation of salvation," and always returns by preference to the unvarnished religion of right-doing. In the notion of moral perfection as the End of creation,—an End realised in God, and destined to be realised in man,—and in the notion of the Church as a corporate unity for the expression of this idea, the world is represented by Kant as an ethical whole, in which atonement is made for the sins of the individual and of the moment. This appears much more emphatically in Hegel.[1] The attainment of reconciliation with God is the motive of all religions; the fact of an accomplished reconciliation is, according to Hegel, the deepest religious truth. It is revealed in the Christian religion. It is at the same time the profoundest insight of philosophy, for it is the expression of the essential nature of Spirit. True religion and true philosophy coincide, for "the absolute content," as Hegel says, must be the same. The notion of Spirit is not the absence of contradiction, for that would mean absolute sameness, which is equivalent to pure nonentity: it is the solution of contradiction, by exhibiting the opposite as held in its own unity. Spirit lives by difference, but in all difference it is still identity with itself. God was first known as Spirit, Hegel says, in the Christian religion, and this is the meaning of its central doctrine of the Trinity. The determination of God as Triune is not to be taken, as Enlightenment takes it, with reference to the number three. Rightly understood, it is a reading of the nature of God, which is fatal to the abstract unit which deistic freethought deems so easy of acceptance. This God-in-himself, as the idea may be styled, has a connection with the world that is purely arbitrary, and serves reason merely as a *point d'appui*. He is nothing more than a name upon our lips; we know nothing of his nature, because, as so conceived, there is nothing to know. To say that God is unknowable, and to say that He is the Supreme Being, are, according to Hegel, identical propositions. God cannot be known apart from the world; He cannot be

[1] Hegel's 'Lectures on the Philosophy of Religion' are contained in vols. xi. and xii. of the 'Werke,' but references to religion occur in almost every one of his works.

said to exist out of that reference. "Without the world, God were not God." "God is the Creator of the world; it belongs to His being, to His essence, to be Creator. . . . That He is Creator is, moreover, not an act undertaken once for all: what is in the Idea is the Idea's own eternal moment and determination."[1] This is expressed in the doctrine of the Trinity, Hegel continues, by saying that from eternity God has begotten a Son, or that He produces Himself eternally in His Son. But this absolute diremption or distinction of Himself from Himself is at the same time perfect identity; and the knowledge of God as the unity of Father and Son is the knowledge of Him as Spirit or as the Triune God. The Holy Ghost is the "eternal love," which expresses this unity—this distinction in which there is no difference. Here is the "still mystery," which is the source of the world's life. It may be otherwise expressed, by saying that it is a necessity of the Absolute to create a world of finite spirits. God is, in the strictest sense, neither more nor less than this self-revelation. Man is as necessary to God as God to man. The true infinity of Spirit is realised in the knowledge of the Infinite as in the finite, and of the finite as in the Infinite, or, as Christianity says, in the oneness of God and man. God is this eternal process or history.

But, so far as we have gone, there seems no room for the disturbance or alienation from God, which is the subjective root of religion. Where there is no estrangement, reconciliation, in the ordinary sense of the term, can have no function. It may fairly be objected to Hegel's account given above, that it moves too much in the clear æther of the Idea, in which distinction is not difference. As Hegel says in the 'Phaenomenology,' the

[1] Hegel, 'Werke,' xii. 181 ('Philosophie der Religion,' vol. ii.)

notion of the divine life as a play of love with itself, even though true, sinks to insipidity if "the seriousness, the pain, the patience and labour of the negative" are not allowed for. The first may be said to be the notion of the universe from the divine standpoint: it is, in fact, in Hegelian terminology, the Idea. The second is the human side of the relation,—the Idea as it appears in history. Here the world is viewed not in its ideal completeness, as the Son who is eternally and essentially one with God, but as the world in the more proper sense of the term, in which the otherness of the relation is accentuated and comes to its right. We have here the other, *as* the other; the world (of nature and of finite spirit) appears as something independent of God and free in itself. It is a mark, Hegel characteristically adds, of the freedom and security of the Idea, that it permits this relative independence without detriment to its ultimate synthesis. Nevertheless, he is somewhat at a loss to find a motive for passing from the perfect Son to the imperfect world. For it is, of course, necessary to suppose that with the freedom there comes also the weakness and the imperfection of separation; it is the fact of "this present evil world" that calls for explanation. This is the point where Hegel approximates most nearly to Schelling. He seems to treat the origin of the finite system of things as a species of *Abfall* or primal apostasy; and as Plato has recourse to the mythical form where clear thought fails him, so we find Hegel falling back on Jacob Böhme. The first begotten, he quotes from Böhme, was Lucifer, the light-bearer, the bright, the clear one; but Lucifer lost himself in his imaginings, and asserted his independence, and fell. "So we pass into the determination of space, of the finite world, of the finite spirit." That, at least, is Hegel's complacent continuation. The whole reminds the reader very much, not to go farther afield, of Schelling's treatise on 'Philosophy and Religion.' But the point is only touched on by Hegel, and the net result is simply that the finite world, as finite, is due to a holding fast of the form of difference. So far as this finitude or difference exists, the restoration of unity appears as a process in time—something to be gradually worked out. Here properly comes in the need of reconciliation and, with the need, the idea.

Reconciliation can be effected only in the sphere of Spirit; and as religion exists only in relation to man or finite spirit, we may concentrate attention on the way in which Hegel interprets alienation here. "This is the place of the conflict of good and evil—the place, too, where this conflict must be fought out."[1] For the rest, we know that Nature is but the theatre or sphere of spirit. But man, as he first appears on that theatre, is simply a part of Nature. Man in a state of nature is a complexus of animal desires, which he fulfils in turn as they arise. But the notion or destiny of man is to be intelligent and free; therefore his existence as a merely natural being is in itself, as inadequate to his notion, evil. The state of nature or "immediacy" is simply a starting-point, which is to be left behind. Consciousness brings the knowledge of this breach between the "is" and the "ought-to-be," and with knowledge comes guilt. In this connection we have the well-known Hegelian interpretation of the Fall, which occurs in various parts of the Works. The connection between evil and knowledge in the story is, according to Hegel, essential. Man *was* evil in his merely natural state—*i.e.*, he was not as he ought to be; but with the dawn of consciousness he *knows* that he is

[1] 'Werke,' xii. 62.

evil. The knowledge of his state opens up to him the possibility of escape from it, and he becomes responsible for further continuance in it. The "absolute demand" made upon man is, that he do not continue in this state; and though the content of the newly awakened will is, to begin with, simply the full play of the man's animal desires, yet the conviction grows that this ought not so to be. In other words, consciousness brings with it a separation between the subject and the natural basis of desires with which he was formerly identical; and the separation means (in the long-run) the knowledge that the true will or self is not to be found in the mere satisfaction of the wants of the natural individual. It means the knowledge of a higher rational Self, of an obligation to realise it, and an infinite falling short of attainment. The breach between the natural man and that which he necessarily regards as his essence or destiny, is the source (also in the long-run) of an infinite pain; and out of pain and unworthiness springs religion with its conception of reconciliation.

Hegel turns to history for the verification of his thesis. The sense in man of failure to realise his vocation, and the consequent misery of alienation from his true good, is what religion calls the consciousness of sin. This consciousness continued to deepen in the human heart; and of the various religions that appeared on the earth none had more than a partial cure for it. It was necessary that the lowest depths of suffering should be fathomed, before any healing could be effectual; for it is a principle of universal application, that a contradiction must be strained to its utmost before it can be successfully solved. So it was with the religious consciousness. The extreme of abandonment and despair was reached in the Roman world before "the fulness of time" came and the word of reconciliation could be spoken. Profoundly dissatisfied with the existent world, men tried, in Stoicism and kindred systems, to escape from it by withdrawing wholly within themselves. But this flight from the world could not be the world's salvation; it is in itself merely a confession of discomfiture. In my relation to the world consist my duties; Stoicism is the renunciation of these, and so remains barren. The principle that is destined to transform the world bears another aspect. "I pray not that thou shouldest take them out of the world, but that thou shouldest keep them from the evil." To a distracted humanity Christ whispers the tidings of the nearness of God. In the midst of unworthiness and helplessness there springs up the new consciousness of reconciliation. Man, with all his imperfections on his head, is still the object of the loving purpose of God. God *is* reconciled, if only man will strip off his painful individuality and believe it. There *is* a victorious purpose in the world, if only he will find himself in it, and work joyfully in its light. With this assurance in the depth of his heart comes the peace of essential unity with what, to his individual effort, is still a flying goal. His subjective frailty and shortcomings simply do not count, when weighed against the active perception of unity with God which is the substance or element of his life.

As a matter of fact, the reconciliation must still be worked out on the stage of the individual life and of universal history. Faith without works, as we know, is dead; it is an idea which lacks its embodiment in reality. But the faith must be there, if man is to work from a proper vantage-ground. Hence Christianity teaches God's reconciliation of the world with himself as a fact or as an eternal truth; and this becomes a presupposition for the individual. It is something that is "finished," and in the strength of which he works. This accomplished reconciliation is the basis of the Church or the Christian community (Gemeinde); it is taught in the Church's doctrine, and the Church is itself the outward expression of the truth. The relation of the subject to the problem of salvation is, therefore, essentially different, according as he is, or is not, born within the pale of the Christian community. This is expressed by the Church in the sacrament of Baptism. Baptism says in symbol that the child is not born into a hostile world, but that his world, from the beginning, is the Church, which is built upon the consciousness of reconciliation. The Church is, in its notion, a society where the virtual conquest over evil is already achieved, and where, therefore, the individual is spared such bitter conflict and outcast wretchedness as preceded the formation of the community. The education which the Church bestows smooths his path for him; and, in every respect, he essays the individual problem under more favourable conditions. The last and most solemn expression of the Church's life is in the Eucharist, or the sacrament of the Supper. Here the Church celebrates its sense of present reconciliation, and the conscious unity of the subject with God.

But so long as this unity is realised only in the Church, there remains an opposition between the Church and the world. The Church, in these circumstances, may be said to represent rather the idea than the reality of reconciliation, inasmuch as it is faced by a hostile power in which its principles have no application. This opposition is the distinctive mark of Mediæval Christianity, in which Christianity resembled rather a flight from the world than the subjugation of the world to God. The virtues of the Church were celibacy and poverty. The world was denounced as unholy; and, as a natural consequence of the stigma set upon it, it actually was unholy. Men's consciences convicted them of sin, when they tampered with the accursed thing. But this unhealthy dualism could not last, and, in the end, the spirit of worldliness possessed itself also of the Church. Instead of universal corruption, however, this was the signal for the appearance of the true conception of reconciliation, on which modern life is built. The Reformation is, in one aspect, the denial of that dualism between the Church and the world, between religion and secular life, which is the mark of Mediævalism in all its forms. The relations of the Family and the State are restored to the divineness that belongs to them; or rather, their divineness is, for the first time, consciously realised. In the laws and customs of the rational or freely moving State, the Church first penetrates the real world with its principles. The State is "the true reconciliation, whereby the divine realises itself in the field of reality." This final stage of realisation in the world must not, of course, be held to supersede the inward function of religion;[1] but we recognise here the point to which Hegel always returns. As he says in the 'Philosophy of History,' "The State is the Divine Idea as it exists on earth." The secular life

[1] It would be a misinterpretation of the Hegelian law of stages to suppose that the final stage abolishes those that dialectically precede it. Hegel's positions are often represented in a false and repulsive light under the influence of this idea. The 'Philosophie des Rechts,' for example, is represented as if the ultimate stage of *Sittlichkeit* were meant entirely to supersede the subjective function of *Moralität* or conscience. It is obvious that the two sides must continue to co-exist; the only thing that is superseded is the abstract conscience that ignores the actual, and insists on judging everything anew. So here, the objective reconciliation effected in the true State is not intended to supersede, for the individual, the subjective life of devotion.

of the modern world has been built up by Christianity; it is founded upon Christian conceptions of the dignity and the rights of man. The secular, therefore, is itself divine. This is, in Hegel's view, at once the principle of Protestantism and the last principle of thought.

As may be imagined from the elaborate parallelism, or rather identity, which he seeks to establish between his own philosophical positions and the leading doctrines of the Christian Church, Hegel has no sympathy with the prevalent modern aversion to theological dogma. He aims rather at a philosophic rehabilitation of dogmatic Christianity;[1] and he is never more in his element than when running out his heavy guns against the theology of feeling. The basis of a Church must be a system of doctrines, and with their withdrawal the community lapses into an aggregation of atoms. It is only principles or beliefs that can be held *in common;* feeling, as such, is purely subjective, and can afford no bond of union. Feeling is certainly indispensable in religion. Religion must be realised in the element of feeling, if it is to have active force in the life. But feeling is in itself a mere form; it is indifferent to its content, and will attach itself, for the matter of that, to any content. It is of the utmost importance, then, to understand that religion, like philosophy, must found upon "a substantial,

[1] "Die Wiederherstellung der ächten Kirchenlehre muss von der Philosophie ausgehen,"—'Werke,' xi. 10. Elsewhere he deplores the state to which theology has sunk, when it becomes necessary for philosophy to undertake the defence of the dogmas of the Church against the orthodox theologians themselves. There is a flavour of the humorous perceptible in the unction with which he takes Tholuck to task for the slackness of his zeal in defending the doctrine of the Trinity. See in particular the Preface to the second edition of the 'Encyclopædia,'—'Werke,' vi. p. xi *et seq.*

objective content of truth."[1] This content, as the theory of the relations of God and man, is the absolute content; that is to say, it is an expression, in its last terms, of the process of the universe, and, as such, is necessarily identical in both. But from what has been seen of Hegel's statement of the "eternal" content of religion, it is evident that the doctrines of ordinary Christianity undergo a considerable transformation in the process of philosophic interpretation. And this, according to Hegel, is no more than we need expect; this is, in fact, Hegel's fundamental distinction between *Vorstellung* and *Begriff*. Religion is truth for all; it is easy of comprehension. "The poor heard Him gladly." Philosophy is truth for those who are capable of the prolonged effort of thought which it implies. Philosophy presents truth essentially for the intellect—truth, therefore, in its exact, scientific, ultimate form. Religion presents the same synthesis, but primarily for the heart—presents it, therefore, in a form calculated to affect the feelings, and through them to work upon the moral will. Religious enlargement speaks the language of imagination; it is saturated with feeling. But its statements cannot be pressed as scientifically exact. Religion, Hegel says, is *reason thinking naïvely.*[2] It has got hold of vital and eternal principles; but the form in which it presents them, while best suited to its own purpose, is not adequate to the principles themselves. Facts of the Notion, constitutive of the universe as such, it treats as pieces of contingent history, which have been,

[1] 'Werke,' xvii. 299 (Preface to Hinrich's 'Religionsphilosophie'). This Preface, written in 1822, and now printed among the "Vermischte Schriften," throws much light on Hegel's attitude towards religion, towards the historical element in Christianity, &c. It contains also a bitter polemic against Schleiermacher, without, however, mentioning names.

[2] 'Werke,' xi. 117.

and are no more. So with the Fall, so again with the Reconciliation; its form is throughout pictorial and narrative. All this Hegel means by saying that religion appears in the form of *Vorstellung*. The distinction between the *Vorstellung* and the *Begriff* is all-important, he contends, for it keeps us from confounding the living principles of religion with the historical form in which they are conveyed. A certain historical form is necessary; but the historical, as such, is contingent, and cannot, therefore, form part of the essential religious content. That content, when separated from its contingent setting, is found to be identical with notional truth, or with the *Begriff*. The *Begriff*, however, Hegel seems to say, can never, for the mass of mankind, supersede the *Vorstellung*.

This opens up the whole question of Hegel's relation to historical Christianity. A memorable utterance of his own may be taken as the authoritative text of what follows: Religion must contain nothing but religion; it contains, as such, only eternal truths of the spirit.[1] A certain historical form, as just mentioned, is necessary. The true religion must appear, must *be*. The idea must have the side of reality, otherwise it is a mere abstraction; and reality implies the circumstantial surroundings of space and time. Or, to put it less abstrusely, the historical or sensuous form was essential, if the truth was ever to become a common possession of mankind. "The unity of the divine and human is the *thought* (Gedanke) of man; but it was necessary that this should first be believed as true of one individual Man." "The consciousness of the Absolute Idea is produced, in the first instance, not for the standpoint of philosophical speculation, but in the form of certainty for mankind."[2] It is a universal rule that we set out from sensuous certainty,

[1] 'Werke,' xi. 152.

[2] 'Werke,' xii. 237, 238.

from something given, something positive. But the given has always to be intelligised; its *meaning* has to be reached. So the external world is given to us in sensation; but it is not a world till we have constructed sensations into a rational system. Religion also comes to us as something given, something positive,—to the child in the form of education, to the race in the form of revelation. But the attitude of thought to sense, or to what is merely given, is always negative: we pass from it, and retain only the rational content of which it is the bearer. By the fact of a historical appearance (recognised as a necessary element of the truth) we must not, therefore, be misled into elevating the particulars of that history to the rank of divine verities. The frame, though necessary, does not stand on the same level as the work of art that it encloses.[1] The particulars of history are always contingent—that is, they may be *so* or they may be otherwise; no truth of reason is involved in their being either. In this way, Hegel says, the whole question of miracles ought not to trouble us. We neither attack them nor defend them; but the testimony they could afford to religious truth was confined to the age in which they are said to have been wrought. The spiritual cannot be attested by the external or unspiritual, and, in regard to miracles, the main point is that we set them aside.[2] The demonstration of the spirit is the only testimony that can be ultimately accepted.

The sensuous history in which Christianity first appeared is thus merely the point of departure (Ausgangspunkt) for the spirit, for faith. The doctrine of the Church is neither the external history of its Founder, as

[1] 'Werke,' xvii. 283.

[2] Ibid., xii. 160,—"Die Hauptsache in dieser Seite der Wunder ist, dass man sie in dieser Weise auf die Seite stellt."

such, nor His own immediate teachings.[1] It is the meaning of the history, as apprehended in the consciousness of the Christian Church. It is not to the point to say that this meaning is contained in the Bible, and that the whole doctrine is, as it were, spelled out of this text. The Bible is merely another form of the "given"; and as soon as we depart from the words of the sacred text, we have transformed it. Here, as elsewhere, the spirit is active in its receptivity. It is the Church's exegesis of the Bible that is the foundation of faith, and not the words of the Bible, as such. The necessity of this passing away of the sensuous, or, at all events, of its transformation by the spirit, is clearly perceived by the author of the Fourth Gospel. The Johannine Christ expresses this insight in pregnant words, when he makes the growth of the Church dependent on his own departure. "It is expedient for you that I go away. . . . The hour is come that the Son of man should be glorified. Verily, verily, I say unto you, Except a corn of wheat fall into the ground and die, it abideth alone: but if it die, it bringeth forth much fruit. . . . Greater works than these shall he [the believer] do, *because* I go to my Father." Hence, according to Hegel, the importance of so far detaching the content of Christianity from its first sensuous presentment as to regard it in itself as "eternal truth." "The true content of Christian faith is to be justified by philosophy, not by history."[2] Why, then, should we be always returning to the garments of flesh from which the spirit has passed? We get thus but a dead Christ; the living Christ is to be found in the Church that He has founded, and in the doctrines of the

[1] "Christus Lehre kann, als diese unmittelbare, nicht christliche Dogmatik, nicht Lehre der Kirche sein,"—'Werke,' xii. 241.

[2] 'Werke,' xii. 266.

relation of God and man, of which it is the visible symbol.

The whole position may perhaps be put more generally. From the religious point of view, the value or worth of a history lies solely in the circumstance that it is the vehicle of such and such truths. Strip it of this significance and the history is no more than any other bit of fact; it ceases to have any religious bearing at all. A history affects us only when read in the light of the eternal purpose of God. It is that purpose, therefore, which moves us, not the bare recital of events; and by any events the divine purpose must be inadequately represented or set forth. All spiritual effects must have spiritual causes. It is by eternal principles or truths that the mind is influenced; and though certain narratives may have proved themselves specially efficacious in bringing home these truths to men's minds, still that is no reason for insisting that the narratives, as they stand, are scientifically maintainable in all their particulars. That the majority of men find their account in holding to the original sense of the narratives, is likewise a very inadequate reason for believing this to be the ultimate form of the truth. The mass of men are habitually unaware of the true theory of what they nevertheless perform with sufficient correctness. The truth which the narratives convey reaches them and influences them, without their being able to indicate exactly how it does so. The *rationale* of the process remains obscure, but the edification is a fact. Beyond this fact the ordinary man does not, as a rule, travel; and when he does, his reasonings on spiritual causation are as likely to be wrong as his reasonings on natural causation. The *post hoc ergo propter hoc* is the prevalent form of argumentation in both cases. He does not sift the antecedents. All the prominent circumstances that preceded the spiritual phenomenon are massed together as its cause; and he is as likely as not to point out as the essential element in the causation precisely the most contingent and indifferent circumstance. Spiritual instinct is unerring in the choice of its proper food; but it is helpless when asked to explain how that food nourishes it.

Nor is it anything to the point that a great number of those who derive benefit from the narratives and religious symbols in question perceive no conflict between their literal sense and the prerogative of reason in other spheres. The ordinary man, as Spinoza says, is slow to perceive contradictions, because he does not *bring them together*. His thinking is not continuous; it is often, indeed, interrupted and casual to the last degree —here a little and there a little. And so it comes that he passes from the religious half of his life to the secular half without observing any inconsistency between his presuppositions and general habit of thought in the two spheres. But sooner or later the contradiction comes to light. So long as a spirit of simple, unaffected piety prevails, it does not appear; for piety passes, as if instinctively, to the inner content, and really lays no stress on the finite particulars. They are there, and the thought of calling them in question has not arisen; but to the unsophisticated religious consciousness they in no wise constitute the foundation of faith. In one aspect, it is their unimportance which has saved them from question. But when the genuine spirit of religion fades out of the Church, its place is taken by an abstract logic and a philosophy of the understanding without insight into the things of God. Orthodoxy in this form, having no root in itself, begins to lay a disproportionate weight on the external and historical.

It insists on making all these indifferent details a matter of faith. But here it is met by the *Aufklärung*, or the spirit of scientific enlightenment and historical criticism. In a historical reference, this is the movement specially associated with the activity of the eighteenth century, though it goes on still, and in many quarters may be said to be only beginning. It is to be noted that Hegel does not dispute the place and function of the negative here. He speaks of the Enlightenment as "the better sense" of mankind rising in revolt against the pretensions of a pettifogging orthodoxy; and as regards the contingent matter to which this orthodoxy would pin our faith, he unhesitatingly acknowledges the victory of the *Aufklärung* over its adversary.[1] Individual utterances in this connection may be ambiguous—sometimes, perhaps, studiously so,—but the general tenor of Hegel's thought is, I think, not to be mistaken. The calmness with which he regards the *Aufklärung* is due to the fact that, on one side, he is prepared to admit all its contentions. What he disputes is the inference which Enlightenment draws from these admissions. He complains that it knows only the negative, and makes no distinction between the external or circumstantial, and the true or divine. In short, he denies the presupposition on which both ordinary orthodoxy and ordinary rationalism proceed—viz., that the peculiarly Christian doctrines stand or fall with the provable extra-naturalness of certain facts. The condemnation of the *Aufklärung* in an absolute regard is that its tendency is to sweep away religion altogether along with its finite forms. Mere enlightenment is no substitute for religion, and the inquiries on which its

[1] "Diese [die *Aufklärung*] ist Meister geworden über diesen Glauben," —'Werke,' ix. 150.

champions spend their energies are likewise essentially non-religious. Hence Hegel considered that the *Aufklärung* had done its work: it had given its gift to the world, and was henceforth barren. Like Kant, therefore, he deprecates, in a religious interest, the perpetual renewal of useless controversy. Wanton attacks upon the sacred books of Christianity indicate a defect in culture quite as much as in religious sense. The Church is right, he holds, from its own standpoint, in fighting shy of investigations into matters of fact undertaken in a non-religious interest.[1] The reason is, that such investigations lend an exaggerated importance to the merely historical — an importance which it does not possess as treated by the Church. This is, of course, not the way in which the Church formulates its opposition: it is Hegel's sympathetic interpretation of her attitude. Hegel's sympathies are essentially religious, and this sometimes communicates a tone of undue depreciation to his remarks on the *Aufklärung*. But, as we have seen, he does not send Enlightenment away without the portion of goods that falls to its share. He considers his own position as a vantage-ground beyond both traditional orthodoxy and ordinary rationalism. In the strife, therefore, which still goes on between these two, Hegel can be invoked on neither side. His thoroughgoing distinction of *Vorstellung* and *Begriff* absolves him from descending into the noisy arena. "Thought justifies the content of religion, and recognises its forms,—that is to say, the determinateness of its historical appearance; but, in the very act of doing so, it recognises also the limita-

[1] 'Werke,' xii. 260,—"So thut die Kirche insofern Recht daran, wenn sie solche Untersuchungen nicht annehmen kann." He instances the case of investigations into the reality of the reported appearances of Christ after his death.

tions of the forms."[1] This sentence from the conclusion of the 'Philosophy of Religion' is well adapted to summarise the whole attitude of the Hegelian philosophy towards the question at issue.

Such, then, in outline, is the Hegelian Philosophy of Religion. So far as it trenches on technically theological ground, I am not called upon to criticise it here. Historically, its direct affiliation to the Kantian position is not to be mistaken. The relation of Hegel to Kant in his theory of religion is, indeed, an exact parallel to the relation between them in respect of the doctrine of knowledge. In both cases the sameness is more striking than the difference. Kantianism seems everywhere on the point of casting off the presuppositions which bind it to the old metaphysic. In evidence of this it is only necessary to specify, in the present case, Kant's whole attitude to positive religion, his treatment of the Fall, and even, to some extent, of the idea of Reconciliation. But the new metaphysic developed by Hegel out of Kantianism does away with the abstract distinction between God and man which still remains at the Kantian standpoint. God is recognised, Hegel says, "not as a Spirit beyond the stars, but as Spirit in all spirits"; and so the course of human history is frankly identified with the course of divine self-revelation. The culmination of this religious development[2] is reached in Christianity; and

[1] 'Werke,' xii. 286.

[2] The limits and the plan of this sketch make impossible even an outline of the course of this development in the historical religions of humanity. Hegel's characterisations of the different faiths are mines of thought, especially in the later stages, where he comes to compare Judaism, Hellenism, and the prosaic secularism of Rome, with "the absolute religion" for which they were destined to make way.

Christianity reveals nothing more than that God is essentially this revelation of Himself.[1] In this connection it is that a new significance is given to the doctrine of the Trinity, which thereby becomes fundamental for the Hegelian Philosophy of Religion. This attitude towards the course of history, and towards Christianity in particular, is the only one which is permissible to an Absolute philosophy. However fenced about with explanations, the thesis of such a philosophy must always be—"The actual is the rational."

The difficulties of such a system are always found in accounting for contingency, for imperfection, for suffering and evil. It would not be fair to leave the subject without pointing out in a word or two where the strain comes upon Hegelianism, when it is conceived as such a final and absolute system. Hegelianism, it may be premised, has, in the individual reflection of its author, no other basis than the bit-by-bit experience on which empiricism builds. This is a matter of course, which ought not to require stating; nevertheless, owing to the form which Hegel has given his thoughts, it is frequently ignored. Though the particulars, or the "given," must necessarily come first *in ordine ad individuum*, yet, the principle of synthesis having been divined, the Hegelian method does not present its results as a collection of inductions or deductions, more or less fragmentary, from experience. The subjective process by which the results are reached is, as it were, suppressed; and an attempt is made to lay before us the *system* of the actual—the actual as it exists *in ordine ad universum*, or from a divine standpoint. It is essential to the success of such an undertaking that the system

[1] 'Werke,' xii. 158.

round itself in itself. What we get must be a perfect system of mutual relativity, and like the Divine Labourer we must be able at the end to pronounce all things very good. That is just equivalent to saying that it must actually *be* a system, and not the *disjecta membra* of one. The idea of perfection — Optimism, not as a hope, but as a reality—is the very nerve of such a synthesis. The world must be seen, as it were, to have its genesis in divine perfection, and it must be sealed up there again at the close. In other words (that all suspicion of an emanation hypothesis be avoided in the expression), there must be no hitch, no flaw, in the system, which might be inconsistent with the perfection of the whole.

Now the objections to which Hegel's synthetic or genetic mode of presentment has given rise—that his philosophy is an *a priori* system, a metaphysical cobweb spun in flagrant disregard of experience, and so forth—may be summarily dismissed, for they have their root in misconception and ignorance. But it is impossible to deny that it is precisely when Hegelianism presents itself in system, as a self-cohering explanation of the whole, that we are apt to be least satisfied with it. The thoughts of the reader will revert instinctively, in the present case, to the hardly disguised failure of the transition from the Son to the world of finite men and things.[1] Hegel is perfectly at home in describing the triune relations of the Idea; but as soon as their transparency or pellucidity is blurred by real difference, the strain comes upon him. The transition here is, in its way, an instructive counterpart to the unsatisfactory phrases in which the passage is made, in the 'Encyclopædia,' from the necessity of the logical Idea to the contingency of

[1] Cf. p. 273 *supra*.

Nature. In its general aspect, the problem is no less than to show how the existence of an imperfect world is compatible with divine perfection; and, of course, when we start from the perfect, the difficulty of explanation is enhanced. Hegel seems to gain the imperfect by a leap. When he has once gained it, he is much more successful in exhibiting the process of regeneration. His treatment of evil as an essential element in the consciousness of a sensuous being, for example, is profound and fundamental; but it manifestly presupposes the fact of the manifestation of reason in a sensuous creature like man. All imperfection may flow from the combination, but why should this combination itself be necessary? So, too, there is no point which Hegel is fonder of emphasising than the *labour* of the Spirit. The world-spirit, he says, has had the patience to undertake "the prodigious labour of the world's history": only subjective impatience demands the attainment of the goal without the means. His reference to "the seriousness, the pain, the patience and labour of the negative," has been already quoted. It would be an egregious mistake, therefore, to suppose that Hegel's Optimism is born of a superficial glance that ignores the darker sides of existence. Throughout, indeed, it takes the shape much more of a deliverance from evil than of the unimpeded march of a victorious purpose. In this respect, it is a much closer transcript of the course of the actual than most Optimistic systems are. But the inevitable question rises—Whence the necessity of this pain and labour in the all-perfect? And if we lose our grasp of this idea of an all-perfect whole, can we be said still to possess the imposing synthesis which Hegel lays claim to? Hegel might answer, that our difficulty is created by the abstract idea of perfection with which we start.

Such pure perfection would be colourless nonentity: there is no victory possible without an adversary, and existence is, in its very essence, this conflict of opposites. His own position, he might say, is demonstrably identical with that of religion, which maintains that evil is "permitted" for the sake of the greater good, or, as philosophy expresses it, is involved in its possibility. Evil that is the means to good, a dualism that yet is overcome, Optimism upon a ground of Pessimism,—such, he might say, is the character of existence as it reveals itself to us. God is this eternal conquest or reconciliation. We have no right to make unto ourselves other gods, or to construct an imaginary world, where good shall be possible without evil, result without effort. Whether Hegel would accept what is here put into his mouth, and whether, if he would, the position amounts to an absolute philosophy, are questions too wide to discuss further in a work whose object is mainly expository. But I probably express the conviction of many students when I say that the strength of Hegelianism lies not so much in the definite answer it gives to any of the questions which are supposed to constitute philosophy, as in its criticism of history. In history, whether it be the history of philosophies, of religions, or of nations, Hegel is like Antæus on his mother earth: his criticisms are invincible, and his interpretations are ever fresh.

PHILOSOPHY AS CRITICISM OF CATEGORIES.

A HUNDRED years have passed[1] since Kant, in a note to the preface of the first 'Critique,' declared his age to be pre-eminently the age of an all-embracing criticism, and proceeded therewith to sketch the outlines of what he called the Critical philosophy. The latter has grown to be a great fact even in that dim general consciousness in which humanity keeps record of the deeds of its past. But a hundred years have apparently not been long enough for commentators and critics to make clear to a perplexed public the exact import of what Kant came to teach. And if Kant had survived to dip into the literature of the centenary and see the different doctrines with which he is credited, one can fancy the indignant disclaimers that would have filled the literary journals. The agreement is general that Kant's contribution to philosophy forms a bridge between one period of thought and another; but opinion is sadly divided as to the true philosophic succession. Hence it is probably better, in any treatment which aims at philosophical persuasion, to regard Kant not so much with reference to the systems of which his own has been the germ, as with reference to the whole period

[1] This essay was published in 1883 in the volume 'Essays on Philosophical Criticism.' See Preface.

which he closed. If we get in this way to see what notions it was that he destroyed, then we may possibly reach a certain unanimity about the principles and outlines of the new philosophy. When we know on what ground we stand, and what things are definitely left behind, we are in a position to work for the needs of our own time, taking help where it is to be found, but without entangling ourselves in the details of any particular post-Kantian development.

An unexceptionable clue to the way in which Kant was accustomed to regard his own philosophic work is furnished by the use he makes of the term criticism. Criticism, as every one knows, is generally mentioned by Kant in connection with Dogmatism and Scepticism, as a third and more excellent way, capable of leading us out of contradiction and doubt into a reasoned certainty. The term thus contains, it may be said, Kant's own account of his relation to his predecessors. That account — often repeated in the Kantian writings — bears a striking similarity, at first sight, to Locke's description of his discovery that most of the questions that perplex mankind have their source in the want of "a survey of our own understandings." "Were the capacities of our understandings well considered, the extent of our knowledge once discovered, and the horizon found which sets the bounds between the enlightened and dark parts of things—between what is and what is not comprehensible by us,—men would perhaps with less scruple acquiesce in the avowed ignorance of the one, and employ their thoughts and discourse with more advantage and satisfaction in the other" ('Essay,' Book I., chap. i., § 7).

But Locke was a man of the world rather than a philosopher by profession; and, being an Englishman, he had not been much troubled by the metaphysical system-builders. Kant, on the other hand, has the latter continually before his mind: "the celebrated Wolff," in particular, had made a deep impression upon him. But he perceived that not one of the metaphysicians was able to establish his system as against the equally plausible construction of others, or in the face of the sceptical objections brought against such systems in general. The disputes of the Schools seemed best likened to the bloodless and unceasing combats of the heroes in Walhalla. A scepticism like David Hume's appeared the natural end of these ineffectual efforts to extend our knowledge. Profoundly convinced, however, that scepticism is not a permanent state for human reason, Kant tried to formulate to himself the necessary causes of the failure of the best-meant of these attempts to construct a philosophy. This is how he differentiates his own work from Hume's. Hume, he says, was satisfied with establishing the fact of an actual failure on the part of metaphysics, but he did not show conclusively how this must be so. Hence, in the general discredit which he threw upon the human faculties, he involved much of the knowledge of the natural world which no one disputes, but which it is impossible to vindicate on the principles of Humian scepticism. Besides, though an effectual solvent of preceding systems, Hume's method offers no guarantee that other philosophers will not arise, more subtle and persuasive, winning many to accept their constructions, and calling for a second Hume to repeat the work of demolition. What is essential is to set the bounds between our necessary knowledge and our equally necessary ignorance. We must submit to critical evaluation, not *facta* of reason, but reason itself. Proof must be had not merely of limitation or finitude in general, but of a determinate boundary line that shuts off knowledge from the field of the unknown and unknowable. That is, we demonstrate, on grounds of principle, not only our ignorance in respect to this or that subject, but our ignorance in respect to all possible questions of a certain class. There is no room for conjecture. In the region of complete certitude alone can reason take up its abode, and to mark out the firm "island" of truth is the task of Criticism.[1]

All the conclusions of the system-builders are vitiated, Kant explains, by the fact that they have not submitted the conceptions and principles which they employ to a preliminary criticism in order to discover the range of their validity. Conceptions which are familiar to us from daily use we assume to be of universal applicability, without considering what are the conditions of our present experience, and whether these conditions may not be of essential import in determining for conceptions the range of their application. Conceptions quite unimpeachable under these conditions may be quite unmeaning when these conditions are removed. A metaphysic which is oblivious to such considerations Kant calls Dogmatic. Thus when philosophers conclude that the soul is immortal because it is a substantial unit and therefore indiscerptible, their argument is altogether in the air, for they have omitted to consider whether such a conception as substance can have any meaning except as applied to a composite object in space. Similarly, when Locke attempts to prove the existence of God by the "evident demonstration that from eternity there has been something," he is importing the conceptions of time and causality into the relations

[1] Cf. Kant's "Methodenlehre" at the end of the 'Critique of Pure Reason.' The special reference is to the second section of the first chapter.

between God and the universe, without reflecting whether time and causality are available ideas when we venture beyond the context of our sense-experience.

Nothing could well be more satisfactory than this. But in such an undertaking everything depends upon the thoroughness with which the idea of criticism is applied, and Kant, unfortunately, left the most fundamental conception of all uncriticised. He dogmatically assumed the conception of the mind as acted upon by something external to it. In other words, the mechanical category of reciprocity, which psychology and ordinary thought may justifiably employ for their own purposes, was taken by him as an adequate or philosophic representation of the relation of the knowing mind to the objective world. The distinction between mind and the world, which is valid only from a certain point of view, he took as an absolute separation. He took it, to use a current phrase, abstractly—that is to say, as a mere fact, a fact standing by itself and true in any reference. And of course when two things are completely separate, they can only be brought together by a bond which is mechanical, external, and accidental to the real nature of both.

Hence it comes (in spite of the inferior position to which Kant explicitly relegates empirical psychology) that the 'Critique of Pure Reason' sets out from a psychological standpoint and never fairly gets beyond it. "In what other fashion is it to be supposed that the knowing faculty could be roused to exercise, if not by objects which affect our senses?" Kant hardly waits to hear the answer, so much does it seem to him a matter of course. Such a self-revelation is too naïve to be got rid of by saying that this sentence in the first paragraph of the Introduction expresses no more than a provisional adoption of the standpoint of ordinary thought, in order to negate it and rise above it by the progressive criticism of the remainder of the book. That this point of view *is* negated and surmounted in the 'Critique' I do not in the least doubt; but it is just as certain that Kant did not mean to express here a merely provisional standpoint from which he could intelligibly launch his own universe upon the reader. The passage may be matched by many others taken from any stage of Kant's speculations. They recur too often to be explained otherwise than by the admission that, while his new method is the conclusive refutation of the claims of psychology to function as philosophy, Kant himself never consciously called in question the fundamental presupposition of psychological philosophy, much less subjected it to the criticism which his principles demanded.

Many untenable Kantian distinctions, to which students —and especially students trained in English philosophy— take exception at the outset, are connected in principle with this initial psychological dualism. Such are, for example, the sheer distinction drawn between the form and the matter of experience, between *a priori* and *a posteriori*, and the equally abstract way in which Kant uses universality and necessity as the criteria of formal or perfectly pure cognition. Since the whole of Kant's scheme of thought appears to rest upon these distinctions, it is not to be wondered at if many conclude that the rest of the system must be entirely in the air. It is not the less true, however, that this is a case in which the pyramid does not stand upon its apparent base.

Such disjunctions in Kant are due to the effort of reflection to escape from the unlimited contingency of the Humian position, while retaining the ultimate presupposition of the unrelatedness of mind and things, from which the scepticism of the earlier thinker resulted. What the mind learns from things must necessarily, on this hypothesis, be so many bare facts or atoms of impression cohering simply as they have been accidentally massed in the piecemeal process of acquisition. Kant unhesitatingly endorses Hume's conclusion on this point: that "experience" cannot yield universality and necessity is the ground common to both Kant and Hume, which furnishes the starting-point of the 'Critique.' On the one hand, Kant found himself faced by this assumption; on the other, by the existence of judgments continually made, and whole sciences constructed, whose universal and necessary application it would be mere affectation to deny. The lines of his own theory were virtually settled by these two admissions. If the necessity which we find in experience is confessedly not derivable from the atomic data furnished to the mind by things, then it must be infused into these data by the action of the mind itself. We have thus the spectacle of experience as the product of an interaction taking place between "the mind" and things. The element contributed by the action of things Kant calls the "matter" of experience; the contribution of the mind he calls the "form." On his own principles, the "matter" ought to be pure matter or unlimited contingency, containing in itself no germ of methodical arrangement, while the "forms" of the mind should compel this mass into order and system. But it is, of course, impossible for Kant to maintain himself at the point of view of a distinction which in this case simply does not exist. He is forced to admit that, for the particular applications of the general forms or laws imposed on experience by the mind, we remain dependent upon things. But in such cases, if the particular application is given in the matter, then *a fortiori* the law or principle in its general form must be so given. It must be possible, by an ordinary process of generalisation and abstraction, to formulate in its generality the principle which the specific instances exemplify. In other words, Kant admits that what is "given" to the mind is not pure matter, not mere particulars, but matter already formed, particulars already universalised—that is to say, related to one another, and characterised by these relations. The task of the knower is simply to read off, or at most laboriously to bring to light, what is *there* complete before him in his material. There is not the slightest doubt that, when we remain at the point of view of the abstract distinction between mind and the world which we have signalised in Kant, empiricists are correct in insisting that not the matter of his experience only, but the form as well, is derived by the individual from the world with which he is set in relation. The mind is not the seat of universals and the world a jumble of particulars, the former being superimposed upon the latter for the production of knowledge. Neither mind nor the world has any existence as so conceived. How, for example, can the unfilled mind of the child be regarded as creatively producing order in a chaos of pelting impressions, or what do we mean by postulating a mind at all in such a case? If they prove nothing else, such considerations prove the complete impossibility of treating knowledge from a psychological standpoint. We conclude, therefore, that matter and form are shifting distinctions relative to the point of view from which they are contemplated; and the same is true of the world and the mind, of which opposition, indeed, the other is only another form. From the standpoint of a theory of knowledge it will be found that the mind and the world are, in a sense, convertible terms. We may talk indifferently of the one or of the other; the content of our notion remains in both cases the same.

A similar criticism applies to the criteria of universality and necessity as employed by Kant. No sooner are the words uttered than people begin to ransack their minds in order to discover whether, as a matter of fact, they ever make such judgments as are here attributed to them. The absolute necessariness which Kant affirms of certain judgments becomes a species of mystic quality. Some thinkers persuade themselves that they recognise this quality in the judgments in question; others, more cautious, maintain that whatever stringency the judgments possess may be sufficiently accounted for without resorting to what they brand as an "intuition." Thus, when a conscientious associationist like Mill comes forward and denies that he finds any absolute universality and necessity whatever in his experience, Kant's argument is brought to a complete standstill. The question of fact on which he builds being denied, there is no common ground between him and his opponent. Few things can be imagined more unfortunate than this reduction of the controversy between Kant and empiricism to a discussion about the existence or non-existence of some mystical necessity in the propositions of geometry. Yet this actually happened in the earlier stages of Kantian study in England. Wherever "intuitions" come into play, the point in dispute is referred to a merely subjective test, and controversy necessarily fritters itself away into a bandying of "yes" or "no" from the opposite sides. No one who has learned Kant's lesson so as to profit by it, should have any hesitation in finding Mill's hypothetical theory of demonstration to be truer in conception than any theory which insists on a difference of kind between the necessity of geometrical and that of any other scientific propositions. All necessity is hypothetical or relative, and simply expresses the dependence of one thing upon another. No truth is necessary except in relation to certain conditions, which being fulfilled, the truth always holds good. The more general or simple the conditions on which any truth depends, the wider is the range of its validity; and truths which, like those of geometry, depend only on the most rudimentary elements or conditions of experience, will of course be universally and necessarily valid *for all experience depending on these conditions.* This, as every student ought to know, is the only necessity which Kant's theory eventually leads him to attribute to the propositions of geometry. It is the more unfortunate that he should seem to base his argumentation upon the assertion of an abstract or absolute necessity. But this is only one of many instances in which the true sense of Kantian terms must be defined by the completed theory. Necessity of the latter type —absolute necessity—is not so much doubtful in fact as it is contradictory in notion. "Necessity" invariably raises the question "Why?" and the answer must consist in showing the conditions. Something may be necessary in relation to conditions which are themselves of limited application: in that case we never speak of it as necessary unless when these conditions are themselves under consideration. When we speak of anything as being necessary in a pre-eminent sense, we mean that our assertion depends for its validity on nothing more than the system of conditions on which experience is founded. There is no abstract opposition, therefore, between the necessary and the contingent, such as Kant presents us with: the difference is not one of kind, but of degree.

This interpretation of necessity is particularly worth

keeping in mind in connection with the Kantian categories or conceptions of the understanding; for Kant's treatment of these so-called *a priori* elements as the contribution of the mind has again led him into false issues—or at least it has led many of his followers and opponents. It is supposed, for example, that the whole question turns upon the mental origin of certain conceptions, and this, as has been seen, is a fact which may very properly be denied. It appears to be forgotten, amid the *pros* and *cons* of such an argument, that mental origin is in itself no clue to the function of a conception or the range of its validity, unless we connect our assertion with a whole theory as to the nature of experience in general. This, it must be allowed, Kant has not neglected to do; and his ultimate proof of the necessity of conceptions like substance and cause is simply that without them experience would be impossible. They are the most general principles on which we find a concatenated universe to depend. Their mental origin falls in such a deduction completely into the background; and Kant is only obliged to assert it because of the absolute opposition which he set up between the necessary and the contingent, and the presupposition with which he started, that experience can give us nothing but contingency. The conceptions derive their necessity from their relation to experience as a whole. Kant proceeds, indeed, to describe the conceptions in this relation as modes of mental combination, according to which the Ego lays out the variety poured in upon it from without. As nothing can come within experience except so far as it fits itself into the structure of the mental mould, the necessary validity for experience of these conceptions is evident. But nothing is gained by isolating these conditions, principles, or categories from the experience in which they are disclosed to us, and hypostatising them as faculties or modes of faculties—methods of action inherent in the mind. On the contrary, this is essentially a mischievous step; for when we talk thus, we are inevitably held to refer to the individual mind; and the difficulties, or rather absurdities, of such a position have already come under our notice. It is to be regretted, therefore, that Kant frequently described his undertaking as a criticism of faculties, instead of keeping by the more comprehensive and less misleading title (which, as we have seen, he also employs) of a criticism of conceptions. Unfortunately, this is not merely a verbal inconsistency; it represents two widely different views of the Critical philosophy.

Kant's general scheme is sufficiently well known to render any minute account of it superfluous in this connection. It was framed, as has been seen, to account for the fact of universal and necessary judgments, and its form was conditioned by the previous acceptance of Hume's fundamental assumptions. Kant's way out of the difficulty was contained in what he called his Copernican change of standpoint. If there is no necessity to be got by waiting on the world of things, let us try what success attends us if objects are made to wait upon us for their most general determinations. The form or "ground-plan" of experience which Kant discovers in following out this idea, consists of twelve categories, conceptions, or methods of combination, according to which the matter of sense is arranged in the perceptive or imaginative spectra of space and time, the process of arrangement being ultimately guided by three ideals of intellectual completeness, and being referable at every point to the unity of the transcendental Ego. Or in Kant's psychological language, the mind is furnished, first, with the *a priori* forms of space and time, in which all its impressions must be received; and secondly, with twelve principles of intellectual synthesis, by submission to which the impressions of sense first become objects in a world of related things. The relations of space and of objects in space,[1] as dependent upon the nature of the mind-form and of the mind-imposed laws of combination, may evidently thus be known with complete certainty. We are in a position, so far as these points are concerned, to anticipate experience: universality and necessity are saved. But the counter-stroke is obvious. We anticipate experience—and to that extent, as Kant paradoxically puts it, legislate for nature—simply because it is our own necessity, and not the necessity of things, which is reflected back to us from the face of this mind-shaped world. We purchase the sense of certainty in our knowledge at the cost of being told that our knowledge is not in a strict sense real knowledge at all. The world of real objects (improperly so called, inasmuch as they never *are* objects), on which Kant represents us as waiting for the matter of our experience, is necessarily cut off from us by the constitution of our powers of knowing. Here Kant draws the line which he says Hume neglected to draw—the line dividing the region of complete certitude from that of necessary and eternal ignorance. The first region is the field of phenomena, related to one another in space and time—the context of possible experience, consisting of the mind-manipulated data of sense. The second, from which our faculties debar us, is the world of things-in-

[1] Time, Kant proves in the 'Refutation of Idealism,' is knowable only in relation to space. He says elsewhere that inner sense receives its whole filling from outer sense. The correlation of time and space being necessary, the limitation of knowledge is correctly described in the text as limitation to the contents of space.

themselves, considered not merely as the unknown region where our sense-experience takes its rise, but as a world in which room may possibly be found for such non-spatial entities as God and the soul, and the aspects of human life which seem to depend on these ideas.

The nature of these results determines the special sense which the term Criticism assumes in Kant's hands. The term originally describes merely the method of procedure, but it naturally becomes descriptive also of the definite view of the universe to which his method leads him. The Critical philosopher, accordingly, is one who clearly apprehends what is implied in calling the deduction of the categories *transcendental.* A transcendental deduction is one undertaken solely with reference to experience,—one which leaves us, therefore, without justification for employing the deduced conceptions in any other reference. And if it be considered that experience in this connection implies for Kant the relation of the mind to an unknown object—means, in fact, the application of the categories to the matter derived from that object,—it is evident that when the latter element falls away, the conceptions must become so many empty words. Experience so conceived is called sense-experience, in order to describe our partially receptive attitude and the compound character of our knowledge. It yields us a knowledge only of material things and their changes; and the attempt to gain any other species of knowledge by means of the categories Kant compares to the flapping of wings in the unsupporting void. Criticism means, then, the recognition of this limitation, and it pronounces experience so limited to be merely phenomenal in character. Experience actual and possible represents, in other words, not things as they are in themselves, but only a certain relation of the human mind towards the world of reality. Our ignorance in this respect is inevitable and final; and if there are other avenues by which—in the case of the Self and God—we may penetrate to noumenal existence, yet the conviction we reach is not such that we can rightly speak of it as knowledge. All knowledge remains in the Kantian scheme phenomenal,—phenomenal in the sense that there is a reality behind, which we do not know.

If now it be asked, by what right Kant draws the line exactly where he does, and cuts off from knowledge everything but a spatial world of interacting substances, the answer must be that his exclusion depends ultimately on his uncritical acceptance of the dualistic assumption of preceding philosophy. We express the same thing in another form, when we say that the result is due to the attempt to construct a theory of knowledge from the standpoint of psychology. This standpoint brings with it the distinction between "sense" as the source of the data of knowledge, and "understanding" as a faculty of "comparing, connecting, and separating" the material supplied by sense. This is Locke's distinction, and it is Kant's too.[1] Kant minimises the contribution of sense; he speaks of it on occasion as a mere blur, and in itself no better than nothing at all. But the *amount* referred to sense

[1] As it happens, Kant's phraseology in the opening paragraph of the Introduction corresponds exactly with the account Locke gives of knowledge in Book II., chap. xii., of the 'Essay.' "The materials being such as he has no power over, either to create or destroy, all that a man could do is either to unite them together, or to set them one by another, or wholly separate them." Kant's language looks like a reminiscence of this passage, when he speaks of impressions producing ideas, and rousing "the faculty of the understanding to *compare, connect, and separate* these, and so to work up the raw material of sensuous impressions into a knowledge of objects." Of course, Kant's "raw material" turns out afterwards not to mean so much as Locke's "simple ideas."

does not affect the principle of the distinction: so far as it is made in this form at all, its consequences will be essentially the same—either with Hume, the denial that (so far as we know) any real world exists, or with Kant, the denial that such a world can ever be revealed to us by knowledge. Hence the importance of observing that the distinction is not a deduction from the theory of knowledge, but a presupposition drawn from another sphere. The division of the mind into receptivity and spontaneity is the mere correlate of that view of the universe from which the Kantian criticism was ultimately destined to set us free—the view which represents the relation of the world to consciousness as a case of interaction between two substances.

The effect of the distinction on the form of the Kantian theory appears in the separation of the Æsthetic from the Analytic, and the hard and fast line drawn in consequence between space and time, as forms of sensibility, and the categories, as functions of the understanding. Kant gets the perceptive forms in the Æsthetic by an independent set of arguments, while in the first part of the Analytic his categories seem to drop at his feet as pure intellectual conceptions. Hence the categories do not appear to him as limited or inadequate *in their own nature*, but because of their subsequent association with sense and its forms. It would be nearer the truth to say that the Kantian categories are themselves the reason why the world appears to us in space: space is merely the abstraction or the ghost of the world of interacting substances which these categories present us with. If the Kantian categories can give us nothing beyond a world of material things, the defect is in their own intellectual quality, and not in any limitation extraneously attached to them. They are bonds of connection, yet they may be said to leave the elements they connect still independent of one another. The categories of quantity, while in one sense they express a connection between all things, express even more emphatically the complete indifference of every individual point to its neighbours; and though the categories of relation—summed up, as they may be, in reciprocity—undoubtedly express a system of elements in which this mutual indifference is overcome, yet the individuals brought into connection are not seen to have any necessary relation to one another in the sense of being members together of one whole. The individuals appear endlessly determined by their relations to one another, but there is involved in this very endlessness an unavoidable sense of contingency. If we are to have a real whole and real parts—parts, that is, whose existence can be understood only through the whole that determines them—we must have recourse to other categories than these. But the imperfect relatedness just referred to is the essential mark of what we call the world of sense; and for a theory of knowledge, if it retain the term sensible world, that world is definable simply by this characteristic, and not by an imaginary reference of its contents to an impressing cause. It is defined, in other words, by the categories that constitute it, and by the relation of these categories to the other modes in which the mind endeavours to harmonise the world. With reference to Kant, then, the point to be insisted on is, the categories which he offers as the only categories are *inherently* inadequate to express a synthesis more intimate than the mutual relatedness and mutual externality of things in space. The world, therefore, necessarily presents this aspect when viewed solely by their light. They are not got independently of sense (we might reply to Kant) and afterwards immersed in it; they are the categories *of* sense. Their true deduction is not from the table of logical judgments; it is given in the "system of principles" in the second part of the Analytic, where they are proved to be the ultimate conditions on which a coherent sense-experience depends. In Kant's technical language, the categories do not require to be schematised, because, apart from schematisation, they do not exist even as conceptions. The conception of substance, for example, means just that relation of a permanent to shifting (or conceivably shifting) attributes which is familiar to us in the sensible world. The logical relation of subject and predicate, which Kant seems to say is the pure category before it is soiled by sense, is merely the image of this real relation expressed in language.[1]

There is thus no justification for a separation of space from the categories, space being the ultimate appearance of a world constructed on these categories alone. When this is admitted, the mere fact that we perceive things *in space* is no imputation upon the reality of our knowledge. In itself space is no limitation; it is an intellectual bond, it is one point of view from which we may represent the world as one. This mode of knowledge becomes limited and unreal only when it claims to be the ultimate aspect from which the universe is to be regarded. The nature of space affords no grounds, then, for a division of knowledge into absolutely phenomenal and absolutely noumenal, such as we find in Kant. The so-called phenomenal world of sense is as real as the so-called noumenal world of ethics—that is to say, its account of the universe is as legitimate so far as it goes; but to claim for either an absolute truth is the essential mark of dogmatism, whether the claim be

[1] The relation of the table of logical judgments to the Kantian categories (where it actually exists and is not a matter of forced interpretation) is thus seen to be reversed.

advanced by the man of science or the metaphysician. Both are accounts which the mind gives to itself of the world,—relatively justified points of view from which experience may be rationalised. It is the province of a theory of knowledge to point out the relation of the one point of view to the other, and, in general, while showing the partial and abstract nature of any particular point of view, to show at the same time how it is related to the ultimate or concrete conception of the universe which alone admits of being thought out without self-contradiction. The opposition between phenomenal and noumenal worlds is thus replaced by one between more abstract and more concrete points of view. That is to say, the opposition itself is no longer of the rigid and absolute nature which it was before. The truth of the one point of view does not interfere with the truth of the other: the higher may rather be regarded as the completion or fulfilment of the lower.

Let us now see how far Kant helps us towards such a philosophical conception. Reasons have been given for disallowing his absolute limitation of knowledge by erecting behind it a realm of unknowables. These unknowables are simply the impressing things of preceding philosophy, uncritically assumed, and removed into a somewhat deeper obscurity. But the theory which derives knowledge from impressions is essentially a psychological theory which we, as spectators, form of the rise of knowledge in an organised individual placed in relation to a world which we already describe under all the categories of knowledge. What we observe is, strictly, an interaction between two things which are themselves objects in a known world. And if we afterwards extend inferentially to our own case the conclusions which our observations suggest, we are still simply repeating the picture of a known environment acting on a known organism. The relation is between phenomenal things and a phenomenal organism in which they set up affections, not between a transcendent or metempirical somewhat and intelligence as such. In other words, when we have formed our notion of the world, and of our own position as individuals in it, we can give even to such a misleading metaphor as impression a certain intelligible meaning; but to step outside of the world of knowledge altogether and characterise it by reference to something beyond itself—this is the type of all impossibility. Yet it is no less than this that Kant and some of his followers undertake to do when they pronounce our knowledge to be only phenomenal, implying by that term the existence of something hidden from us in its own transcendency. While adhering, therefore, in the fullest manner to Kant's position that the categories are only of immanent use for the organisation of experience, we deny altogether that the existence of transcendent entities may be justly inferred from such a statement. Only to those who are haunted by the ghosts of the old metaphysic can the proposition appear in the light of a limitation of human reason: to others adhesion to Kant's position, so far as it asserts immanence, becomes a matter of course. What they combat in Kant's scheme is the assumption that his twelve categories are the only categories implied in our experience, and the belief, corresponding to this assumption, that they give a completely coherent and exhaustive account of that experience.

Kant himself, however, is prone to confess that experience is not exhausted by these categories, if by experience is understood the whole life of man. The world of ethical action (to take his own crucial instance) remains completely unintelligible when viewed from the standpoint of mechanism. Determination by ends is the characteristic feature of this world; and action so determined cannot be understood, Kant says, except under the idea of freedom. That is to say, the attempt to explain it by the categories of natural causality is equivalent to a denial of the existence of the facts in question. Such a procedure means that in our levelling zeal we obliterate the specific difference between two sets of facts; whereas in reality the difference is the fundamental feature of the case which calls upon us for a *rationale* of its possibility. Now it is a matter of common knowledge that for Kant himself moral experience was *the* reality. In the Preface to the 'Critique of Practical Reason' he speaks of the idea of freedom as the "topstone of the whole edifice of a system of pure reason, *speculative as well as practical*"; and no attentive reader of the first Critique can fail to notice the vista, ever and anon opened up, of a world of supersensible reality into which we are eventually to be carried by the march of the argument. The whole Critical scheme of sense-experience is thereby invested with a palpably preparatory character. Kant fully recognises, and indeed enforces, this aspect of his work when he comes to review its scope and method in the Preface to the second edition. The whole investigation is there represented as merely "making room" for the extension of our knowledge on the basis of practical data: Criticism simply fulfils the function of "a police force" in keeping the unregulated activity of the speculative reason within bounds.

It might well seem, then, as if, in going on to treat the presuppositions of morality, we were merely passing from one sphere of rational experience to another. Kant's method, too, is essentially the same in all three Critiques. It is an analysis of certain experiences with a view to determine the conditions of their possibility. One would expect, therefore, that the different sets of conceptions to which his analysis leads him would be treated impartially, and on their own merits, or looked at merely in their relation to one another as parts of one rational explanation of experience. If there is no flaw in our deduction of the conceptions, it seems very like stultifying the transcendental method to talk of differences between them in respect of objective truth or validity. Kant, however, as is well known, draws a variety of such distinctions. Thus, in the 'Critique of Judgment,' he finds the idea of organisation to be as essential to a complete account of nature as he had previously found the conception of substance to be for a narrower range of experience. Yet he arbitrarily holds the former to be of merely regulative utility—a fiction or contrivance of the mind to aid it in investigation, —while the latter is allowed to be constitutive of nature as such. And so, again, Kant restricts the terms experience and knowledge to the sense-phenomena of the first Critique, while the presuppositions of ethical experience are made at most matters of rational belief or moral certainty. It is impossible to decorate the one with pre-eminent titles without a corresponding disparagement of the others. The term experience is in these circumstances a question-begging epithet. When such distinctions are drawn it inevitably tends to make men regard the 'Critique of Pure Reason' as alone embodying Kant's substantive theory of the world. The categories of life, of beauty, and of morality come to be looked on as appendices of a more or less uncertain character, the acceptance or rejection of which does not interfere with the finality of the categories of sense. This is unquestionably the form in which Kantian results are most widely current at present. It is a form for which Kant himself is chiefly responsible, through his habit of "isolating" different spheres of experience for the purpose of his analysis, and neglecting afterwards to exhibit their organic relation to one another. None the less is it a form which ignores explicit intimations like those quoted from above from the two Prefaces, and one which is based upon that very notion of the relation of mind to reality which Kant came to destroy. After all, too much stress has probably been laid upon the difference of nomenclature which Kant adopts, and it ought to be remembered that though he refuses to call his moral faith knowledge, he yet holds that it, and it alone, brings him into contact with reality.

If we now return to Kant's account of the phenomenal nature of our knowledge, and abstract altogether from the illegitimate reference of our sense-objects to the transcendent thing-in-itself, another meaning of the phenomenality of sense-experience begins to emerge. The opposition is no longer between the world of sense and its unknown correlate (or cause), but between the world of sense as nature or the realm of causal necessity, and the "intelligible world," as Kant calls it, or the realm of ends, in which the will determines itself by its own law. Noumenal personality and freedom are reached in the notion of the self-legislative and self-obedient will. The condemnation of phenomenality comes upon the world of sense because of the contrast which its externality of connected part and part offers to the self-centred finality of a conception like the self-determining will. If this is not the meaning of phenomenality which is most prominent in the 'Critique of Pure Reason,' still it is continually appearing there also; and in proportion as it comes into the foreground, the other reference of objects to their transcendental correlates tends to lose its importance and almost to disappear. Any one may convince himself of this by turning to Kant's official chapter "On the ground of division of all objects into phenomena and noumena." He will find that the conception of noumena or non-sensuous objects is there defined as a "Grenzbegriff," a limitative conception, or, more exactly, as a conception which sets bounds to the sphere of sense (ein die Sinnlichkeit in Schranken setzender Begriff). The conception is problematical, Kant says, inasmuch as it does not give us a knowledge of intelligible or non-sensuous objects as actually existing, but merely affirms their possibility. Its utility lies in the fact that by it we prevent sense-knowledge from laying claim to the whole of reality. Evidently it would be unfair to interpret the term problematical here as if Kant meant by using it to throw doubt on the actual existence of what he sometimes calls "the non-sensuous cause" of our ideas. "In what other fashion is it to be supposed that the knowing faculty should be roused to exercise," he might repeat, "if not by objects which affect our senses?" The question of the origin of the matter of sense remains for Kant just where it was, but he is speaking here in quite another connection, and that problem has fallen out of view for the time. He is engaged in limiting sense so as to "make room" for the *mundus intelligibilis* which he is afterwards to produce as guaranteed by the Practical Reason. It is the existence of freedom and its implicates that is declared to be, in the meantime, merely problematical. The phrase "intelligible world" is never used by Kant, so far as I know, except of the world of ethically determined agents,—an additional proof that we are right in attributing to him here a point of view which judges the inadequacy of sense, not by reference to a somewhat beyond the confines of intelligible experience altogether, but by reference to a higher phase of experience itself. The lower point of view is not, strictly speaking, abolished by the higher; but it is perceived that to try to take the sensible world absolutely or by itself would be to render it unintelligible. Isolated in this way, the world of interacting substances would have all the irrationality of a series that cannot be summed, of multiplicity without unity, of externality without internality. It is impossible, in Kant's language, to treat nature as an End-in-itself, as something there on its own account; yet reason demands this notion of the self-sufficing and self-justifying, as that in which alone it can rest. Kant recognises that it is only intelligence, and especially intelligence in its moral aspect, that supplies the lacking notion; nature itself, he says, assumes a unity which does not otherwise belong to it, and becomes a "realm" or system, when viewed in relation to rational beings as its end.[1]

It is thus on account of its incomplete and self-less character that the *mundus sensibilis* appears phenomenal, when regarded from the standpoint of the intelligible world. And reason is compelled, Kant says, to pass beyond the phenomenal and occupy such a standpoint, "if we are not to deny to man the consciousness of himself as intelligence, *i.e.*, as rational and through reason active, in other words, as a free cause."[2] The importance

[1] Cf. 'Grundlegung zur Metaphysik der Sitten.' 'Werke,' iv. 286.

[2] 'Werke,' iv. 306. The expression "Standpunkt" is used significantly by Kant himself in this context.

of the change in the point of view can hardly be overestimated. Self-consciousness is here put forward explicitly as the one noumenon to which all phenomena are referred, and by which they are, as it were, judged, and declared to be phenomenal. This is the real Copernican change of standpoint which Kant effected, or which at least he puts us in the way of effecting; and it must be pronounced fundamental, seeing that it reverses the whole notion of reality on which the old metaphysic was built. The dominating categories of philosophy in the present day are still, it is to be feared, those of inner and outer, substance and quality, or in their latest and most imposing garb, noumenon and phenomenon. And these are so interpreted as to represent the intellect clinging round the outside of things, getting to know only the surface of the world, and pining for the revelation of that intense reality, the "support of accidents," which yet is unrevealable and mocks our cries. A true metaphysic teaches that if we so conduct ourselves, we do in very truth "pine for what is not." This unapproachable reality is entirely a fiction of the mind; there is nothing transcendent, no unknowable, if we once see that a phenomenal world is a permissible phrase only when taken to mean something in which reason cannot rest, and that the ultimate noumenon is to be found in self-consciousness, or in the notion of knowledge and its implications. The centre of the world lies then in our own nature as self-conscious beings, and in that life with our fellows which, in different aspects, constitutes alike the secular and divine community. The spirit fostered by physical science, and the mood familiar to all of us—the mood which weighs man's paltry life and its concerns against the "pomp of worlds" and the measureless fields of space—is in reality less philosophical than that of the poet and humanist, to whom this pomp is barren save as the background of the human drama. Ordinary people get most of their metaphysics through religion or through poetry, and they probably often come nearer the truth in that way than if they went to the professed philosophers.

Kant's ethics are part, therefore, of the strength and not of the weakness of their author. They are not to be regarded as a calling in of faith to repair the breaches of knowledge; on the contrary, they are founded on Kant's deepest philosophical conceptions. But for all that, the superstructure contains much questionable material; and as we are not engaged on a question of hermeneutics, it is essential to arrive for ourselves at a general notion of how the ethical point of view stands related to the mechanical. This will serve as an illustration of the main thesis of this essay, the distinction of categories or points of view. It is at the same time the more necessary in the present case, as Kant has expressed the relation chiefly by negations, and has left the sensible and intelligible systems separated by an apparently impassable gulf. The positive predicate of freedom which he applies to the ethical world is, on the other hand, so ambiguous, and to men of scientific training so ominous, that it has been more productive of misconception than of enlightenment. It may be said at once, then, that if Kant's account of freedom contains anything which seems to lift man, as it were, out of all the influences and surroundings that make him what he is, and from this height makes him hurl a decisive and solely self-originated fiat into the strife of motives beneath—then, undoubtedly, this idea is not only at variance with the teaching of physical and social science, but is fatal to all rational connection in the universe. But the self in such a conception is a bare unit, an abstraction which has no existence in fact. So long as we take up with such notions of the self, we must inevitably seem to be battered about by the shocks of circumstance. The man whose self could be emptied of all its contents and reduced to this atomic condition would be, in a strict sense, no more than the moving point which exemplifies the composition of forces. In reducing the abstract self to this position, and so abolishing it, determinism is entirely within its rights: it is in vain that the upholders of "free-will" try to save for this self even a power of directing attention on one motive rather than another. But happily the real self is not this ghost of argumentative fancy. A man cannot be separated from the world which lies about him from his infancy—and long before it,—moulding him after its own image, and supplying him with all sorts of permanent motives in the shape of creeds and laws, customs and prejudices, creating, in a word, the concrete personality we are held to refer to when, in ordinary speech, we name this or the other individual. The self-conscious individual is not something identical with himself alone, and different from everything else: he is not even exclusive as one thing in nature is exclusive of other things. The whole past and the whole present are transformed, as it were, by self-consciousness into its own nature. A man's motives do not seem to him, therefore, to come to him from without: they are the suggestions of his good or evil self. And if he reviews his past experience, when his self, as others might say, was in the making, he cannot himself take this external view. It is impossible to him, because it abolishes the one presupposition from which he cannot depart: it abolishes himself. Much rather he will say that he has made himself what he is: he identifies himself necessarily with all his past, and of every deed he can say, " Alone I did it."

In short, though the external view with its tabulation of motives may be useful for statistical purposes, and may yield scientific results that are not to be despised, it is absolutely valueless in ethics or the explanation of moral experience as such. The presupposition of ethical action, as of intelligence generally, is the Ego. It is true that, as explained above, we do not suppose the Ego, in action, to bring an inexplicable force into play, any more than we suppose it, as intellect, to add any determinations to things which were not there already. But just as any metaphysic which does not base itself on self-consciousness, as the fundamental presupposition and the supreme category of thought, is forced openly or tacitly to deny the conscious life, so a science of ethics which does not assume as its basis the self-determination of the rational being, remains outside of moral experience altogether. Moral experience consists entirely in this self-reference; if this be destroyed, the whole ethical point of view vanishes. Let us contrast with this the point of view of physical science from which we started. From this standpoint every moral action is simply an event, and, as an event, forms a term in a series of mechanical transformations. This is certainly one way of regarding the actions in question: they *are* such events, and for science that is the legitimate and true method of treating them. All that we contend is that the scientific explanation does not exhaust their significance; so far as they are actions, that is, related to the moral consciousness, it gives no account of them at all. The world of ethics is superimposed therefore upon that of science, not as contradicting it, but as introducing a totally new order of conceptions, by which actions which are for science mere factual units in a series become elements in a life guided by the notion of End, or Ought. Their sole ethical meaning is in relation to this ideally judging consciousness, and to that extent they cease to be facts conditioned by other facts. The ethical consciousness identifies itself with each of its actions, and each therefore is immediately referred to the standard of duty. Ethically, that is to say, the action is not referred backward in time to the circumstances and predispositions of which, as motives, it is the legitimate outcome; but the man brings his action face to face with a "Thou shalt," which he finds within him,[1] and according to its conformity or want of conformity with this law he approves or condemns his conduct. The former method of looking at his actions is appropriate to a spectator—a psychologist, a statistician, a scientific educator, &c.—but not to the man himself. As soon as an individual begins to seek excuses for his "fault," by showing how natural it was in the circumstances, he has fallen from the ethical point of view. He is assuming the position of a spectator or scientific observer, and however justifiable this standpoint may be for others, it certainly means the destruction of the ethical consciousness in him who deliberately adopts it in his own regard. The proper category of ethics is not cause and effect, but End, with its correlative Obligation.

The realm of ethical ends, however, is only one of the conceptions or points of view by which reason makes the world intelligible to itself; and by treating it as the sole antithesis of the world of sense, Kant ran

[1] The "matter" which the law commands, depends of course upon his social environment and his past; but the "form" of law exists wherever consciousness exists, since rights and duties are involved in the most rudimentary notion of society.

the risk, as was hinted above, of falling into a fresh dualism. It is not even well to speak of the one as "intelligible" by pre-eminence, lest the sensible world lose its reference to consciousness altogether. We might do worse than recall in this connection Kant's demonstration of the intellectual elements in sense-experience. We do not get "facts" given to us in the mechanical scheme of science, and in ethics a point of view from which to regard this factual world. Bare facts in this sense have no existence save for an abstract thought which conceives them as the pegs on which relations may be hung. The process of knowledge does not consist in the discovery of such *individua*, but in the progressive overthrowal of such ideas of the nature of the actual. In this process, the scientific account of things forms one of the ways in which the mind seeks to present the world as an intelligible whole: it is a *theorising* of the world, and as it turns out, the theorising is incomplete and ultimately contradicts itself. Such considerations prepare us to expect a progress by more gradual stages from the less to the more complete conception of the universe than is found in Kant's great leap from mechanism to morality. Here again Kant helps us on the way. The 'Critique of Judgment,' according to his own account of it, is intended to bridge over the gulf between the world of the understanding, outlined in the first Critique, and the world of reason or of free determination, outlined in the second. There is, as usual, much that is artificial in the scheme of faculties with which Kant connects his investigation. So far as we are concerned here, the best method of approaching the 'Critique of Judgment' is simply by reference to the aspects of nature which it endeavours to explain. Its importance lies in its recognition of certain points of view which are continually recurring in our contemplation of the world, but which find no place in the Critical idea of nature, as so far expounded. These are the æsthetic and the teleological judgment of things, or, in less technical language, the phenomena of beauty and of organisation.[1]

The weakness of the book lies in the presupposition on which it proceeds, that the record of objectivity has been definitely closed in the first Critique. In other words, Kant believes knowledge to be limited by the imagination; nothing is real (in the domain of knowledge) unless what can be constructed in relations of space. Now the 'Critique of Judgment' consists virtually in the production of two sets of negative instances: a living body and an object considered as beautiful are not exhausted in the space-relations which constitute them. Imagination knows only parts that are external to one another, and to that extent independent of one another; but in the organism this externality and independence disappear. The parts are only parts through the whole of which they are parts. Part and whole acquire, in fact, a meaning in which their necessary correlation is for the first time apparent,—a correlation or union so intimate as to be inadequately expressed by terms which contain, like part and whole, a quantitative suggestion. Similarly, the category of cause breaks down when applied to the organism, for all the parts are mutually cause and effect; and the organism as a whole is its own cause and its own effect (*causa sui*). It organises

[1] To avoid confusion, the significance of the æsthetic judgment, or of the categories of art, for our ultimate notion of the world, is not touched upon in the present essay.

itself. In all this, Kant's description of organic phenomena is unexceptionable; he pleads the case well against himself. But unfortunately the negative instances he produces did not lead to a recasting of his theory. They only led to a fresh distinction. The new aspects of nature could not be recognised as constitutive or objectively valid, but they might be accepted as regulative points of view for the investigation of phenomena. But as there is no ground for this distinction except in presuppositions which have been shown to be irrelevant we shall make no scruple of ignoring it, and treating the relation of organism to mechanism not as subjectivity to objectivity, but as a more adequate to a less adequate interpretation of the same facts.

It must be observed that the notion of organism given above constitutes no assertion of the existence of a vital force as a separate cause of the phenomena of life. This is the kind of deduction which metaphysicians of the kind that have brought the name into disrepute were quick to draw. But it is easy to see that by explanations of this sort we are just setting up a duplicate of the thing to be explained, or, in other words, hypostatising it as its own cause. Besides, when the physiologist comes to close quarters with a living body, he finds everywhere a mechanism of parts connected with one another and communicating with the surrounding world. Motion is handed on from one member of this system to another without the intervention of any other than mechanical contrivances; and so far from a necessity arising for a transcendent cause, there is nowhere a gap to be found in the circle of mechanical motions where its introduction could be effected. The physiologist, in short, in describing the action of the different parts of the organism, is in precisely the same position as the psychologist in giving an account of mental states and processes. The empirical psychologist analyses the most complex states into their elements, and builds up ethical and religious sentiment out of desires and aversions, and all by a process essentially mechanical, without any reference to the unity of the conscious life for which these states exist. Just as the psychologist has neither occasion nor right to consider any special power which he calls the Ego, so the physiologist in the case of the organism. He works within the conditions of organic existence, as the psychologist within those of consciousness, but neither requires for the purpose of his special science to make any explicit reference to these conditions. Hence it comes that physiology, so far as it treats the living body as a whole, represents it as merely a mechanical conjunction of parts in space. The abstraction is not only defensible but necessary: none the less, however, is it a complete abstraction from the significance of the same parts viewed as members of a living system. Viewed organically, or in their relation to the whole, they are seen to be mutually implicative, and within certain limits, mutually creative. The presuppositions of mechanism are so far overthrown that at the organic standpoint the mutual exclusiveness of the parts disappears: the organism, *quâ* organism, is not in space at all. If we persist, therefore, in looking at the parts abstractly or in their separateness, and if we tender this as the complete account of them, we are leaving out of sight the very fact which constitutes the phenomenon to be explained.

So far from mechanism being objective and the notion

of organism only subjective, we should be compelled, if we were in the way of talking in this strain, to reverse the relation. For even as applied to mechanical things, if the category of causality be thought out into reciprocity, and if reciprocity be conceived as complete, the result is that we arrive at a closed circle of perfect mutual conditionedness, in which all play of actual causality is brought to a standstill. The universe becomes like the sleeping-palace of Dornröschen; there is no point where movement might be introduced into the dead picture. We sublate in this way the conceptions with which we started, and only find the contradiction solved for us (at least temporarily) in the notion of the organism.

If the categories of reciprocity and abstract individuality fail us in speaking of the living body, still less will they serve us when they come to treat of conscious individuals and of what is called the social organism. Step by step we have combated the intellectual vice of abstraction, but it is when we reach self-consciousness that the nature of this fault becomes fully apparent. When we examine the conceptions of ordinary and scientific thought in the light thrown upon them by that supreme category, of which they are all the imperfect reflections, the whole series of stages from which the individual knower views the world appears as a gradual deliverance from an abstract individualism, or, as Spinoza said, from the imaginative thought which insists on taking the individual as a thing by itself. When we reach the only true individual, the self-conscious being, we find that individuality is not the exclusive thing we had imagined it to be. The self is individual only to the extent that it is at the same time universal. It knows itself, *i.e.*, it *is* itself, just because it includes within its knowledge not only one particular self, as an object in space and time, but also a whole intelligible world embracing many such selves. A mere individual, supposed for a moment possible, would be a self-less point; and it was the assumption of the reality of such self-less points that led us into contradiction at a lower stage. In the notion of the self we find that what is outside of, or different from, a man in the narrow sense, yet enters into and constitutes his self in such a way, that without it he would cease to be anything more than the imaginary point just referred to. The individual is individualised only by his relations to the totality of the intelligible world. In a more restricted sense, his individuality is constituted by the social organism of which he is a member: he cannot be an individual except so far as he is a member of society. If this is the relation of society to the individual, it is at once apparent how false any theory must be which tries to take the individual as a mere individual, and regards society as an aggregate of such beings combined together for mutual advantage. The doctrine of *laissez-faire* and the theory of the police state are immediate deductions from the individualistic premisses. It is natural from such a point of view that the State should be treated as a mechanism external to the individuals, and constructed by them merely that they may live at ease and enjoy their goods. But the logic of practice refutes both these principles. The economic doctrine has been largely modified even by those who promulgated it, little as their professed philosophical principles give them a right to do so; and the external view of the State is refuted not only by its practical action in numberless spheres of life, but by every patriotic emotion that passes over individuals or peoples. If the State is the artificial aggregate it is represented as being, how shall we explain Shakespeare's impassioned apostrophe to

> "This happy breed of men, this little world,
> This precious stone set in the silver sea, . . .
> This blessed spot, this earth, this realm, this England, . . .
> This land of such dear souls, this dear, dear land"?

This little world—a more felicitous phrase could hardly be desired to describe what the true State must always be to its citizens. The State is not Leviathan, as Hobbes supposed, swallowing up the individual, but the ethical cosmos into which he is born, and by which his relation to the wider cosmos of universal experience is mediated. These, however, are considerations which are being recognised, one is glad to see, in many quarters, even though it be as yet without a consciousness of their ultimate philosophical bearing. Still we are not entitled to depart from individualistic metaphysics in one point, unless we recognise the fallaciousness of its method everywhere. We need not fear by so doing to sacrifice what are called the rights of individuality. Socialism, for example, is the recoil from individualism, not the refutation of it. Individualism and socialism are alike refuted by the true notion of self-consciousness, which combines all-inclusiveness with intensest concentration in a way which might have seemed impossible, had we been engaged in an abstract argument and not simply in an analysis of concrete reality. While this notion is held fast, the members in whom the social organism is realised will not cease to know themselves as personalities, and to demand that the free play of their lives be not sacrificed to imaginary needs of the body politic.

Our whole criticism of categories thus leads us up to the notion of self-consciousness or knowledge. Here we may connect ourselves for the last time with Kant. The shortcomings of his theory of knowledge have been somewhat severely criticised in the earlier part of the essay. It has been seen that he vitiated his analysis to a great extent by confusing a psychological or a spectator's account of the growth of knowledge with a transcendental analysis of its conditions. It has also been shown how the presuppositions that sprang from this confusion prevented him from seeing the mutual relations of the categories in their true light, as simply stages or phases of explanation (of greater or less abstractness) which necessarily supersede one another in the development of knowledge. But in spite of the absolute line which Kant drew at reciprocity, he explicitly announced the emancipation of the category of categories—the unity of apperception—from the dominion of the conceptions which were its own creatures. It can be compassed, he says, by none of them; it can be known only through itself. Knowledge is related as such to a universally synthetic principle which calls itself "I," and which is described by Kant as the transcendental Ego, to distinguish it from the empirical consciousness which constitutes, as it were, the matter of this formal unity. Kant's view of this unity as merely logical and merely human prevented him from recognising that he had found the true noumenon here as well as in the ethical sphere. Nevertheless, his assertion of the unity of the subject as the ultimate principle of thought leads directly to the conception of knowledge as necessarily organic to a subject, and as constituting in this form the complete Fact from which all so-called facts are only abstractions.

Here the line between Dogmatism and Criticism may be drawn, without prejudice to Kant's essential meaning.

Dogmatism, or the use of uncriticised conceptions, means practically the unquestioning application of the categories of mechanism to the relation between consciousness and things. Mind and matter are hypostatised, and the category of reciprocity is employed to describe their union in knowledge. How far Kant was himself a Dogmatist in this sense has been already considered; at all events, the whole of modern philosophy before Kant is based upon this conception. "In order to make his theory work," says Professor Fraser in his article on Locke in the 'Encyclopædia Britannica,' "he [Locke] begins by assuming a *hypothetical duality* beneath phenomena—some phenomena referable to external things, others referable to the conscious self,—and in fact confesses that this dual experience is *the* ultimate fact, the denial of which would make it impossible to speak about the growth and constitution of our thoughts." It is to be noted that what is spoken of is not a duality with reference to knowledge—in which case knowledge itself would be the ultimate fact; there is an assumption of two facts or things, out of whose (contingent) relation to one another a third fact arises as something additional. The derivative fact acts as a mirror in which actuality, consisting of the first two facts, is reflected. Now if we start with the notion of a mind-substance (existing prior to the self-consciousness which constitutes the real existence of a *self*) and of an independently existing world, it is easy to make a watershed of experience in the fashion indicated, and so to appear to establish the hypothetical duality with which we started. This, as Professor Fraser says, is what Locke did; and all psychological philosophy does so still. As speculation becomes more acute, it is necessarily led, as idealism or materialism, to dissolve one of these substances into a series of changes in the other, while scepticism calmly points out to both disputants that the arguments which apply in the one case apply in the other also. But idealism, materialism, and Humism have meaning only with reference to the assumption of a duality of self-existing substances to which experience is referred as to its causes. These theories exist as the denial of one of the factors, or as the assertion of the impossibility of proving either, but they do not attack the abstraction on which this hypothesis of dual existence was originally founded. Hume is a sceptic because he cannot prove either mind or matter to be real in the sense in which Cartesian and Lockian metaphysics understood reality. But if such realities are no more than fictions of abstract thought, then a sceptical disproof of our knowledge of them is so far from being a final disproof of the possibility of any real knowledge, that it is rather to be taken as indispensably preliminary to the attainment of a true notion of what reality is.

Such a notion is attainable only through a transcendental analysis of knowledge—an analysis, that is, which shall regard knowledge simply as it is in itself, without any presupposition of existences which give rise to it. An analysis of this sort, so far as it remains true to its transcendental standpoint, will not be tempted to substantiate the conditions of knowledge apart from the synthesis in which it finds them. It will simply relate them to one another as different elements in—or better, perhaps, as different aspects of—the one concrete reality. This is why Kant's treatment of the "I think" is so different from Descartes' procedure with his "Cogito." Kant, like Descartes, finds the presupposition of knowledge and of intelligible existence in an "I think"; but he never forgets that it is only in relation to the world, or as the synthesis of intelligible elements, that the self exists or can have a meaning. A world without this unifying principle would fall asunder into unrelated particulars; the synthetic principle itself, apart from the world which it unifies, would be no more than the barren identity, I = I. Even this consciousness of self-identity is reached only through the synthesis of objects to which it stands in relation. This necessity of correlation may be treated without injustice as the fundamental feature of the transcendental method. So far is it from being a figure of speech that the self exists only *through* the world and *vice versa*, that we might say with equal truth the self *is* the world and the world is the self. The relation between them is that of subject to predicate when the predication is supposed to be exhaustive. The subject is identical with its completed predicate without remainder. So the self and the world are only two sides of the same reality: they are the same intelligible world looked at from two opposite points of view. But, finally, it must not be forgotten that it is only from the point of view of the self or subject that the identity can be grasped: this, therefore, is the ultimate point of view which unifies the whole.

It will be easily understood that, in speaking thus of the self of knowledge, abstraction is made from any particular self in experience. No one who has mastered Kant's distinction between the transcendental and empirical Ego is likely to have any difficulty here. At the same time, the theory of knowledge makes no assertion of the existence of the transcendental self otherwise than as the form of these empirical individuals. To raise the question of existence in this shape is to fall back once more into mechanical or spatial categories, and to treat the ultimate synthesis of thought as if it were a thing that could exist here or there. Separate facts, however, are the type of reality only to that abstract thought which has faced us in every sphere. The transcendental self, as the implicate of all experience, is, for a theory of knowledge, simply the necessary point of view from which the universe can be unified—that is, from which it becomes an universe.

Thus the Kantian criticism with its claim to map out knowledge and ignorance has assumed under our hands the less pretentious form of a criticism of categories. The attempt is no longer made to determine the validity of reason as such; the trustworthiness of knowledge is and must be an assumption. But this does not mean that every reasoned conclusion is true. Knowledge is not a collection of facts known as such once for all, and to which we afterwards add other facts, extending our knowledge as we might extend an estate by adding acre to acre. This is not a true picture of the march of knowledge. On the contrary, every advance of science is a partial refutation of what we supposed we knew; we undertake in every new scientific theory a criticism and rectification of the conceptions on which the old was constructed. On the largest scale, the advance of knowledge is neither more nor less than a progressive criticism of its own conceptions. And, as we have seen, this is not all. Besides the continual self-criticism carried on by the individual sciences, there is the criticism which one science or department of inquiry passes upon another. The science of life cannot move hand or foot without the category of development which, in its biological conception, is foreign to the inorganic world; and the science of conduct is founded upon the notion of duty, of which the whole world of nature knows nothing. But so long as this mutual criticism is left in the hands of the separate sciences themselves, it tends to degenerate into a strife in which there is no umpire. Philosophy, as theory of knowledge, can alone arbitrate between the combatants, by showing the relation of the different points of view to one another, and allowing to each a sphere of relative justification. When physical science, for example, begins to formulate its own results and to put them forward as an adequate theory of the universe, it is for philosophy to step in and show how these results depend entirely upon preconceptions drawn from a certain stage of knowledge and found to be refuted in the further progress of thought. Philosophy in the capacity of a science of thought should possess a complete survey of its categories and of their dialectical connection; but this "Wissenschaft der Logik" will probably never be completely written. In the meantime, it is perhaps better if philosophy, as critic of the sciences, is content to derive its matter from them and to prophesy in part. Examples of this progress and connection among conceptions or points of view have been given in the preceding pages, and whether we apply to them the name of dialectic or not is of little matter. This critical office, in which philosophy acts, as it were, as the watch-dog of knowledge, is important enough not to compromise the dignity even of the queen of the sciences. She is critic not only of the special sciences, but especially of all metaphysics and systems of philosophy.

Most men of science believe that metaphysics consist in the elaboration of transcendent entities like an extraneous Deity, or Mr Spencer's Unknowable, or the noumena of those who describe our knowledge as "merely" phenomenal. But the theory of knowledge teaches us that all such constructions in the void have their genesis in a belief that the substance is something different from all its qualities, or that the cause is not identical with the sum of its effects. We learn, on the contrary, that cause and effect, substance and quality, and all similar conceptions, are not the names of two different things, but necessary aspects of the same object, and that therefore, when we are dealing, not with limited objects, but with the universe as the synthesis of all objects, it is a mere repetition to invent a cause of this synthesis. To be delivered from bad metaphysics is the first step and the most important one towards the true conception of the science. True metaphysic lies, as we have tried to show, in that criticism of experience which aims at developing out of the material of science and of life the completed notion of experience itself.

THE END.

PRINTED BY WILLIAM BLACKWOOD AND SONS.

Catalogue

of

Messrs Blackwood & Sons'

Publications

CATALOGUE

OF

MESSRS BLACKWOOD & SON'S

PUBLICATIONS.

ACTA SANCTORUM HIBERNIÆ; Ex Codice Salmanticensi.
Nunc primum integre edita opera CAROLI DE SMEDT et JOSEPHI DE BACKER, e Soc. Jesu, Hagiographorum Bollandianorum; Auctore et Sumptus Largiente JOANNE PATRICIO MARCHIONE BOTHAE. In One handsome 4to Volume, bound in half roxburghe, £2, 2s.; in paper cover, 31s. 6d.

ADAMSON.

The Development of Modern Philosophy. With other Lectures and Essays. By ROBERT ADAMSON, LL.D., late Professor of Logic in the University of Glasgow. Edited by Professor W. R. SORLEY, University of Cambridge. In 2 vols. demy 8vo, 18s. net.

The Development of Greek Philosophy. Edited by Professor SORLEY and R. P. HARDIE, M.A. Demy 8vo. [*In the press.*

AIKMAN.

Manures and the Principles of Manuring. By C. M. AIKMAN, D.Sc., F.R.S.E., &c., formerly Professor of Chemistry, Glasgow Veterinary College, and Examiner in Chemistry, University of Glasgow, &c. Second Impression. Crown 8vo, 6s. 6d.

Farmyard Manure: Its Nature, Composition, and Treatment. Crown 8vo, 1s. 6d.

ALISON.

History of Europe. By Sir ARCHIBALD ALISON, Bart., D.C.L.

1. From the Commencement of the French Revolution to the Battle of Waterloo.
   LIBRARY EDITION, 14 vols., with Portraits. Demy 8vo, £10, 10s.
   ANOTHER EDITION, in 20 vols. crown 8vo, £6.
   PEOPLE'S EDITION, 13 vols. crown 8vo, £2, 11s.
2. Continuation to the Accession of Louis Napoleon.
   LIBRARY EDITION, 8 vols. 8vo, £6, 7s. 6d.
   PEOPLE'S EDITION, 8 vols. crown 8vo 34s.

Epitome of Alison's History of Europe. Thirtieth Thousand, 7s. 6d.

Atlas to Alison's History of Europe. By A. Keith Johnston.
LIBRARY EDITION, demy 4to, £3, 3s.
PEOPLE'S EDITION, 31s. 6d.

ANCIENT CLASSICS FOR ENGLISH READERS. Edited by Rev. W. LUCAS COLLINS, M.A. Price 1s. each net. *For List of Vols. see p. 2.*

ARMYTAGE. Maids of Honour. By A. J. GREEN-ARMYTAGE. Crown 8vo, 10s. 6d. net.

ATKINSON. Local Government in Scotland. By MABEL ATKINSON, M.A. In 1 vol. demy 8vo, 5s. net.

AYTOUN.

Lays of the Scottish Cavaliers, and other Poems. By W. EDMONDSTOUNE AYTOUN, D.C.L., Professor of Rhetoric and Belles-Lettres in the University of Edinburgh. New Edition. Fcap. 8vo, 3s. 6d.

CHEAP EDITION. 1s. Cloth, 1s. 3d.

An Illustrated Edition of the Lays of the Scottish Cavaliers From designs by Sir NOEL PATON. Cheaper Edition. Small 4to, 10s. 6d.

BADEN-POWELL. Ballooning as a Sport. By Major B. BADEN-POWELL. With Illustrations. Crown 8vo, 3s. 6d. net.

BANKS. The Ethics of Work and Wealth. By D. C. BANKS. Crown 8vo, 5s. net.

BARBOUR. Thoughts from the Writings of R. W. BARBOUR. Pott 8vo, limp leather, 2s. 6d. net.

BARBOUR. A History of William Paterson and the Darien Company. With Illustrations and Appendices. By JAMES SAMUEL BARBOUR. Crown 8vo, 6s. net.

BARCLAY. A New Theory of Organic Evolution. By JAMES W. BARCLAY. In 1 vol. crown 8vo, 3s. 6d. net.

"BARFLEUR" Naval Policy. A Plea for the Study of War. By "Barfleur." Demy 8vo, 7s. 6d. net.

BARRINGTON.

The King's Fool. By MICHAEL BARRINGTON. Crown 8vo, 6s.

The Reminiscences of Sir Barrington Beaumont, Bart. A Novel. Crown 8vo, 6s.

BARTLETT.

The Siege and Capitulation of Port Arthur. By E. ASHMEAD BARTLETT. Demy 8vo, 21s. net.

The Immortals and the Channel Tunnel: A Discussion in Valhalla. Demy 8vo, 1s. net.

BELLESHEIM. History of the Catholic Church of Scotland. From the Introduction of Christianity to the Present Day. By ALPHONS BELLESHEIM, D.D., Canon of Aix-la-Chapelle. Translated, with Notes and Additions, by D. OSWALD HUNTER BLAIR, O.S.B., Monk of Fort Augustus. Cheap Edition. Complete in 4 vols. demy 8vo, with Maps. Price 21s. net.

BLACK. The Scots Churches in England. By KENNETH MACLEOD BLACK. Crown 8vo, 5s. net.

BLACKBURN.

A Burgher Quixote. By DOUGLAS BLACKBURN, Author of 'Prinsloo of Prinsloosdorp.' Second Impression. With Frontispiece. Crown 8vo, 6s.

Richard Hartley: Prospector. Crown 8vo, 6s.

BLACKWOOD.

Annals of a Publishing House. William Blackwood and his Sons; Their Magazine and Friends. By Mrs OLIPHANT. With Four Portraits. Third Edition. Demy 8vo. Vols. I. and II. £2, 2s.

Annals of a Publishing House. Vol. III. John Blackwood. By his Daughter Mrs BLACKWOOD PORTER. With 2 Portraits and View of Strathtyrum. Demy 8vo, 21s.

Blackwood's Magazine, from Commencement in 1817 to June 1906. Nos. 1 to 1088, forming 179 Volumes.

Tales from Blackwood. First Series. Price One Shilling each in Paper Cover. Sold separately at all Railway Bookstalls.

They may also be had bound in 12 vols., cloth, 18s. Half calf, richly gilt, 30s. Or the 12 vols. in 6, roxburghe, 21s. Half red morocco, 28s.

BLACKWOOD.

Tales from Blackwood. Second Series. Complete in Twenty-four Shilling Parts. Handsomely bound in 12 vols., cloth, 30s. In leather back, roxburghe style, 37s. 6d. Half calf, gilt, 52s. 6d. Half morocco, 55s.

Tales from Blackwood. Third Series. Complete in Twelve Shilling Parts. Handsomely bound in 6 vols., cloth, 15s.; and in 12 vols. cloth, 18s. The 6 vols. in roxburghe 21s. Half calf, 25s. Half morocco, 28s.

Travel, Adventure, and Sport. From 'Blackwood's Magazine. Uniform with 'Tales from Blackwood.' In Twelve Parts, each price 1s. Handsomely bound in 6 vols., cloth, 15s. And in half calf, 25s.

New Educational Series. *See separate Educational Catalogue.*

New Uniform Series of Novels (Copyright).

Crown 8vo, cloth. Price 3s. 6d. each. Now ready:—

WENDERHOLME. By P. G. Hamerton.
THE STORY OF MARGRÉDEL. By D. Storrar Meldrum.
MISS MARJORIBANKS. By Mrs Oliphant.
THE PERPETUAL CURATE, and THE RECTOR By the Same.
SALEM CHAPEL, and THE DOCTOR'S FAMILY. By the Same.
A SENSITIVE PLANT. By E. D. Gerard.
LADY LEE'S WIDOWHOOD. By General Sir E. B. Hamley.
KATIE STEWART, and other Stories. By Mrs Oliphant.
VALENTINE AND HIS BROTHER. By the Same.
SONS AND DAUGHTERS. By the Same.
MARMORNE. By P. G. Hamerton.
REATA. By E. D. Gerard.
BEGGAR MY NEIGHBOUR. By the Same.
THE WATERS OF HERCULES. By the Same.
FAIR TO SEE. By L. W. M. Lockhart.
MINE IS THINE. By the Same.
DOUBLES AND QUITS. By the Same.
ALTIORA PETO. By Laurence Oliphant.
PICCADILLY. By the Same. With Illustrations.
LADY BABY. By D. Gerard.
THE BLACKSMITH OF VOE. By Paul Cushing.
MY TRIVIAL LIFE AND MISFORTUNE. By A Plain Woman.
POOR NELLIE. By the Same.

Standard Novels. Uniform in size and binding. Each complete in one Volume.

FLORIN SERIES, Illustrated Boards. Bound in Cloth, 2s. 6d.

TOM CRINGLE'S LOG. By Michael Scott.
THE CRUISE OF THE MIDGE. By the Same.
CYRIL THORNTON. By Captain Hamilton.
ANNALS OF THE PARISH. By John Galt.
THE PROVOST, &c By the Same.
SIR ANDREW WYLIE. By the Same.
THE ENTAIL. By the Same.
MISS MOLLY. By Beatrice May Butt.
REGINALD DALTON. By J. G. Lockhart.
PEN OWEN. By Dean Hook.
ADAM BLAIR. By J. G. Lockhart.
LADY LEE'S WIDOWHOOD. By General Sir E. B. Hamley.
SALEM CHAPEL. By Mrs Oliphant.
THE PERPETUAL CURATE. By the Same.
MISS MARJORIBANKS. By the Same.
JOHN: A Love Story. By the Same.

SHILLING SERIES, Illustrated Cover. Bound in Cloth, 1s. 6d.

THE RECTOR, and THE DOCTOR'S FAMILY. By Mrs Oliphant.
THE LIFE OF MANSIE WAUCH. By D. M. Moir
PENINSULAR SCENES AND SKETCHES. By F. Hardman.
SIR FRIZZLE PUMPKIN, NIGHTS AT MESS, &c.
THE SUBALTERN.
LIFE IN THE FAR WEST. By G. F. Ruxton.
VALERIUS: A Roman Story. By J. G. Lockhart.

BON GAULTIER'S BOOK OF BALLADS. A new Edition, with Autobiographical Introduction by Sir THEODORE MARTIN, K.C.B. With Illustrations by Doyle, Leech, and Crowquill. Small quarto, 5s. net.

BOWHILL. Questions and Answers in the Theory and Practice of Military Topography. By Major J. H. BOWHILL. Crown 8vo, 4s. 6d. net. Portfolio containing 34 working plans and diagrams, 3s. 6d. net.

BRUCE. In the Footsteps of Marco Polo. Being the Account of a Journey Overland from Simla to Pekin. By Major CLARENCE DALRYMPLE BRUCE. With Illustrations. Demy 8vo, 21s. net.

BRUCE. Life of John Collingwood Bruce. By Right Hon. Sir GAINSFORD BRUCE. Demy 8vo, 5s. net.

BRUCE. Our Heritage: Individual, Social, and Religious. By W. S. BRUCE, D.D., Croall Lecturer for 1903. Crown 8vo, 2s. 6d. net.

BUCHAN.

The Watcher by the Threshold, and other Tales. By JOHN BUCHAN. Second Impression. Crown 8vo, 6s.

A Lodge in the Wilderness. Second Impression. Short demy 8vo, 6s.

BURBIDGE.

Domestic Floriculture, Window Gardening, and Floral Decorations. Being Practical Directions for the Propagation, Culture, and Arrangement of Plants and Flowers as Domestic Ornaments. By F. W. BURBIDGE. Second Edition. Crown 8vo, with numerous Illustrations, 7s. 6d.

BURTON.

The History of Scotland: From Agricola's Invasion to the Extinction of the last Jacobite Insurrection. By JOHN HILL BURTON, D.C.L., Historiographer-Royal for Scotland. Cheaper Edition. In 8 vols. Crown 8vo, 2s. 6d. net each. Being issued in Monthly volumes.

The Book-Hunter. A New Edition, with specially designed Title-page and Cover by JOSEPH BROWN. Printed on antique laid paper. Post 8vo, 3s. 6d.

The Scot Abroad. Uniform with 'The Book-Hunter.' Post 8vo, 3s. 6d.

BUTE.

The Roman Breviary: Reformed by Order of the Holy Œcumenical Council of Trent; Published by Order of Pope St Pius V.; and Revised by Clement VIII. and Urban VIII.; together with the Offices since granted. Translated out of Latin into English by JOHN, MARQUESS OF BUTE, K.T. New Edition, Revised and Enlarged. In 4 vols. crown 8vo, and in 1 vol. crown 4to. [*In the press.*

The Altus of St Columba. With a Prose Paraphrase and Notes By JOHN, MARQUESS OF BUTE, K.T. In paper cover, 2s. 6d.

Sermones, Fratris Adæ, Ordinis Præmonstratensis, &c. Twenty-eight Discourses of Adam Scotus of Whithorn, hitherto unpublished; to which is added a Collection of Notes by the same, illustrative of the rule of St Augustine. Edited, at the desire of the late MARQUESS OF BUTE, K.T., LL.D., &c., by WALTER DE GRAY BIRCH, LL.D., F.S.A., of the British Museum, &c. Royal 8vo, 25s. net.

Catalogue of a Collection of Original MSS. formerly belonging to the Holy Office of the Inquisition in the Canary Islands. Prepared under the direction of the late MARQUESS OF BUTE, K.T., LL.D., by WALTER DE GRAY BIRCH, LL.D., F.S.A. 2 vols. royal 8vo, £3, 3s. net.

BUTE, MACPHAIL, AND LONSDALE. **The Arms of the** Royal and Parliamentary Burghs of Scotland. By JOHN, MARQUESS OF BUTE, K.T., J. R. N. MACPHAIL, and H. W. LONSDALE. With 131 Engravings on wood, and 11 other Illustrations. Crown 4to. £2, 2s. net.

BUTE, STEVENSON, AND LONSDALE. The Arms of the Baronial and Police Burghs of Scotland. By JOHN, MARQUESS OF BUTE, K.T., J. H. STEVENSON, and H. W. LONSDALE. With numerous Illustrations. Crown 4to, £2, 2s. net.

CAIRD. Sermons. By JOHN CAIRD, D.D., Principal of the University of Glasgow. Seventeenth Thousand. Fcap. 8vo, 5s.

CALDWELL. Schopenhauer's System in its Philosophical Significance (the Shaw Fellowship Lectures, 1893). By Professor WILLIAM CALDWELL, D.Sc., M'Gill University, Montreal. Demy 8vo, 10s. 6d. net.

CALLWELL.

The Effect of Maritime Command on Land Campaigns since Waterloo. By Lt.-Col. C. E. CALLWELL, R.G.A. With Plans. Post 8vo, 6s. net.

Tactics of To-day. Sixth Impression. Crown 8vo, 2s. 6d. net.

Military Operations and Maritime Preponderance: Their Relations and Interdependence. Demy 8vo, 15s. net.

CAMPBELL. Balmerino and its Abbey. A Parish History, With Notices of the Adjacent District. By JAMES CAMPBELL, D.D., F.S.A. Scot., Minister of Balmerino; Author of 'A History of the Celtic Church in Scotland.' A New Edition. With an Appendix of Illustrative Documents, a Map of the Parish, and upwards of 40 Illustrations. Demy 8vo, 30s. net.

CAREY.

Monsieur Martin: A Romance of the Great Northern War. By WYMOND CAREY. Crown 8vo, 6s.

"No. 101." Third Impression. Crown 8vo, 6s. Cheap Edition, royal 8vo, paper covers, 6d.

CARLYLE. A History of Mediæval Political Theory in the West. By R. W. CARLYLE, C.I.E., Balliol College, Oxford; and A. J. CARLYLE, M.A., Chaplain and Lecturer (late Fellow) of University College, Oxford. In 3 vols. demy 8vo. Vol. I.—A History of Political Theory from the Roman Lawyers of the Second Century to the Political Writers of the Ninth. By A. J. CARLYLE. 15s. net.

CHESNEY. The Dilemma. By General Sir GEORGE CHESNEY, K.C.B. A New Edition. Crown 8vo, 2s.

CHURCH SERVICE SOCIETY.

A Book of Common Order: being Forms of Worship issued by the Church Service Society. Seventh Edition, carefully revised. In 1 vol. crown 8vo, cloth, 3s. 6d.; French morocco, 5s. Also in 2 vols. crown 8vo, cloth, 4s.; French morocco, 6s. 6d.

Daily Offices for Morning and Evening Prayer throughout the Week. Crown 8vo, 3s. 6d.

Order of Divine Service for Children. Issued by the Church Service Society. With Scottish Hymnal. Cloth, 3d.

CLIFFORD.

Sally: A Study; and other Tales of the Outskirts. By HUGH CLIFFORD, C.M.G. Crown 8vo, 6s.

Bush-Whacking, and other Sketches. Second Impression. Crown 8vo, 6s.

CLODD. Thomas Henry Huxley. "Modern English Writers." By EDWARD CLODD. Crown 8vo, 2s. 6d.

CLOUSTON.

The Lunatic at Large. By J. STORER CLOUSTON. Fourth Impression. Crown 8vo, 6s. CHEAP EDITION, royal 8vo, paper cover, 6d.

Count Bunker: Being a Sequel to 'The Lunatic at Large.' Crown 8vo, 6s. CHEAP EDITION, royal 8vo, papers covers, 6d.

The Adventures of M. D'Haricot. Second Impression. Crown 8vo, 6s. CHEAP EDITION, royal 8vo, paper cover, 6d.

Our Lady's Inn. Crown 8vo, 6s.

Garmiscath. Crown 8vo, 6s.

CONNELL. The Young Days of Admiral Qulliam. By F. NORREYS CONNELL. Crown 8vo, 6s.

CONRAD.

Lord Jim. A Tale. By JOSEPH CONRAD, Author of 'The Nigger of the Narcissus,' 'An Outcast of the Islands,' 'Tales of Unrest,' &c. Second Impression. Crown 8vo, 6s.

Youth: A Narrative; and Two other Stories. Second Impression. Crown 8vo, 6s.

COOPER. Liturgy of 1637, commonly called Laud's Liturgy. Edited by the Rev. Professor COOPER, D.D., Glasgow. Crown 8vo, 7s. 6d. net.

CORNFORD. R. L. Stevenson. "Modern English Writers." By L. COPE CORNFORD. Second Edition. Crown 8vo, 2s. 6d.

COUNTY HISTORIES OF SCOTLAND. In demy 8vo volumes of about 350 pp. each. With Maps. Price 7s. 6d. net.

Fife and Kinross. By ÆNEAS J. G. MACKAY, LL.D., Sheriff of these Counties.

Dumfries and Galloway. By Sir HERBERT MAXWELL, Bart., M.P. Second Edition.

Moray and Nairn. By CHARLES RAMPINI, LL.D., Sheriff of Dumfries and Galloway.

Inverness. By J. CAMERON LEES, D.D.

Roxburgh, Selkirk, and Peebles. By Sir GEORGE DOUGLAS, Bart.

Aberdeen and Banff. By WILLIAM WATT, Editor of Aberdeen 'Daily Free Press.'

Perth and Clackmannan. By JOHN CHISHOLM, M.A., Advocate. [*In the press.*

CRAIK. A Century of Scottish History. From the Days before the '45 to those within living Memory. By Sir HENRY CRAIK, K.C.B., M.A. (Oxon.), Hon. LL.D. (Glasgow). 2 vols. demy 8vo, 30s. net.

CRAWFORD. **Saracinesca. By F. MARION CRAWFORD, Author of 'Mr Isaacs,' &c., &c. Crown 8vo, 3s. 6d.** Also at 6d.

CROSS.

Impressions of Dante and of the New World. By J. W. CROSS. Post 8vo, 6s.

The Rake's Progress in Finance. Crown 8vo, 2s. net.

CUMMING.

Memories. By C. F. GORDON CUMMING. Demy 8vo. Illustrated, 20s net.

At Home in Fiji. Post 8vo. Illustrated. Cheap Edition, 6s.

A Lady's Cruise in a French Man-of-War. Post 8vo. Illustrated. Cheap Edition. 6s.

Fire-Fountains. 2 vols. post 8vo. Illustrated, 25s.

Granite Crags. Post 8vo. Illustrated. Cheap Edition. 6s.

Wanderings in China. Small post 8vo. Cheap Edition. 6s.

DAVIDSON. Herbart's Psychology and Educational Theory. By JOHN DAVIDSON. Demy 8vo, 5s. net.

DAVIS. "When Half-Gods Go." By JESSIE AINSWORTH DAVIS. Crown 8vo, 6s.

DILNOT. Scoundrel Mark. By FRANK DILNOT. Crown 8vo, 6s.

DIVER. Captain Desmond, V.C. By M. DIVER. Crown 8vo, 6s.

DODDS AND MACPHERSON. The Licensing Acts (Scotland) Consolidation and Amendment Act, 1903. Annotated by Mr J. M. DODDS, of the Scottish Office; Joint-Editor of the 'Parish Council Guide for Scotland,' and Mr EWAN MACPHERSON, Advocate, Legal Secretary to the Lord Advocate. In 1 vol. crown 8vo, 5s. net.

DOUGLAS.

The Ethics of John Stuart Mill. By CHARLES DOUGLAS, M.A., D.Sc., M.P., late Lecturer in Moral Philosophy, and Assistant to the Professor of Moral Philosophy in the University of Edinburgh. Post 8vo, 6s. net.

John Stuart Mill: A Study of his Philosophy. Crown 8vo, 4s. 6d. net.

DOWNEY. Charles Lever: His Life in his Letters. By EDMUND DOWNEY. With Portraits. Demy 8vo, 2 vols., 21s. net.

DUFF. An Exposition of Browning's 'Sordello.' With Historical and other Notes. By DAVID DUFF, B.D. Demy 8vo, 10s. 6d. net.

ECCOTT.

Fortune's Castaway. By W. J. ECCOTT. Crown 8vo, 6s.

His Indolence of Arras. Crown 8vo, 6s. Cheap Edition, royal 8vo, paper cover, 6d.

Hearth of Hutton. Crown 8vo, 6s.

ELIOT.

The New Popular Edition of George Eliot's Works, with Photogravure Frontispiece to each Volume, from Drawings by William Hatherell, R.I., Edgar Bundy, R.I., Byam Shaw, R.I., A. A. Van Anrooy, Maurice Greiffenhagen, Claude A. Shepperson, R.I., E. J. Sullivan, and Max Cowper. Each Work complete in One Volume. Handsomely bound, gilt top. 3s. 6d. net. Ten Volumes in all.

ADAM BEDE.
SCENES OF CLERICAL LIFE.
THE MILL ON THE FLOSS.
FELIX HOLT, THE RADICAL.
MIDDLEMARCH.
SILAS MARNER; BROTHER JACOB; THE LIFTED VEIL.
ROMOLA.
DANIEL DERONDA.
THE SPANISH GYPSY; JUBAL.
ESSAYS; THEOPHRASTUS SUCH.

George Eliot's Life. With Portrait and other Illustrations. New Edition, in one volume. Crown 8vo, 7s. 6d.

Life and Works of George Eliot (Warwick Edition). 14 volumes, cloth, limp, gilt top, 2s. net per volume; leather, limp, gilt top, 2s. 6d. net per volume; leather gilt top, with book-marker, 3s. net per volume.

ADAM BEDE. 826 pp.
THE MILL ON THE FLOSS. 828 pp.
FELIX HOLT, THE RADICAL. 718 pp.
ROMOLA. 900 pp.
SCENES OF CLERICAL LIFE. 624 pp.
SILAS MARNER; BROTHER JACOB; THE LIFTED VEIL. 560 pp.
MIDDLEMARCH. 2 vols. 664 and 630 pp.
DANIEL DERONDA. 2 vols. 616 and 636 pp.
THE SPANISH GYPSY; JUBAL
ESSAYS; THEOPHRASTUS SUCH.
LIFE. 2 vols., 626 and 580 pp.

Works of George Eliot (Standard Edition). 21 volumes, crown 8vo. In buckram cloth, gilt top, 2s. 6d. per vol.; or in roxburghe binding, 3s. 6d. per vol.

ADAM BEDE. 2 vols.—THE MILL ON THE FLOSS. 2 vols.—FELIX HOLT, THE RADICAL. 2 vols.—ROMOLA. 2 vols.—SCENES OF CLERICAL LIFE. 2 vols.—MIDDLEMARCH. 3 vols.—DANIEL DERONDA. 3 vols.—SILAS MARNER. 1 vol.—JUBAL. 1 vol.—THE SPANISH GYPSY. 1 vol.—ESSAYS. 1 vol.—THEOPHRASTUS SUCH. 1 vol.

Life and Works of George Eliot (Cabinet Edition). 24 volumes, crown 8vo, price £6. Also to be had handsomely bound in half and full calf. The Volumes are sold separately, bound in cloth, price 5s. each.

Novels by George Eliot. Popular Copyright Edition. In new uniform binding, price 3s. 6d. each.

ADAM BEDE.
THE MILL ON THE FLOSS.
SCENES OF CLERICAL LIFE.
ROMOLA.
FELIX HOLT, THE RADICAL.
SILAS MARNER; THE LIFTED VEIL; BROTHER JACOB.
MIDDLEMARCH.
DANIEL DERONDA.

Essays. New Edition. Crown 8vo, 5s.

Impressions of Theophrastus Such. New Edition. Crown 8vo, 5s.

The Spanish Gypsy. New Edition. Crown 8vo, 5s.

The Legend of Jubal, and other Poems, Old and New. New Edition. Crown 8vo, 5s.

Silas Marner. **New Edition, with Illustrations by Reginald** Birch. Crown 8vo, 1s. 6d. net. Cheap Edition, 2s. 6d. Cheap Edition, royal 8vo, paper cover, price 6d.

Scenes of Clerical Life. Pocket Edition, 3 vols. pott 8vo, 1s. net each; bound in leather, 1s. 6d. net each. Cheap Edition, 3s. Illustrated Edition, with 20 Illustrations by H. R. Millar, crown 8vo, 2s.; paper covers, 1s. Cheap Edition, royal 8vo, in paper cover, price 6d.

Felix Holt. Cheap Edition. Royal 8vo, in paper cover, 6d.

Adam Bede. Pocket Edition. In 1 vol. pott 8vo, 1s. net; bound in leather, in 3 vols., 4s. 6d. net. Cheap Edition, royal 8vo, in paper cover, price 6d. New Edition, crown 8vo, paper cover, 1s.; crown 8vo, with Illustrations, cloth, 2s.

ELIOT.
The Mill on the Floss. Pocket Edition, in 1 vol. pott 8vo, 1s. net, limp leather, 4s. 6d. net. Cheap Edition, royal 8vo, in paper cover, price 6d. New Edition, paper covers, 1s.; cloth, 2s.
Romola. Cheap Edition. Royal 8vo, in paper cover, price 6d.
Silas Marner; Brother Jacob; Lifted Veil. Pocket Edition. Pott 8vo, cloth, 1s. net; limp leather, 2s. 3d. net.
Wise, Witty, and Tender Sayings, in Prose and Verse. Selected from the Works of George Eliot. New Edition. Fcap. 8vo, 3s. 6d.

ELLIS.
Barbara Winslow, Rebel. By Beth Ellis. Crown 8vo, 6s.
Madame, Will You Walk? Crown 8vo, 6s.
Blind Mouths. Crown 8vo, 6s.

ELTON. **The Augustan Ages. "Periods of European Literature."** By Oliver Elton, B.A., Lecturer in English Literature, Owen's College, Manchester. Crown 8vo, 5s. net.

EVERARD. History of the Royal and Ancient Golf Club, St Andrews. By H. S. C. Everard. With Eight Coloured Portraits, and many other Unique Illustrations. Crown 4to, 21s. net.

FAHIE. A History of Wireless Telegraphy. Including some Bare-wire Proposals for Subaqueous Telegraphs. By J. J. Fahie, Member of the Institution of Electrical Engineers, London, and of the Société Internationale des Electriciens, Paris; Author of 'A History of Electric Telegraphy to the Year 1837,' &c. With Illustrations. Third Edition, Revised. Crown 8vo, 6s.

FERGUSSON. Scots Poems. By Robert Fergusson. With Photogravure Portrait. Pott 8vo, gilt top, bound in cloth, 1s. net; leather, 1s. 6d. net.

FERRIER. **Philosophical Remains.** Crown 8vo, 14s.

FLINT.
Philosophy as Scientia Scientiarum. A History of Classifications of the Sciences. By Robert Flint, Corresponding Member of the Institute of France, Hon. Member of the Royal Society of Palermo, Professor in the University of Edinburgh, &c. 12s. 6d. net.
Studies on Theological, Biblical, and other Subjects. 7s. 6d. net.
Historical Philosophy in France and French Belgium and Switzerland. 8vo, 21s.
Agnosticism. Demy 8vo, 18s. net.
Theism. Being the Baird Lecture for 1876. Tenth Edition, Revised. Crown 8vo, 7s. 6d.
Anti-Theistic Theories. Being the Baird Lecture for 1877. **Fifth Edition. Crown 8vo, 10s. 6d.**
Sermons and Addresses. Demy 8vo, 7s. 6d

FOREIGN CLASSICS FOR ENGLISH READERS. Edited by Mrs Oliphant. Price 1s. each net. *For List of Volumes, see page 2.*

FORREST.
History of the Indian Mutiny. By G. W. Forrest, C.I.E. Ex-Director of Records, Government of India. 2 vols. demy 8vo, 38s. net.
Sepoy Generals: Wellington to Roberts. With Portraits. Crown 8vo, 6s.

FORSTER.

Where Angels Fear to Tread. By E. M. FORSTER. Crown 8vo, 6s.

The Longest Journey. Crown 8vo, 6s.

FOULIS.

Erchie: My Droll Friend. By HUGH FOULIS. Paper covers, 6d.; cloth, 1s. 6d. net.

The Vital Spark. Illustrated. 1s. net.

FRANKLIN. My Brilliant Career. By MILES FRANKLIN. Fourth Impression. Crown 8vo, 6s.

FRASER.

Philosophy of Theism. Being the Gifford Lectures delivered before the University of Edinburgh in 1894-96. By ALEXANDER CAMPBELL FRASER, D.C.L. Oxford; Emeritus Professor of Logic and Metaphysics in the University of Edinburgh. Second Edition, Revised. Post 8vo, 6s. 6d. net.

Biographia Philosophica. In 1 vol. demy 8vo, 6s. net.

FRENCH COOKERY FOR ENGLISH HOMES. Third Impression. Crown 8vo, limp cloth, 2s. 6d. Also in limp leather, 3s.

FULTON. The Sovereignty of the Sea. An Historical Account of the Claims to the exclusive Dominion of the British Seas and of the Evolution of the Territorial Waters, with special reference to the Rights of Fishing. By T. WEMYSS FULTON, M.D., F.R.S.E. With numerous Illustrations and Maps. Demy 8vo. [*In the press.*

GALLOWAY. Studies in the Philosophy of Religion. By GEORGE GALLOWAY, B.D. Demy 8vo, 7s. 6d. net.

GENERAL ASSEMBLY OF THE CHURCH OF SCOTLAND.

Scottish Hymnal, With Appendix Incorporated. Published for use in Churches by Authority of the General Assembly. 1. Large type, cloth, red edges, 2s. 6d.; French morocco, 4s. 2. Bourgeois type, limp cloth, 1s.; French morocco, 2s. 3. Nonpareil type, cloth, red edges, 6d.; French morocco, 1s. 4d. 4. Paper covers, 3d. 5. Sunday-School Edition, paper covers, 1d., cloth, 2d. No. 1, bound with the Psalms and Paraphrases, French morocco, 8s. No. 2, bound with the Psalms and Paraphrases, cloth, 2s.; French morocco, 3s.

Prayers for Social and Family Worship. Prepared by a Special Committee of the General Assembly of the Church of Scotland. Entirely New Edition, Revised and Enlarged. Fcap. 8vo, red edges, 1s. 6d. net.

Prayers for Family Worship. A Selection of Four Weeks' Prayers. New Edition. Authorised by the General Assembly of the Church of Scotland. Fcap. 8vo, red edges 1s. net.

One Hundred Prayers. Prepared by the Committee on Aids to Devotion. 16mo, cloth limp, 6d.

Morning and Evening Prayers for Affixing to Bibles. Prepared by the Committee on Aids to Devotion. 1d. for 6, or 1s. per 100.

Prayers for Soldiers and Sailors. Prepared by the Committee on Aids to Devotion. Thirtieth Thousand. 16mo, cloth limp. 2d. net.

Prayers for Sailors and Fisher-Folk. Prepared and Published by Instruction of the General Assembly of the Church of Scotland. Fcap. 8vo, 1s. net.

GERARD.

Reata: What's in a Name. By E. D. GERARD. Cheap Edition. Crown 8vo, 3s. 6d.

Beggar my Neighbour. Cheap Edition. Crown 8vo, 3s. 6d.

GERARD.

The Waters of Hercules. Cheap Edition. Crown 8vo, 3s. 6d.

A Sensitive Plant. Crown 8vo, 3s. 6d.

GERARD.

Honour's Glassy Bubble. By E. GERARD. Crown 8vo, 6s.

A Foreigner. An Anglo-German Study. Crown 8vo, 6s.

GERARD.

One Year. By DOROTHEA GERARD (Madame Longard de Longgarde). Crown 8vo, 6s.

The Impediment. Crown 8vo, 6s.

A Spotless Reputation. Third Edition. Crown 8vo, 6s.

The Wrong Man. Second Edition. Crown 8vo, 6s

Lady Baby. Cheap Edition. Crown 8vo, 3s. 6d. Cheap Edition, royal 8vo, paper cover, 6d.

Recha. Crown 8vo, 6s.

A Forgotten Sin. Crown 8vo, 6s.

GIBBON.

Souls in Bondage. By PERCEVAL GIBBON. Crown 8vo, 6s. Cheap Edition, royal 8vo, paper cover, 6d.

The Vrouw Grobelaar's Leading Cases. Crown 8vo, 6s.

GILL. The $CHCl_3$-Problem. By RICHARD GILL. 2 vols. crown 8vo, 5s. net each.

GILLANDERS. Forest Entomology. By A. T. GILLANDERS, F.E.S. With Illustrations. Crown 8vo. [*In the press.*

GILLESPIE. The Humour of Scottish Life. By Very Rev. JOHN GILLESPIE, LL.D. Crown 8vo, 3s. 6d. net.

GLEIG. The Subaltern. By Rev. G. R. GLEIG. Fcap. 8vo, 1s. net.

GRAHAM.

Manual of the Elections (Scot.) (Corrupt and Illegal Practices) Act, 1890. With Analysis, Relative Act of Sederunt, Appendix containing the Corrupt Practices Acts of 1883 and 1885, and Copious Index. By J. EDWARD GRAHAM, Advocate. 8vo, 4s. 6d.

A Manual of the Acts relating to Education in Scotland. (Founded on that of the late Mr Craig Sellar.) Demy 8vo, 18s.

GRAHAM AND PATERSON. True Romances of Scotland. By E. MAXTONE GRAHAM and E. PATERSON. Illustrations. Crown 8vo, 5s. net.

GRAND.

A Domestic Experiment. By SARAH GRAND, Author of 'The Heavenly Twins,' 'Ideala: A Study from Life.' Crown 8vo. 6s.

Singularly Deluded. Crown 8vo, 6s.

GRIER.

In Furthest Ind. The Narrative of Mr EDWARD CARLYON of Ellswether, in the County of Northampton, and late of the Honourable East India Company's Service, Gentleman. Wrote by his own hand in the year of grace 1697. Edited, with a few Explanatory Notes. By SYDNEY C. GRIER. Post 8vo, 6s.

His Excellency's English Governess. Third Impression. **Cr. 8vo, 6s.**

GRIER.

An Uncrowned King: A Romance of High Politics. Third Impression. Crown 8vo, 6s.

Peace with Honour. Third Impression. **Crown 8vo, 6s.**

A Crowned Queen: The Romance of a Minister of State. Third Impression. Crown 8vo, 6s.

Like Another Helen. Second Impression. Crown 8vo, 6s.

The Kings of the East: A Romance of the near Future. Second Impression. Crown 8vo, 6s.

The Warden of the Marches. Third Impression. Crown 8vo, 6s. Cheap Edition, paper cover, 6d.

The Prince of the Captivity. Second Impression. Crown 8vo, 6s.

The Advanced-Guard. Third Impression. Crown 8vo, 6s.

The Great Proconsul: The Memoirs of Mrs Hester Ward, formerly in the family of the Hon. Warren Hastings, Esquire, late Governor-General of India. Crown 8vo, 6s.

The Heir. Crown 8vo, 6s.

The Letters of Warren Hastings to his Wife. Demy 8vo, 15s. net.

GRIERSON. The First Half of the Seventeenth Century. (Periods of European Literature.) By Professor H. J. C. GRIERSON. Crown 8vo, 5s. net.

GRIFFIN.

Lady Sarah's Deed of Gift. By E. ACEITUNA GRIFFIN. Crown 8vo, 6s.

A Servant of the King. Crown 8vo, 6s.

GROOT.

Jan Van Dyck. By J. MORGAN-DE-GROOT. Crown 8vo, 6s.

The Bar Sinister. Crown 8vo, 6s.

A Lotus Flower. Crown 8vo, 6s.

HAMLEY.

The Operations of War Explained and Illustrated. By General Sir EDWARD BRUCE HAMLEY, K.C.B., K.C.M.G. Second Edition of Fifth Edition. With Maps and Plans. 4to, 30s. Also in 2 parts: Part I., 10s. 6d.; Part II., 21s.

A New Edition, brought up to the latest requirements. By Colonel L. E. Kiggell. [*In the press*

Thomas Carlyle: An Essay. Second Edition. Crown 8vo, 2s. 6d.

On Outposts. Second Edition. **8vo, 2s.**

Lady Lee's **Widowhood. New Edition.** Crown 8vo, 2s.

Our Poor Relations. A Philozoic Essay. With Illustrations, chiefly by Ernest Griset. Crown 8vo, cloth gilt, 3s. 6d.

HANNAY. The Later Renaissance. "Periods of European Literature." By DAVID HANNAY. Crown 8vo, 5s. net.

HARRADEN.

Ships that Pass in the Night. By BEATRICE HARRADEN. Illustrated Edition. Crown 8vo, 3s. 6d.

HARRADEN.

The Fowler. Illustrated Edition. Crown 8vo, 3s. 6d. Cheap Edition, paper cover, 6d.

In Varying Moods: Short Stories. Illustrated Edition. Crown 8vo, 3s. 6d.

Untold Tales of the Past. With 40 Illustrations by H. R. Millar. Square crown 8vo, gilt top, 5s. net.

Katharine Frensham. Crown 8vo, 6s. Cheap Edition, paper cover, 6d.

HARRIS.

The Disappearance of Dick. By WALTER B. HARRIS. With 17 Illustrations. Crown 8vo, 5s.

The Career of Harold Ensleigh. Crown 8vo, 6s.

HARTLEY. Wild Sport with Gun, Rifle, and Salmon-Rod. By GILFRID W. HARTLEY. With numerous Illustrations in photogravure and half-tone from drawings by G. E. LODGE and others. Demy 8vo, 6s. net.

HAY-NEWTON. Readings on the Evolution of Religion. By Mrs F. HAY-NEWTON. Crown 8vo, 5s.

HEMANS.

The Poetical Works of Mrs Hemans. Copyright Edition. Royal 8vo, with Engravings, cloth, gilt edges, 5s.

Select Poems of Mrs Hemans. Fcap., cloth, gilt edges, 3s.

HENDERSON. The Young Estate Manager's Guide. By RICHARD HENDERSON, Member (by Examination) of the Royal Agricultural Society of England, the Highland and Agricultural Society of Scotland, and the Surveyors' Institution. With an Introduction by R. Patrick Wright, F.R.S.E., Professor of Agriculture, Glasgow and West of Scotland Technical College. With Plans and Diagrams. Crown 8vo, 5s.

HENDERSON. The Minstrelsy of the Scottish Border. By Sir WALTER SCOTT. A New Edition. Edited by T. F. Henderson, Author of 'A History of Scottish Vernacular Literature.' With a New Portrait of Sir Walter Scott. In 4 vols., demy 8vo, £2, 2s. net.

HERFORD. Browning (Modern English Writers). By Professor HERFORD. Crown 8vo, 2s. 6d.

HERKLESS AND HANNAY. The College of St Leonard's. By JOHN HERKLESS and ROBERT KERR HANNAY. Post 8vo, 7s. 6d. net.

HEWISON. The Isle of Bute in the Olden Time. With Illustrations, Maps, and Plans. By JAMES KING HEWISON, D.D., R.S.A. (Scot.), Minister of Rothesay. Vol. I., Celtic Saints and Heroes. Crown 4to, 15s. net. Vol. II., The Royal Stewards and the Brandanes. Crown 4to, 15s. net.

HINTS ON HOCKEY. With Plans and Rules. New Edition Fcap. 8vo, 1s.

HOME PRAYERS. By Ministers of the Church of Scotland and Members of the Church Service Society. Second Edition. Fcap. 8vo, 3s.

HUME. The Globular Jottings of Griselda. By E. DOUGLAS HUME. With Illustrations. Demy 8vo, 10s. net.

HUME. Dialogues concerning Natural Religion. By DAVID HUME. Reprinted, with an Introduction by BRUCE M'EWEN, D.Phil. Crown 8vo, 3s. 6d. net.

HUNT. A Handy Vocabulary: English-Afrikander, Afrikander-English. For the Use of English-speaking People in South Africa. By G. M. G. HUNT. Small 8vo, 1s.

HUTCHINSON. Hints on the Game of Golf. By HORACE G. HUTCHINSON. Twelfth Edition, Revised. Fcap. 8vo, cloth, 1s.

HUTTON. Italy and the Italians. By EDWARD HUTTON. With Illustrations. Second Edition. Large crown 8vo, 6s.

IDDESLEIGH. Life, Letters, and Diaries of Sir Stafford Northcote, First Earl of Iddesleigh. By ANDREW LANG. With Three Portraits and a View of Pynes. Third Edition. 2 vols. post 8vo, 31s. 6d.

POPULAR EDITION. With Portrait and View of Pynes. Post 8vo, 3s. 6d.

INCHBOLD. Phantasma. By A. C. INCHBOLD. Crown 8vo, 6s.

INNES.

Free Church Union Case. Judgment of the House of Lords. With Introduction by A. TAYLOR INNES. Demy 8vo, 1s. net.

The Law of Creeds in Scotland. A Treatise on the Relations of Churches in Scotland, Established and not Established, to the Civil Law. Demy 8vo, 10s. net.

INTELLIGENCE OFFICER.

On the Heels of De Wet. By THE INTELLIGENCE OFFICER. Sixth Impression. Crown 8vo, 6s. Cheap Edition, royal 8vo, paper cover, 6d.

The Boy Galloper. With Illustrations. In 1 vol. cr. 8vo, 6s.

The Yellow War. Crown 8vo, 6s. Cheap Edition, paper cover, 6d.

IRONS. The Psychology of Ethics. By DAVID IRONS, M.A., Ph.D., Professor of Philosophy in Bryn Mawr College, Penn. Crown 8vo, 5s. net.

JAMES. William Wetmore Story and his Friends. From Letters, Diaries, and Recollections. By HENRY JAMES. With 2 Portraits. In two vols. post 8vo, 24s. net.

JAMES.

Modern Strategy. By Lieut.-Col. WALTER H. JAMES, *P.S.C.*, late R.E. With 6 Maps. Second Edition, thoroughly revised and brought up to date. Royal 8vo, 16s. net.

The Campaign of 1815, chiefly in Flanders. Demy 8vo, 10s. 6d. net.

The Development of Tactics from 1740 to the Present Day. Demy 8vo. [*In the press.*

JOHNSTON.

Elements of Agricultural Chemistry. An entirely New Edition from the Edition by Sir CHARLES A. CAMERON, M.D., F.R.C.S.I. &c. Revised and brought down to date by C. M. AIKMAN, M.A., B.Sc., F.R.S.E., Professor of Chemistry, Glasgow Veterinary College. 17th Edition. Crown 8vo, 6s. 6d.

Catechism of Agricultural Chemistry. An entirely New Edition from the Edition by Sir CHARLES A. CAMERON. Revised and Enlarged by C. M. AIKMAN M.A &c. 95th Thousand. With numerous Illustrations. Crown 8vo, 1s.

JOHNSTON. Agricultural Holdings (Scotland) Acts, 1883 to 1900; and the Ground Game Act, 1880. With Notes, and Summary of Procedure, &c. By CHRISTOPHER N. JOHNSTON, M.A., Advocate. Fifth Edition. Demy 8vo, 6s. net.

JOKAI. Timar's Two Worlds. By MAURUS JOKAI. Authorised Translation by Mrs HEGAN KENNARD. Cheap Edition. Crown 8vo, 6s.

JONES. A Maid of Normandy: A Romance of Versailles. By DORA M. JONES. Crown 8vo, 6s.

KENNEDY. Hurrah for the Life of a Sailor! Fifty Years in the Royal Navy. By Admiral Sir WILLIAM KENNEDY, K.C.B. With Illustrations from Sketches by the Author. Fifth Impression. Demy 8vo, 12s. 6d.

CHEAPER EDITION, small demy 8vo, 6s.

KER. The Dark Ages. "Periods of European Literature." By Professor W. P. KER. In 1 vol. crown 8vo. 5s. net.

KERR.

Memories: Grave and Gay. By JOHN KERR, LL.D. With Portrait and other Illustrations. Cheaper Edition, Enlarged. Crown 8vo, 2s. 6d. net.

Other Memories: Old and New. Crown 8vo. 3s. 6d. net.

KINGLAKE.

History of the Invasion of the Crimea. By A. W. KINGLAKE. Complete in 9 vols., crown 8vo. Cheap reissue at 3s. 6d. each.

—— Abridged Edition for Military Students. Revised by Lieut.-Col. Sir GEORGE SYDENHAM CLARKE, K.C.M.G., R.E. Demy 8vo, 15s. net.

———— Atlas to accompany above. Folio, 9s. net.

History of the Invasion of the Crimea. Demy 8vo. Vol. VI. Winter Troubles. With a Map, 16s. Vols. VII. and VIII. From the Morrow of Inkerman to the Death of Lord Raglan. With an Index to the Whole Work. With Maps and Plans. 28s

Eothen. A New Edition, uniform with the Cabinet Edition of the 'History of the Invasion of the Crimea.' 6s.

CHEAPER EDITION. With Portrait and Biographical Sketch of the Author. Crown 8vo, 2s. 6d. net.

KNEIPP. My Water-Cure. As Tested through more than Thirty Years, and Described for the Healing of Diseases and the Preservation of Health. By SEBASTIAN KNEIPP. With a Portrait and other Illustrations. Authorised English Translation from the Thirtieth German Edition, by A. de F. With an Appendix, containing the Latest Developments of Pfarrer Kneipp's System, and a Preface by E. Gerard. Crown 8vo, 3s. 6d.

LANG.

A History of Scotland from the Roman Occupation. By ANDREW LANG. Vol. I. With a Photogravure Frontispiece and Four Maps. Second Edition. Demy 8vo, 15s. net.

Vol. II. With a Photogravure Frontispiece. 15s. net.
Vol. III. With a Photogravure Frontispiece. 15s. net.
Vol. IV. With a Photogravure Frontispiece. 20s. net.

Tennyson. "Modern English Writers." 2nd Ed. Cr. 8vo, 2s. 6d.

Life, Letters, and Diaries of Sir Stafford Northcote, First Earl of Iddesleigh. With Three Portraits and a View of Pynes. Third Edition. 2 vols. post 8vo, 31s. 6d.

POPULAR EDITION. With Portrait and View of Pynes. Post 8vo, 3s. 6d.

The Highlands of Scotland in 1750. From Manuscript 104 in the King's Library, British Museum. With an Introduction by ANDREW LANG. Crown 8vo, 5s. net.

LANG.

The Expansion of the Christian Life. The Duff Lecture for 1897. By the Rev. J. MARSHALL LANG, D.D., Principal of the University of Aberdeen. Crown 8vo, 5s.

The Church and its Social Mission. Being the Baird Lecture for 1901. Crown 8vo, 6s. net.

LAWSON.

British Economics in 1904. By W. R. LAWSON. Crown 8vo, 6s. net.

American Finance. Part First—Domestic. Crown 8vo, 6s. net.

LEHMANN. **Crumbs of Pity, and other Verses; to which are** added Six Lives of Great Men. By R. C. LEHMANN, author of 'Anni Fugaces,' &c. Crown 8vo, 5s. net.

LEIGHTON. **The Life History of British Serpents, and their** Local Distribution in the British Isles. By GERALD R. LEIGHTON, M.D. With 50 Illustrations. Crown 8vo, 5s. net.

LEISHMAN. **The Westminster Directory. Edited, with an Intro**duction and Notes, by the Very Rev. T. LEISHMAN D.D. Crown 8vo 4s. net.

LINDSAY.

Recent Advances in Theistic Philosophy of Religion. By Rev. JAMES LINDSAY, M.A., B.D., B.Sc., F.R.S.E., F.G.S., Minister of the Parish of St Andrew's, Kilmarnock. Demy 8vo, 12s. 6d. net.

The Progressiveness of Modern Christian Thought. Crown 8vo, 6s.

Essays, Literary and Philosophical. Crown 8vo, 3s. 6d.

The Significance of the Old Testament for Modern Theology. Crown 8vo, 1s. net.

The Teaching Function of the Modern Pulpit. Crown 8vo, 1s. net

"LINESMAN." Words by an Eyewitness: The Struggle in Natal. By "LINESMAN." Eleventh Impression, with Three Additional Chapters. Crown 8vo, 6s.

LITURGIES AND ORDERS OF DIVINE SERVICE (CHURCH SERVICE SOCIETY).

The Second Prayer Book of King Edward the Sixth (1552). With Historical Introduction and Notes by the Rev. H. J. WOTHERSPOON, M.A., of St Oswald's Edinburgh; and THE LITURGY OF COMPROMISE. Used in the English Congregation at Frankfort. From an Unpublished MS. Edited by the Rev. G. W. SPROTT, D.D., of North Berwick. 4s. net.

Book of Common Order. Commonly called Knox's Liturgy. Edited by Rev. G. W. SPROTT, D.D. 4s. 6d. net.

Scottish Liturgies of the Reign of James VI. Edited by Rev. G. W. SPROTT, D.D. 4s. net.

Liturgy of 1637. Commonly called Laud's Liturgy. Edited by the Rev. Professor COOPER, D.D. 7s. 6d. net.

The Westminster Directory. Edited by Very Rev. T. LEISHMAN, D.D. 4s. net.

Euchologion. A Book of Common Order: Being Forms of Prayer, and Administration of the Sacraments, and other Ordinances of the Church. Edited by the Rev. G. W. SPROTT, D.D., of North Berwick. 4s. 6d. net.

LOBBAN. An Anthology of English Verse from Chaucer to the Present Day. By J. H. LOBBAN, M.A. Crown 8vo, gilt top, 5s.

LOCKHART.

Doubles and Quits. By LAURENCE W. M. LOCKHART. Cheap Edition. Royal 8vo, paper covers, 6d.

Mine is Thine. New Edition. Crown 8vo, 3s. 6d.

LORIMER. The Author's Progress: or, The Literary Book of the Road. By ADAM LORIMER. Crown 8vo, 5s. net.

LYNDEN-BELL. A Primer of Tactics, Fortification, Topography, and Military Law. By Lieut.-Colonel C. P. LYNDEN-BELL. With Diagrams. Crown 8vo, 3s. net.

MABIE.

Essays on Nature and Culture. By HAMILTON WRIGHT MABIE. With Portrait. Fcap. 8vo, 3s. 6d.

Books and Culture. Fcap. 8vo, 3s. 6d.

M'AULAY. The Safety of the Honours. By ALLAN M'AULAY. Crown 8vo, 6s.

MACDONALD. A Manual of the Criminal Law (Scotland) Procedure Act, 1887. By NORMAN DORAN MACDONALD. Revised by the LORD JUSTICE-CLERK. 8vo, 10s. 6d.

MACKAY. The Return of the Emigrant. By LYDIA MILLER MACKAY. Crown 8vo, 6s.

MACKENZIE. Studies in Roman Law. With Comparative Views of the Laws of France, England, and Scotland. By LORD MACKENZIE, one of the Judges of the Court of Session in Scotland. Seventh Edition, Edited by JOHN KIRKPATRICK, M.A., LL.B., Advocate, Professor of History in the University of Edinburgh. 8vo, 21s.

MACLEOD. The Doctrine and Validity of the Ministry and Sacraments of the National Church of Scotland. By the Very Rev. DONALD MACLEOD, D.D. Being the Baird Lecture for 1903. Crown 8vo, 6s. net.

MACPHERSON.

Books to Read and How to Read Them. By HECTOR MACPHERSON. Second Impression. Crown 8vo, 3s. 6d. net.

A Century's Intellectual Development. Crown 8vo, 6s. net.

MACPHERSON. A Century's Progress in Astronomy. By HECTOR MACPHERSON, Jun. Short demy 8vo, 6s. net.

MAIN. Three Hundred English Sonnets. Chosen and Edited by DAVID M. MAIN. New Edition. Fcap. 8vo, 3s. 6d.

MAIR.

A Digest of Laws and Decisions, Ecclesiastical and Civil, relating to the Constitution, Practice, and Affairs of the Church of Scotland. With Notes and Forms of Procedure. By the Rev. WILLIAM MAIR, D.D., lately Minister of the Parish of Earlston. New Edition, Revised. In 1 vol. crown 8vo, 12s. 6d. net.

Speaking; or, From Voice Production to the Platform and Pulpit. Third Edition, Revised. Crown 8vo, 3s.

MARSHMAN. **History of India. From the Earliest Period to** the present time. By JOHN CLARK MARSHMAN, C.S.I. Third and Cheaper Edition. Post 8vo, with Map, 6s.

MARTIN.

Poems of Giacomo Leopardi. Translated by Sir THEODORE MARTIN, K.C.B. Crown 8vo, 5s. net.

The Æneid of Virgil. Books I.-VI. Translated by Sir THEO- DORE MARTIN, K.C.B. Post 8vo, 7s. 6d.

Goethe's Faust. Part I. Translated into English Verse. Second Edition, crown 8vo, 6s. Ninth Edition, fcap. 8vo, 3s. 6d.

Goethe's Faust. Part II. Translated into English Verse. Second Edition, Revised. Fcap. 8vo, 6s.

The Works of Horace. Translated into English Verse, with Life and Notes. 2 vols. New Edition. Crown 8vo, 21s.

Poems and Ballads of Heinrich Heine. Done into English Verse. Third Edition. Small crown 8vo, 5s.

The Song of the Bell, and other Translations from Schiller, Goethe, Uhland, and Others. Crown 8vo, 7s. 6d.

Madonna Pia: A Tragedy; and Three Other Dramas. Crown 8vo. 7s. 6d.

Catullus. With Life and Notes. Second Edition, Revised and Corrected. Post 8vo, 7s. 6d.

The 'Vita Nuova' of Dante. Translated with an Introduction and Notes. Fourth Edition. Small crown 8vo, 5s.

Aladdin: A Dramatic Poem. By ADAM OEHLENSCHLAEGER. Fcap. 8vo, 5s.

Correggio: A Tragedy. By OEHLENSCHLAEGER. With Notes. Fcap. 8vo, 3s.

Helena Faucit (Lady Martin). By Sir THEODORE MARTIN, K.C.B., K.C.V.O. With Five Photogravure Plates. Second Edition. Demy 8vo 10s. 6d. net.

MARTIN. **On some of Shakespeare's Female Characters. By** HELENA FAUCIT, Lady MARTIN. *Dedicated by permission to Her Most Gracious Majesty the Queen.* With a Portrait by Lehmann. Seventh Edition, with a new Preface. Demy 8vo, 7s. 6d.

MATHESON.

Can the Old Faith Live with the New? or, The Problem of Evolution and Revelation. By the Rev. GEORGE MATHESON, D.D. Third Edition. Crown 8vo, 7s. 6d.

The Psalmist and the Scientist; or, Modern Value of the Religious Sentiment. Third Edition. Crown 8vo, 5s.

Spiritual Development of St Paul. Fourth Edition. Cr. 8vo, 5s.

The Distinctive Messages of the Old Religions. Second Edition. Crown 8vo, 5s.

Sacred Songs. Third Edition. Crown 8vo, 2s. 6d.

MAUGHAM. Richard Hawkwood. By H. N. MAUGHAM. A Romance. Crown 8vo, 6s.

MAXWELL.

Dumfries and Galloway. By Right Hon. Sir HERBERT MAXWELL, Bart. Being one of the Volumes of the County Histories of Scotland. With Four Maps. Second Edition. Demy 8vo, 7s. 6d. net.

Scottish Land-Names: Their Origin and Meaning. Being the Rhind Lectures in Archæology for 1893. Post 8vo, 6s.

The Chevalier of the Splendid Crest. Third Edition. Crown 8vo, 6s.

MAXWELL. In Malay Forests. By GEORGE MAXWELL. Crown 8vo, 6s. net.

MELDRUM.

The Conquest of Charlotte. By DAVID S. MELDRUM. Third Impression. Crown 8vo, 6s.

Holland and the Hollanders. With numerous Illustrations and a Map. Second Edition. Square 8vo, 6s.

The Story of Margrédel: Being a Fireside History of a Fifeshire Family. Cheap Edition Crown 8vo, 3s. 6d.

Grey Mantle and Gold Fringe. Crown 8vo, 6s.

MELLONE.

Studies in Philosophical Criticism and Construction. By SYDNEY HERBERT MELLONE, M.A. Lond., D.Sc. Edin. Post 8vo, 10s. 6d. net.

Leaders of Religious Thought in the Nineteenth Century. Crown 8vo, 6s. net.

An Introductory Text-Book of Logic. Second Edition, Revised. Crown 8vo, 5s.

MERZ. **A History of European Thought in the Nineteenth Century.** By JOHN THEODORE MERZ. Vol. I., post 8vo, 10s. 6d. net. Vol. II., 15s. net.

MEYNELL. John Ruskin. "Modern English Writers." By Mrs MEYNELL. Third Impression. Crown 8vo. 2s. 6d.

MICHIE. The Englishman in China during the Victorian Era. As Illustrated in the Life of Sir Rutherford Alcock, K.C.B., D.C.L. By ALEXANDER MICHIE. With Illustrations, Portraits, and Maps. 2 vols. demy 8vo, 38s. net.

MICKLETHWAIT. The Licensing Act, 1904. By St J. G. MICKLETHWAIT, M.A., B.C.L., Barrister-at-Law. Crown 8vo, 2s. 6d. net.

MILL.

The Colonel Sahib. A Novel. By GARRETT MILL. Second Impression. Crown 8vo, 6s.

Ottavia. Second Impression. Crown 8vo, 6s.

Mr Montgomery: Fool. Crown 8vo, 6s.

In the Hands of the Czar. Crown 8vo, 6s.

The Cardinal's Secret. Crown 8vo, 6s.

MILLAR. The Mid-Eighteenth Century. "Periods of European Literature." By J. H. MILLAR. Crown 8vo, 5s. net.

MILN. A Woman and Her Talent. By LOUISE JORDAN MILN. Crown 8vo, 6s.

MITCHELL. The Scottish Reformation. Being the Baird Lecture for 1899. By the late ALEXANDER F. MITCHELL, D.D., LL.D. Edited by D. HAY FLEMING, LL.D. With a Biographical Sketch of the Author, by James Christie, D.D. Crown 8vo, 6s.

MODERN ENGLISH WRITERS. In handy crown 8vo volumes, tastefully bound, price 2s. 6d. each.

Matthew Arnold. By Professor SAINTSBURY. Second Impression.

R. L. Stevenson. By L. COPE CORNFORD. Second Impression.

John Ruskin. By Mrs MEYNELL. Third Impression.

Tennyson. By ANDREW LANG. Second Edition.

Huxley. By EDWARD CLODD.

Thackeray. By CHARLES WHIBLEY.

Browning. By Prof. C. H. HERFORD.

In Preparation.

GEORGE ELIOT. By A. T. Quiller-Couch. | FROUDE. By John Oliver Hobbes.

MOIR. Life of Mansie Wauch, Tailor in Dalkeith. By D. M. MOIR. With CRUIKSHANK'S Illustrations. Cheaper Edition. Crown 8vo, 2s. 6d.

MOMERIE.

Dr Alfred Momerie. His Life and Work. By Mrs MOMERIE. Demy 8vo, 12s. 6d. net.

The Origin of Evil, and other Sermons. By Rev. ALFRED WILLIAMS MOMERIE, M.A., D.Sc., LL.D. Eighth Edition, Enlarged. Crown 8vo, 5s.

Personality. The Beginning and End of Metaphysics, and a Necessary Assumption in all Positive Philosophy. Fifth Ed., Revised. Cr. 8vo, 3s.

Agnosticism. Fourth Edition, Revised. Crown 8vo, 5s.

Preaching and Hearing; and other Sermons. Fourth Edition, Enlarged. Crown 8vo, 5s.

Belief in God. Fourth Edition. Crown 8vo, 3s.

The Future of Religion, and other Essays. Second Edition. Crown 8vo, 3s. 6d.

The English Church and the Romish Schism. Second Edition. Crown 8vo, 2s. 6d.

Essays on the Bible. Crown 8vo. [*In the press.*

MONTAGUE. Military Topography. Illustrated by Practical Examples of a Practical Subject. By Major-General W. E. MONTAGUE, C.B., *P.S.C.*, late Garrison Instructor Intelligence Department, Author of 'Campaigning in South Africa.' With Forty-one Diagrams. Crown 8vo, 5s.

MONTAGUE. Tales from the Talmud. By G. R. MONTAGUE. Crown 8vo, 6s.

MUNRO. The Daft Days. By NEIL MUNRO. Crown 8vo, 6s.

Uniform Edition Novels.

John Splendid. The Tale of a Poor Gentleman and the Little Wars of Lorn. Sixth Impression. Crown 8vo, 3s. 6d.

Children of Tempest: A Tale of the Outer Isles. Crown 8vo, 3s. 6d.

Shoes of Fortune. Crown 8vo, 3s. 6d.

The Lost Pibroch, and other Sheiling Stories. Fourth Impression. Crown 8vo, 3s. 6d.

Doom Castle: A Romance. Second Impression. Crown 8vo, 3s. 6d.

Gilian the Dreamer. Crown 8vo, 3s. 6d.

MUNRO.

Rambles and Studies in Bosnia-Herzegovina and Dalmatia. By ROBERT MUNRO, M.A., M.D., LL.D., F.R.S.E. Second Edition, Revised and Enlarged. With numerous illustrations. Demy 8vo, 12s. 6d. net.

Prehistoric Problems. With numerous Illustrations. Demy 8vo, 10s. net.

MUNRO. On Valuation of Property. By WILLIAM MUNRO, M.A., Her Majesty's Assessor of Railways and Canals for Scotland. Second Edition, Revised and Enlarged. 8vo, 3s. 6d.

MY TRIVIAL LIFE AND MISFORTUNE: A Gossip with no Plot in Particular. By A PLAIN WOMAN. Cheap Edition. Crown 8vo, 3s. 6d.

By the SAME AUTHOR.

POOR NELLIE. Cheap Edition. Crown 8vo, 3s. 6d.

MYRES. A Manual of Classical Geography. By JOHN L. MYRES. Crown 8vo. [*In the press.*

NEWCOMBE. Village, Town, and Jungle Life in India By A. C. NEWCOMBE. Demy 8vo, 12s. 6d. net.

NICHOLSON AND LYDEKKER.

A Manual of Palæontology, for the Use of Students. With a General Introduction on the Principles of Palæontology. By Professor H. ALLEYNE NICHOLSON and RICHARD LYDEKKER, B.A. Third Edition, entirely Rewritten and greatly Enlarged. 2 vols. 8vo, £3, 3s.

NICOL. Recent Archæology and the Bible. Being the Croall Lectures for 1898. By the Rev. THOMAS NICOL, D.D., Professor of Divinity and Biblical Criticism in the University of Aberdeen; Author of 'Recent Explorations in Bible Lands.' Demy 8vo, 9s. net.

NISBET. The Forester: A Practical Treatise on British Forestry and Arboriculture for Landowners, Land Agents, and Foresters. By JOHN NISBET, D.Œc. In 2 volumes, royal 8vo, with 285 Illustrations, 42s. net.

NOBLE.

The Edge of Circumstance. By EDWARD NOBLE. Crown 8vo, 6s. Cheap Edition, royal 8vo, paper cover, 6d.

Waves of Fate. Crown 8vo, 6s.

Fisherman's Gat: A Story of the Thames Estuary Crown 8vo, 6s.

NOYES.

Poems by ALFRED NOYES. 7s. 6d. net.

The Forest of Wild Thyme: A Tale for Children under Ninety. Crown 8vo, 5s. net.

Drake: An English Epic. Books I.-III. Crown 8vo, 5s. net.

O. The Yellow War. By O. Crown 8vo, 6s. Cheap Edition. Royal 8vo, 6d.

OLIPHANT.

Masollam: A Problem of the Period. A Novel. By LAURENCE OLIPHANT. 3 vols. post 8vo, 25s. 6d.

Piccadilly. With Illustrations by Richard Doyle. New Edition, 3s. 6d. Cheap Edition, boards, 2s. 6d.

Episodes in a Life of Adventure; or, Moss from a Rolling Stone. Cheaper Edition. Post 8vo, 3s. 6d.

OLIPHANT.

The Autobiography and Letters of Mrs M. O. W. Oliphant. Arranged and Edited by Mrs HARRY COGHILL. With Two Portraits. Cheap Edition. Crown 8vo, 6s.

Annals of a Publishing House. William Blackwood and his Sons; Their Magazine and Friends. By Mrs OLIPHANT. With Four Portraits. Third Edition. Demy 8vo. Vols. I. and II. £2, 2s.

A Widow's Tale, and other Stories. With an Introductory Note by J. M. BARRIE. Second Edition. Crown 8vo, 6s.

Katie Stewart, and other Stories. New Edition. Crown 8vo, cloth, 3s. 6d.

Katie Stewart. Illustrated boards, 2s. 6d.

Valentine and his Brother. New Edition. Crown 8vo, 3s. 6d.

Sons and Daughters. Crown 8vo. 3s. 6d.

OMOND. The Romantic Triumph. "Periods of European Literature." By T. S. OMOND. Crown 8vo, 5s. net.

O'NEILL. Songs of the Glens of Antrim. By MOIRA O'NEILL. Twelfth Impression. Crown 8vo, 3s. 6d.

PAGE.

Intermediate Text-Book of Geology. By Professor LAPWORTH. Founded on Dr Page's 'Introductory Text-Book of Geology.' Crown 8vo, 5s.

Advanced Text-Book of Geology. New Edition. Revised and enlarged by Professor LAPWORTH. Crown 8vo. [*In the press.*

Introductory Text-Book of Physical Geography. Crown 8vo, 2s. 6d.

Advanced Text-Book of Physical Geography. Crown 8vo, 5s.

Physical Geography Examinator. Crown 8vo, sewed, 9d.

PARKER. Miss Lomax: Millionaire. By BESSIE PARKER. Crown 8vo, 6s.

PATERSON. Peggotts; or, The Indian Contingent. By MARGARET PATERSON. Crown 8vo, 6s.

PAUL. History of the Royal Company of Archers, the Queen's Body-Guard for Scotland. By Sir JAMES BALFOUR PAUL, Advocate of the Scottish Bar. Crown 4to, with Portraits and other Illustrations. £2, 2s.

PEARSE. The Hearseys: Five Generations of an Anglo-Indian Family. By Colonel HUGH PEARSE. Demy 8vo, 15s. net.

PERIODS OF EUROPEAN LITERATURE. Edited by Professor SAINTSBURY. *For List of Volumes, see page 2.*

PHILOSOPHICAL CLASSICS FOR ENGLISH READERS. Edited by WILLIAM KNIGHT, LL.D., Professor of Moral Philosophy, University of St Andrews. Cheap Re-issue in Shilling Volumes net.
[*For List of Volumes, see page 2.*

POLLOK. The Course of Time: A Poem. By ROBERT POLLOK, A.M. New Edition. With Portrait. Fcap. 8vo, gilt top, 2s. 6d.

POLLOK. Studies in Practical Theology. By ALLAN POLLOK, D.D., LL.D. Crown 8vo, 5s. net.

PRESTWICH. Essays: Descriptive and Biographical. By GRACE, Lady PRESTWICH, Author of 'The Harbour Bar' and 'Enga.' With a Memoir by her sister, LOUISA E. MILNE. With Illustrations. Demy 8vo, 10s. 6d.

PRINGLE-PATTISON.

Scottish Philosophy. A Comparison of the Scottish and German Answers to Hume. Balfour Philosophical Lectures, University of Edinburgh. By A. SETH PRINGLE-PATTISON, LL.D., Professor of Logic and Metaphysics in Edinburgh University. Third Edition. Crown 8vo, 5s.

Hegelianism and Personality. Balfour Philosophical Lectures. Second Series. Second Edition. Crown 8vo, 5s.

Man's Place in the Cosmos, and other Essays. Second Edition, Enlarged. Post 8vo, 6s. net.

Two Lectures on Theism. Delivered on the occasion of the Sesquicentennial Celebration of Princeton University. Crown 8vo, 2s 6d.

The Philosophical Radicals and Other Essays, including Chapters reprinted on the Philosophy of Religion in Kant and Hegel. Crown 8vo, 6s. net.

PUBLIC GENERAL STATUTES AFFECTING SCOTLAND from 1707 to 1847, with Chronological Table and Index. 3 vols. large 8vo, £3, 3s. Also Published Annually with General Index.

QUESTION OF COLOUR, A. A Study of South Africa. Crown 8vo, 6s. net.

RANJITSINHJI. The Jubilee Book of Cricket. By PRINCE RANJITSINHJI.

POPULAR EDITION. With 107 full-page Illustrations. Sixth Edition. Large crown 8vo, 6s.

SIXPENNY EDITION. With a selection of the Illustrations.

ROBERTSON.

The Poetry and the Religion of the Psalms. The Croall Lectures, 1893-94. By JAMES ROBERTSON, D.D., Professor of Oriental Languages in the University of Glasgow. Demy 8vo, 12s.

ROBERTSON.

A History of German Literature. By JOHN G. ROBERTSON, Professor of German, University of London. Demy 8vo, 10s. 6d. net.

Schiller after a Century. Crown 8vo, 2s. 6d. net.

RONALDSHAY.

On the Outskirts of Empire in Asia. By the EARL OF RONALDSHAY, F.R.G.S. With numerous Illustrations and Maps. Royal 8vo, 21s. net

Sport and Politics under an Eastern Sky. With numerous Illustrations and Maps. Royal 8vo, 21s. net.

RUTLAND.

Notes of an Irish Tour in 1846. By the DUKE OF RUTLAND, G.C.B. (LORD JOHN MANNERS). New Edition. Crown 8vo, 2s. 6d.

Correspondence between the Right Honble. William Pitt and Charles Duke of Rutland, Lord-Lieutenant of Ireland, 1781-1787. With Introductory Note by JOHN DUKE OF RUTLAND. 8vo, 7s. 6d.

The Collected Writings of Janetta, Duchess of Rutland. With Portrait and Illustrations. 2 vols. post 8vo, 15s. net.

Impressions of Bad-Homburg. Comprising a Short Account of the Women's Associations of Germany under the Red Cross. By the DUCHESS OF RUTLAND (LADY JOHN MANNERS). Crown 8vo, 1s. 6d.

Some Personal Recollections of the Later Years of the Earl of Beaconsfield, K.G. Sixth Edition. 6d.

Employment of Women in the Public Service. 6d.

RUTLAND.

Some of the Advantages of Easily Accessible Reading and Recreation Rooms and Free Libraries. With Remarks on Starting and Maintaining them. Second Edition. Crown 8vo, 1s.

A Sequel to Rich Men's Dwellings, and other Occasional Papers. Crown 8vo, 2s. 6d.

Encouraging Experiences of Reading and Recreation Rooms, Aims of Guilds, Nottingham Social Guide, Existing Institutions, &c., &c. Crown 8vo, 1s.

SAINTSBURY.

A History of Criticism and Literary Taste in Europe. From the Earliest Texts to the Present Day. By GEORGE SAINTSBURY, M.A. (Oxon.) Hon. LL.D. (Aberd.), Professor of Rhetoric and English Literature in the University of Edinburgh. In 3 vols. demy 8vo. Vol. I.—Classical and Mediæval Criticism. 16s. net.

Vol. II.—From the Renaissance to the Decline of Eighteenth Century Orthodoxy. 20s. net.

Vol. III.—Nineteenth Century. 20s. net.

Matthew Arnold. "Modern English Writers." Second Edition. Crown 8vo, 2s. 6d

The Flourishing of Romance and the Rise of Allegory (12th and 13th Centuries). "Periods of European Literature." Crown 8vo, 5s. net.

The Earlier Renaissance. **"Periods of European Literature."** Crown 8vo, 5s. net.

"SCOLOPAX." A Book of the Snipe. By SCOLOPAX. Illustrated. Crown 8vo, 5s. net.

SCOTT. Tom Cringle's Log. By MICHAEL SCOTT. New Edition. With 19 Full-page Illustrations. Crown 8vo, 3s. 6d.

SCUDAMORE. Belgium and the Belgians. By CYRIL SCUDAMORE. With Illustrations. Square crown 8vo, 6s.

SELLAR. Recollections and Impressions. By E. M. SELLAR. With Eight Portraits. Demy 8vo, 10s. 6d. net.

SETH. A Study of Ethical Principles. BY JAMES SETH, M.A., Professor of Moral Philosophy in the University of Edinburgh. Eighth Edition, Revised. Post 8vo, 7s. 6d.

SHARPLEY. Aristophanes—Pax. Edited, with Introduction and Notes, by H. SHARPLEY. Demy 8vo, 12s. 6d. net.

SHAW. Securities over Moveables. Four Lectures delivered at the Request of the Society of Accountants in Edinburgh, the Institute of Accountants and Actuaries in Glasgow, and the Institute of Bankers in Scotland, in 1902-3. Demy 8vo, 3s. 6d. net.

SIMPSON. Side-Lights on Siberia. Some account of the Great Siberian Iron Road: The Prisons and Exile System. By J. Y. SIMPSON, M.A., D.Sc. With numerous Illustrations and a Map. Demy 8vo, 16s.

SINCLAIR. The Thistle and Fleur de Lys: A Vocabulary of Franco-Scottish Words. By ISABEL G. SINCLAIR. Crown 8vo, 3s. net.

SKELTON. The Handbook of Public Health. A New Edition, Revised by JAMES PATTEN MACDOUGALL, Advocate, Secretary to the Local Government Board for Scotland, Joint-Author of 'The Parish Council Guide for Scotland,' and ABIJAH MURRAY, Chief Clerk of the Local Government Board for Scotland. In Two Parts. Crown 8vo. Part I.—The Public Health (Scotland) Act, 1897, with Notes. 3s. 6d. net.

SKRINE. Fontenoy, and Great Britain's share in the War of the Austrian Succession. By F. H. SKRINE. With Map, Plans, and Illustrations. Demy 8vo, 21s. net.

SMITH.

The Transition Period. "Periods of European Literature. By G. GREGORY SMITH. Crown 8vo, 5s. net.

Specimens of Middle Scots. Post 8vo, 7s. 6d. net.

SMITH. Retrievers, and how to Break them. By Lieutenant-Colonel Sir HENRY SMITH, K.C.B. With an Introduction by Mr S. E. SHIRLEY, President of the Kennel Club. Dedicated by special permission to H.R.H. the Duke of Cornwall and York. New Edition, enlarged. With additional Illustrations. Crown 8vo, 1s.

SNELL. The Fourteenth Century. "Periods of European Literature." By F. J. SNELL. Crown 8vo, 5s. net.

"SON OF THE MARSHES, A."

From Spring to Fall; or, When Life Stirs. By "A SON OF THE MARSHES." Cheap Uniform Edition. Crown 8vo, 3s. 6d.

Within an Hour of London Town: Among Wild Birds and their Haunts. Edited by J. A. OWEN. Cheap Uniform Edition. Cr. 8vo, 3s. 6d.

With the Woodlanders and by the Tide. Cheap Uniform Edition. Crown 8vo, 3s. 6d.

On Surrey Hills. Cheap Uniform Edition. Crown 8vo, 3s. 6d.

Annals of a Fishing Village. Cheap Uniform Edition. Crown 8vo, 3s. 6d.

SORLEY.

The Ethics of Naturalism. By W. R. SORLEY, M.A., Fellow of Trinity College, Cambridge, Professor of Moral Philosophy, University of Cambridge. Second Edition. Crown 8vo, 6s.

Recent Tendencies in Ethics. Crown 8vo, 2s. 6d. net.

SPROTT.

The Worship and Offices of the Church of Scotland. By GEORGE W. SPROTT, D.D., Minister of North Berwick. Crown 8vo, 6s.

The Book of Common Order of the Church of Scotland, commonly known as John Knox's Liturgy. With Historical Introduction and Illustrative Notes. Crown 8vo, 4s. 6d. net.

Scottish Liturgies of the Reign of James VI. Edited, with an Introduction and Notes. Crown 8vo, 4s. net.

Euchologion: A Book of Common Order. Crown 8vo, 4s. 6d. net.

STEEVENS.

Things Seen: Impressions of Men, Cities, and Books. By the late G. W. STEEVENS. Edited by G. S. STREET. With a Memoir by W. E. HENLEY, and a Photogravure reproduction of Collier's Portrait. Memorial Edition. Crown 8vo, 6s.

STEEVENS.

From Capetown to Ladysmith, and Egypt in 1898. Memorial Edition. Crown 8vo, 6s.

In India. With Map. Memorial Edition. Crown 8vo, 6s.

With Kitchener to Khartum. With 8 Maps and Plans. Memorial Edition. Crown 8vo, 6s.

The Land of the Dollar. Memorial Edition. Crown 8vo, 6s.

Glimpses of Three Nations. Memorial Edition. Cr. 8vo, 6s.

Monologues of the Dead. Memorial Edition. Crown 8vo, 3s. 6d.

With the Conquering Turk. With 4 Maps. Ch. Ed. Cr. 8vo, 6s.

STEPHENS.

The Book of the Farm; detailing the Labours of the Farmer, Farm-Steward, Ploughman, Shepherd, Hedger, Farm-Labourer, Field-Worker, and Cattle-man. Illustrated with numerous Portraits of Animals and Engravings of Implements, and Plans of Farm Buildings. Fourth Edition. Revised, and in great part Re-written, by JAMES MACDONALD, F.R.S.E., Secretary Highland and Agricultural Society of Scotland. Complete in Six Divisional Volumes, bound in cloth, each 10s. 6d., or handsomely bound, in 3 volumes with leather back and gilt top, £3, 3s.

STEWART. Haud Immemor. Reminiscences of Legal and Social Life in Edinburgh and London, 1850-1900. By CHARLES STEWART. With 10 Photogravure Plates. Royal 8vo, 7s. 6d

STEWART AND CUFF. Practical Nursing. By ISLA STEWART, Matron of St Bartholomew's Hospital, London; and HERBERT E. CUFF, M.D., F.R.C.S., Medical Superintendent North-Eastern Fever Hospital, Tottenham, London. With Diagrams. In 2 vols. crown 8vo. Vol. I. Second Edition. 3s. 6d. net. Vol. II., 3s. 6d. net.

Also in 1 Volume, 5s. net.

STIRLING.

Our Regiments in South Africa, 1899-1902. Their Record, based on the Despatches. By JOHN STIRLING. In 1 vol. demy 8vo, 12s. 6d. net.

The Colonials in South Africa, 1899-1902. Their Record, based on the Despatches Demy 8vo, 10s. net.

STODDART. John Stuart Blackie: A Biography. By ANNA M. STODDART. POPULAR EDITION, with Portrait. Crown 8vo, 3s. 6d.

STORMONTH.

Dictionary of the English Language, Pronouncing, Etymological, and Explanatory. By the Rev. JAMES STORMONTH. Revised by the Rev. P. H. PHELP. Library Edition. New and Cheaper Edition, with Supplement. Imperial 8vo, handsomely bound in half morocco, 18s. net.

STORMONTH.

Etymological and Pronouncing Dictionary of the English Language. Including a very Copious Selection of Scientific Terms. For use in Schools and Colleges, and as a Book of General Reference. The Pronunciation carefully revised by the Rev. P. H. PHELP, M.A. Cantab. Sixteenth Edition, Revised. Crown 8vo, pp. 1000. 5s. net.

Handy Dictionary. New Edition, thoroughly Revised. By WILLIAM BAYNE. 16mo, 1s.

STORY. William Wetmore Story and his Friends. From Letters, Diaries, and Recollections. By HENRY JAMES. With 2 Portraits. In 2 vols. post 8vo, 24s. net.

SYNGE. The Story of the World. By M. B. SYNGE. With Coloured Frontispieces and numerous Illustrations by E. M. SYNGE, A.R.E., and Maps. 2 vols, 3s. 6d. each net.

THEOBALD. A Text-Book of Agricultural Zoology. By FRED. V. THEOBALD. With numerous Illustrations. Crown 8vo, 8s. 6d.

THOMSON. Handy Book of the Flower-Garden. By DAVID THOMSON. Crown 8vo, 5s.

THOMSON. A Practical Treatise on the Cultivation of the Grape Vine. By WILLIAM THOMSON, Tweed Vineyards. Tenth Edition. 8vo, 5s.

THOMSON. History of the Fife Light Horse. By Colonel ANSTRUTHER THOMSON. With numerous Portraits. Small 4to, 21s. net.

THORBURN. The Punjab in Peace and War. By S. S. THORBURN. Demy 8vo, 12s. 6d. net.

THURSTON.

The Circle. By KATHERINE CECIL THURSTON. Fifth Impression. Crown 8vo, 6s.

John Chilcote, M.P. Fourteenth Impression, crown 8vo, 6s. Cheap Edition, paper cover, 6d.

The Mystics. With Illustrations. Crown 8vo, 3s. 6d.

TIELE. Elements of the Science of Religion. Part I.—Morphological. Part II.—Ontological. Being the Gifford Lectures delivered before the University of Edinburgh in 1896-98. By C. P. TIELE, Theol. D., Litt.D. (Bonon.), Hon. M.R.A.S., &c., Professor of the Science of Religion, in the University of Leiden. In 2 vols. post 8vo, 7s. 6d. net. each.

TRANSACTIONS OF THE HIGHLAND AND AGRICULTURAL SOCIETY OF SCOTLAND. Published annually, price 5s.

TRAVERS.

The Way of Escape. A Novel. By GRAHAM TRAVERS (Margaret Todd, M.D.) Second Impression. Crown 8vo, 6s.

Mona Maclean, Medical Student. A Novel. Fourteenth Edition. Crown 8vo, 6s. Cheap Edition, royal 8vo, paper cover, 6d.

Windyhaugh. Fourth Edition. Crown 8vo, 6s.

Fellow Travellers. Fourth Edition. Crown 8vo, 6s.

TROTTER.

A Leader of Light Horse. Life of Hodson of Hodson's Horse. By Captain L. J. TROTTER, Author of 'Life of John Nicholson, Soldier and Statesman.' With a Portrait and 2 Maps. Demy 8vo, 16s.

TRUSCOTT. The Marriage of Aminta. By L. PARRY TRUSCOTT. Crown 8vo, 6s.

TULLOCH.

Modern Theories in Philosophy and Religion. By JOHN TULLOCH, D.D., Principal of St Mary's College in the University of St Andrews, and one of her Majesty's Chaplains in Ordinary in Scotland. 8vo. 15s.

TWEEDIE. The Arabian Horse: His Country and People. By Major-General W. TWEEDIE, C.S.I., Bengal Staff Corps; for many years H.B.M.'s Consul-General, Baghdad, and Political Resident for the Government of India in Turkish Arabia. In one vol. royal 4to, with Seven Coloured Plates and other Illustrations, and a Map of the Country. Price £3, 3s. net.

VAUGHAN. The Romantic Revolt. By Professor C. E. VAUGHAN. Crown 8vo, 5s. net.

VOYAGE OF THE "SCOTIA," THE. Being the Record of a Voyage of Exploration in Antartic Seas. By THREE OF THE STAFF. Demy 8vo, 21s. net.

WADDELL.

Christianity as an Ideal. By Rev. P. HATELY WADDELL, B.D. Crown 8vo, 3s. 6d.

Essays on Faith. Crown 8vo, 3s. 6d.

WARREN'S (SAMUEL) WORKS:—

Diary of a Late Physician. Cloth, 2s. 6d.; boards, 2s.

Ten Thousand A-Year. Cloth, 3s. 6d.; boards, 2s. 6d.

Now and Then. The Lily and the Bee. Intellectual and Moral Development of the Present Age. 4s. 6d.

Essays: Critical, Imaginative, and Juridical. 5s.

WATSON. The Skipper. By GILBERT WATSON. Crown 8vo, 6s.

WATT. By Still Waters. By MACLEAN WATT. 1s. 6d. net. Leather, 2s. net.

WENLEY. Aspects of Pessimism. By R. M. WENLEY, M.A., D.Sc., D.Phil., Professor of Philosophy in the University of Michigan, U.S.A. Crown 8vo, 6s.

WHIBLEY.

Thackeray. "Modern English Writers." By CHARLES WHIBLEY. Crown 8vo, 2s. 6d.

William Pitt. With Portraits and Caricatures. Crown 8vo, 6s. net.

WHITE.

The Young Gerande. By EDMUND WHITE. In 1 vol. crown 8vo, 6s.

Bray of Buckholt. Crown 8vo, 6s.

WILLIAMSON. Ideals of Ministry. By A. WALLACE WILLIAMSON, D.D., St Cuthbert's, Edinburgh. Crown 8vo, 3s. 6d.

WILSON. The Prophets and Prophecy to the Close of the Eighth Century B.C. By the Rev. ALEXANDER WILSON, M.A., Minister of Ythan Wells, Aberdeenshire. With Introductory Preface by the Rev. ALLAN MENZIES, D.D., Professor of Biblical Criticism in the University of St Andrews. Fcap. 8vo, 1s. net.

WILSON.

Works of Professor Wilson. Edited by his Son-in-Law, Professor FERRIER. 12 vols. crown 8vo, £2, 8s.

Christopher in his Sporting-Jacket. 2 vols., 8s.

Isle of Palms, City of the Plague, and other Poems. 4s.

Lights and Shadows of Scottish Life, and other Tales. 4s.

Essays, Critical and Imaginative. 4 vols., 16s.

The Noctes Ambrosianæ. 4 vols., 16s.

Homer and his Translators, and the Greek Drama. Crown 8vo, 4s.

WORSLEY.

Homer's Odyssey. Translated into English Verse in the Spenserian Stanza. By PHILIP STANHOPE WORSLEY, M.A. New and Cheaper Edition. Post 8vo, 7s. 6d. net.

Homer's Iliad. Translated by P. S. Worsley and Prof. Conington. 2 vols. crown 8vo, 21s.

WOTHERSPOON.

Kyrie Eleison ("Lord, have Mercy"). A Manual of Private Prayers. With Notes and Additional Matter. By H. J. WOTHERSPOON, M.A., of St Oswald's, Edinburgh. Cloth, red edges, 1s. net; limp leather, 1s. 6d. net.

Before and After. Being Part I. of 'Kyrie Eleison.' Cloth, limp, 6d. net.

The Second Prayer Book of King Edward the Sixth (1552) and the Liturgy of Compromise. Edited by Rev. G. W. SPROTT, D.D. Crown 8vo, 4s. net.

YATE. Khurasan and Sistan. By Lieut.-Col. C. E. YATE, C.S.I., C.M.G., F.R.G.S., Indian Staff Corps, Agent to the Governor-General and Chief Commissioner for Baluchistan, late Agent to the Governor-General of India, and Her Britannic Majesty's Consul-General for Khurasan and Sistan. With Map and 25 Illustrations, and Portraits. Demy 8vo, 21s.

ZACK.

On Trial. By ZACK. Second Edition. Crown 8vo, 6s.

Life is Life, and other Tales and Episodes. Second Edition. Crown 8vo, 6s.

4/07

BY THE SAME AUTHOR.

MAN'S PLACE IN THE COSMOS

AND OTHER ESSAYS.

Second Edition. Revised and Enlarged. Post 8vo, 6s. net.

CONTENTS: Man's Place in the Cosmos—The Present Position of the Philosophical Sciences—The "New" Psychology and Automatism—A New Theory of the Absolute—Mr Balfour and his Critics—The Venture of Theism—The Life and Opinions of Friedrich Nietzsche.

SCOTTISH PHILOSOPHY.

A COMPARISON OF THE SCOTTISH AND GERMAN ANSWERS TO HUME.

Balfour Philosophical Lectures.

Third Edition. Crown 8vo, 5s.

HEGELIANISM AND PERSONALITY.

Balfour Philosophical Lectures.

Second Series. Second Edition. Crown 8vo, 5s.

TWO LECTURES ON THEISM.

DELIVERED ON THE OCCASION OF THE SESQUICENTENNIAL CELEBRATION OF PRINCETON UNIVERSITY.

Crown 8vo, 2s. 6d.

WILLIAM BLACKWOOD & SONS, EDINBURGH AND LONDON.